SOFT TECHNOLOGIES AT WORK-LEARNING SOCIAL/SOFT SKILLS

SOFT TECHNOLOGIES AT WORK-LEARNING SOCIAL/ SOFT SKILLS

Dr. V. R. Katkhede
M.A. Ph.D. – HR
Advisor – Corporate – HR
Uttam Galva Steels Ltd.
Mumbai.

Himalaya Publishing House

MUMBAI • NEW DELHI • NAGPUR • BENGALURU • HYDERABAD • CHENNAI • PUNE • LUCKNOW • AHMEDABAD • ERNAKULAM • BHUBANESWAR • INDORE • KOLKATA • GUWAHATI

First Edition : 2011

Published by : Mrs. Meena Pandey for **Himalaya Publishing House Pvt. Ltd.**, "Ramdoot", Dr. Bhalerao Marg, Girgaon, **Mumbai - 400 004.** Phone: 022-23860170/23863863, Fax: 022-23877178 **E-mail: himpub@vsnl.com; Website: www.himpub.com**

Branch Offices :

New Delhi : "Pooja Apartments", 4-B, Murari Lal Street, Ansari Road, Darya Ganj, New Delhi - 110 002. Phone: 011-23270392, 23278631; Fax: 011-23256286

Nagpur : Kundanlal Chandak Industrial Estate, Ghat Road, Nagpur - 440 018. Phone: 0712-2738731, 3296733; Telefax: 0712-2721215

Bengaluru : No. 16/1 (Old 12/1), 1st Floor, Next to Hotel Highlands, Madhava Nagar, Race Course Road, Bengaluru - 560 001. Phone: 080-32919385; Telefax: 080-22286611

Hyderabad : No. 3-4-184, Lingampally, Besides Raghavendra Swamy Matham, Kachiguda, Hyderabad - 500 027. Phone: 040-27560041, 27550139; Mobile: 09848130433

Chennai : No. 85/50, Bazullah Road, T. Nagar, Chennai - 600 017. Phone: 044-28144004/28144005

Pune : First Floor, "Laksha" Apartment, No. 527, Mehunpura, Shaniwarpeth (Near Prabhat Theatre), Pune - 411 030. Phone: 020-24496323/24496333

Lucknow : Jai Baba Bhavan, Church Road, Near Manas Complex and Dr. Awasthi Clinic, Aliganj, Lucknow - 226 024. Phone: 0522-2339329, 4068914; Mobile: 09305302158, 09415349385, 09389593752

Ahmedabad : 114, "SHAIL", 1st Floor, Opp. Madhu Sudan House, C.G. Road, Navrang Pura, Ahmedabad - 380 009. Phone: 079-26560126; Mobile: 09327324149, 09314679413

Ernakulam : 39/104 A, Lakshmi Apartment, Karikkamuri Cross Rd., Ernakulam, Cochin - 622011, Kerala. Phone: 0484-2378012, 2378016; Mobile: 09344199799

Bhubaneswar : 5 Station Square, Bhubaneswar - 751 001 (Odisha). Mobile: 09861046007

Indore : Kesardeep Avenue Extension, 73, Narayan Bagh, Flat No. 302, IIIrd Floor, Near Humpty Dumpty School, Narayan Bagh, Indore - 452 007 (M.P.). Mobile: 09301386468

Kolkata : 108/4, Beliaghata Main Road, Near ID Hospital, Opp. SBI Bank, Kolkata - 700 010, Phone: 033-32449649, Mobile: 09910440956

Guwahati : House No. 15, Behind Pragjyotish College, Near Sharma Printing Press, P.O. Bharalumukh, Guwahati - 781009, (Assam). Mobile: 09883055590, 09883055536

DTP by : HPH, Editorial Office, Bhandup (Avinash)

Printed at : A to Z Printers, New Delhi

PREFACE

It is experienced that four in the ten are not able to work cooperatively with fellow-workers. More and more organizations are complaining about lack of social skills in young hires. Too many youngsters can't take criticism; they get defensive or hostile when people give them feedback on how they are doing. They react to performance feedback as though it were a personal attack. The problem is not just with youngsters, it is true for seasoned executives as well. The few reasons for such low level cooperativeness, non-involvement are:

1. Arrogance – I know it all and I am already adequately trained.
2. Fear of not being able to learn new ways of working or not being able to do what is taught.
3. Lack of clear concept of new role and hence a failure to recognize the need to learn new skills.

Today we are in a time, with no guarantee of job security, when the very concept of a "job" is rapidly being replaced by portable skills. Employers today are looking for specific technical skills are now less important than underlying ability to learn on the job. Globalization of workforce puts a particular premium on portable skills. As business changes, so do the traits needed to excel. Sometimes, entirely new capabilities have begun to appear as skills. New challenges demand new talents.

Today we are being judged by a new yardstick, not just by how smart we are, or by our training and expertise, but also by how well we handle ourselves and each other in the organization or society at large. The new rules predict who is most likely to become a star performer and who is most prone to derailing.

These rules have little to do with what were told was important in school; academic abilities are largely irrelevant to this standard. The new measure takes for granted having enough intellectual ability and technical know-how to do your jobs; it focuses instead on personal qualities such as initiative, empathy, adaptability and persuasiveness. The research distills with unprecedented precision which qualities mark a star performer. And it is demonstrated which human abilities make up the greater part of ingredients for excellence at work. Whatever your job, understanding how to cultivate these capabilities can be essential for success in your career. Your ability to perform at peak depends to a very great extent on your having these abilities – though almost certainly you never taught them in school. Even so, your career will depend, to a greater or lesser extent; on how well you have mastered these capabilities, communication skills, inter-personal skills and initiative. We are living in a time when our prospects for the future increasingly depend upon managing ourselves and handling our relationships more artfully. This requires adequate back up of soft skills.

Clearly, the business market is providing strong signals about the large gap in our educational system. It is not producing enough people with the essential soft skills the economy needs. It is observed that soft skills make greater impact on clients from across the world rather than a high degree of technical skills. Although several companies, enterprises obtain from providing training to their employees on soft skills, the reality is 'soft skills' has graduated from a 'nice-to-have' category to the 'must have' category for various sectors. It is an important part of individual and management training as it has a significant impact on personality development and organizational development respectively.

The changing world of work expects you to do a lot more for performing your tasks, it expects you to upgrade your skills, productively contribute to works outside your job profile and constantly learn and venture into newer areas. The reason, they say, is the continuous technological changes that various sectors are going through. And this is precisely the reason why many organizations have brought in cross functional training to satiate employees desire to learn and acquire new skills. Emerging technologies have increased the demand for certain skill sets. Cross training equips individuals to work on projects, involving multiple technologies enabling them to possess a diverse skill set, and thus making them imminently employable in a variety of functions. Multi-skilling helps in the technology bandwidth, avoids redundancies in the system and gives the organization a significant competitive advantage in bidding for new business. Also, employees skilled in multiple technologies help the organization make its resource management efficient and cost-effective. Organizations are increasingly indulging in cross training to upgrade their employee's skills not only to satisfy their business interests but also to help employees satisfy their personal need to sharpen their skill sets and broaden their knowledge base. For an employee, it just takes an extra effort from his/her part to acquire new skills. And this additional skill acquired empowers employees and make them valuable to the organization. The workplace philosophy today is no longer about concentrating only on one's own task, but is also about adding value to other functions. As job horizons widen, the need to know and contribute more has become imperative and now organizations are doing, just that by implementing multi-skilling training activities. In the end, employees know the importance of such skill upgradation, acquisition are going to excel their traits at work. So, if you feel the need to learn something new, this book skill at work will prove useful to you. Process of learning from observation, acquisition, development, application to problem-solving, involves a set of activities called 'learning cycle' is well incorporated in this book. It directs learner what he should know about learning and then learn and develop his skill to acquire mastery in particular areas of operation.

This book invites its reader to place themselves individually in a personal development mode to learn about and grow their own skill sets with the stress on the word learning and its linkage with total personality development at work. The objective of this book is on the importance of individual initiative and to achieve excellence at work. Overall, not only will the book contribute to encouraging a personal sense of direction and focus for employee learning, but it will also assist materially with the road map to skill development.

Dr. V. R. Katkhede

ACKNOWLEDGEMENT

This book is the product of my Thirty-two years experience in the areas of training, employee relations, organizational development and performance management. But the forceful single statement of Mr. Beasant Lal Shaw, CMD of NECO Group of Industries, Nagpur has greatly inspired me to undertake writing of this book. Once upon a time in the Sr. Executive meeting he said that, "The difference between what we are doing and what we are capable of doing would solve most of our problems. You must have right mindset and skill set to constantly look for potential in people. Great service provider in the world of work do not always have state-of-the-art technology, rather they have state-of-the-art people skills." This statement (made) in 1994 has changed my mindset and I started collecting, writing and teaching 'people skills' to employees and MBA students. Therefore, I continue to be grateful to him.

My deepest gratitude is to the hundreds of my fellow-employees from the companies, I worked, have shared with me their experiences, feelings and thoughts. This book owes much to them for its insight into what it means to work with soft skills and their results and recognition at workplace.

I am thankful to my personal assistant, Miss. Shraddha Yewale, for her typing and secretarial work. She has always remained supportive and this book could not have been completed without her unfailing faithfulness.

However, no list of acknowledgement would be complete without recognizing the indulgence and moral support provided by my wife Mrs. Kamal, who continuously helped me a lot during preparation of this book.

Dr. V.R. Katkhede

CONTENTS

CHAPTER 1

Introduction

The emphasis on human/social/soft skills was considered important in the past but it is of primary importance today. The ability to get along with people is the most wanted ~ortant skill today. The great English Poet Samuel Butler put it more eloquently "Any fool can paint a picture but it takes a wise man to be able to sell it". If the "fool" is the metaphor for hard skill then the "wise man" would be the soft skill; but the soft skill of the wise man is useless without the hard skill of the fool; the harmonising of both skills sells the picture. Hard as well as soft skills are complementary to each other. Until recently we paid little attention to social/soft skills.

The Industrial Revolution created the need for hard/technology skills. People worked in production line and were not required to think or interact to each other. However, things have changed; instead of standing behind the production lines, they now sit in front of a computer and control a robot who works in the production line. Now, people need more technical skill, but they also need skills to communicate and work within a group. Increasingly success in business life depends not on technical knowledge alone but also on relationship with other people at work.

Traditionally, the word "skill" has been associated with the range of technical job-specific abilities. As a result of the rapid changes in the organisational structure, systems, staffing and the structure of employment, there is a growing recognition that the possession of social/soft skills which are also referred as generic, personal to work effectively in new work pattern. These types of skills are reported to be of increasing important to employers as they relate to a person's ability to operate effectively in the workplace either alone or with others. In an ever more complex, technology-driven society it is imperative that one has the necessary skills to succeed in life. By skills we are not merely referring to the technical skills of one's profession, such as the ability at this moment to properly operate your browser software on the internet. We are actually referring to a whole range of skills, from the very specific technology skills require of life and one's work to the subtle, yet critical inter-personal and psychological skills demanded by life. Generally, skills are classified in three major types.

- **Technical Skills** – The most fundamental type of skills; including the technical skills required in life for e.g., grooming, organizing, planning, etc. As well as the very specific technical skills required of your specific jobs related administrative procedures, machine operations, computer protocol, financial procedures, sales administrations, accounting, auditing, etc. These, skills are also called hard skills. These skills are typically easy to observe, quantify and measure.They are also easy to train, because most of the time skill sets are rand new to the learners and no unlearning is involved; we have both hard skills and soft skills within us, which are part of our personality and emotional make up.

- **Interpersonal Skills** – In addition, you will need to know how to convey information, verbally or non-verbally to people you are in contact with. These are our intet-personal skills. To succeed in life we need to have writing, speaking presentation, communication, management, leadership, organisational skills among others.

- **Psychologica1 Skills** – Perhaps the most important type of skills to succeed in life is psychological skills. The ability to show real concern for others and knowing how to show that concern in interactions with others is a psychological skill. Other psychological skills include the ability to help others develop and grow, the abiuty to create harmony in difficult situations, the ability to know how to motivate others, the ability to understand another's true motives when interacting with them, you increase the motivation and energy of those around you, and you increases your chance to success, joy and happiness in life.

  Soft skills variably referred as generic personal, behavioural skills relate to persons ability to operate in the workplace. The need for these skills is not new but contemporary changes in the organisational behaviour and life, the focus on team-working and the growth in the service, hospitality sectors have increased their importance and they are now emerging as a critical feature for personal and organisational success. Other skills which at times overlap yet are distinguishable from social/soft skills in their use are basic skills – include the fundamental-elements of literacy and numeracy. Core-skills – include communication planning, teamwrork, coaching, mentoring, etc. Key skills covers use of numbers, working with others, self-learning, problems-solving, etc. To sum up social/soft skills are intetr-personal and intra-personal skills required to be effective in the organisational and social-personal life.

SKILLS - DEFINITION

The review of literature indicates that there is no common definition for the term soft skills. It is generally seen those as people-oriented skills and self-management skills.

The situation in everyday life illustrate that it is important to achieve our objectives, maintaining a good atmosphere with our relationships at work and at personal level. Therefore a good definition of social/soft skills would be one that contemplates both aspects: Philips (1978) states that "the degree in which a person can communicate with others in a way that satisfies their own rights, needs, pleasure and obligations with a reasonable degree without damages the rights, needs, pleasures or similar obligation of another person and in which they share with others a free and open interchange". Laballo (1980) says "mixed behaviour emitted by an individual in an adequate way to the situation, respecting other people's behaviour and who generally resolve problems immediately". Soft skills can be defined as:

- A set of skills that influence how we interact with each other.
- The ability of influencing human behaviour positively.
- The expertise of selling your ideas, hopes, dreams to others.
- Treating individuals not as commodities but as individuals with head and hearts and with their own strengths and weaknesses.

When considering the development of the workforce in our business it is necessary to consider all aspects of employee development. There are more things to be considered than employees technical skills. We can interview and hire dozens of employees with Bachelor, master's degree or any other technical qualification, certification, but what differentiates these individuals from each other? Many managers argue that technical skill, competencies in our employees are far more important than their skills at communicating, listening and motivating each other. It is my argument that these soft skills are a vital part of employees make up. It is important that we as managers have a good understanding of organisational behaviour, skills and use it in the workplace. Without this set if soft skills, we set ourselves up to fail.

Hard and soft skills are both important in our work environment and to each individual's success. Soft skills pay a highly important role in workplace as well as in one's own career success. They enable you to standout in a crowd of other equal or higher qualified job seekers and are applicable to almost every field of work. However, there is a distant difference between these two separate skills sets. Soft skills involve how you project yourself and your professional skills to others.

HARD VS. SIFT SKILLS - DIFFERENCE

"Hard skills get YOU hired while soft skills get YOU promoted"
"We are hired for our technical skills. but fired for lack of soft skills"

Today's business graduates have an abundance of technical knowledge. They can do liner programming, calculate a discounted rate of return, develop a sophisticated marketing plan, and crunch numbers on computer spread sheet. They are technically solid, but most lack the inter-personal and social/soft skills necessary to lead people. Microsoft's Bill Gates to be a techno Geek, he is much more than that. He obviously has a vast knowledge of computer programming or windows would not have evolved. But it would have only been one operating system among many if he lacked the ability to think strategically. For individuals and organisations alike to grow, they must invest in good social/soft skills required to prosper.

Our hard skills are our primary skills; technical, administrative, professional that are needed to perform a particular job. They are tangible, observable and easily measureable. Hard skills are acquired through training and education. Hard skills are account payable, accounts receivable, financial analysis, data entry, library science, scientist, counsellor, computer technician, programming, teacher, executive, nurse, sales forecasting, project management, recruitment. etc. Hard skills are academic degrees, pertinent licenses, certifications, etc. Naturally, there will always be a need for hard skills in the job. But you will find that an employer will generally list hard skills in a job description, why? Because when hiring a man, certain job requirements must be described a list a particular skill needed as to grab the attention of interested candidate. It does not mean that they don't need soft skills. Employer may list soft skill requirements description to attract certain candidates and narrow the search. Bear in mind that your soft skills are as equally important at workplace. No doubt, your hard skills may. Some of the job opportunities may required that an individual possess soft skills as problem-solving, analytical thinking, communication skills, leadership skill, influencing people, team-building, etc., keep in mind that recruiters look for certain keywords when receiving resumes for positions. Unless you have these skills listed your resume will not catch their attention. Overall your hard skills will help land you an interview with potential employer and your soft skills will help you advance in the company if hired. Factor like qualification, education, technical skills, training, opportunities and luck breaks certainly contribute to one's success. But they are not enough. Success whether, at individual or group level at workplace or home is much more than achievement of an objective. To be able to enjoy success it is important to have the proximity of satisfied, happy and cooperative people. The question arises how? The answer is acquisition and learning of soft skills. Moreover, whenever and wherever we work, world does not operate in ideal conditions. There will be always situation where classroom theory is at best left behind. It is in such situation soft skills help people to go ahead. It is also said that knowledge skill can give you break, but it is social, soft skill that enhances your smooth sailing through that break. Research findings have amply proved that the higher you rise in the rank, soft skills are the most important to your success, because technicarl/hard skills alone are not sufficient when it comes to progressing up the ladder. Soft skills like leadership, decision-making, conflict resolution, negotiation, etc. Skills are essential for entrepreneurial success and for maximizing humk resources in any organisation. When balanced with a good management team and an effective management system, soft skills provide a way to the highest return on the investment in terms of human resources. While professional/hard/technical skills may open the door of opportunity, soft skills keep you in the driver's seat.

There is a general recognition of the important of "soft skills" in improving the productivity of the workforce; but there is still quite a degree of a ambiguity in dealing their boundaries. In general, soft skills were seen as people-oriented skills and self-management skills. The following four competence type frameworks develop by Bunk (1994) was found to be valuable for understanding the range of competencies and skills required in the world of work.

Specified Competence	Methodological Competence	Social Competence	Participatory Competence
Delivers **CONTITUITY** Knowledge, Skills and Abilities	Delivers **FLEXIBILITY** Procedures	Delivers **SOCIABILITY** Modes of Behaviour	Delivers **PARTICIPATION** Structuring Methods
Occupation Specific • External, vertical and horizontal knowledge about the occupation Enterprise specific Experience Specific	Variable Working Methods • Situated solutions • Problem-solving solution • Independent thinking and working • Planning, assessing and executing work • Adaptability	Individuals Social Skills: • Willingness to achieve flexibility and adaptability • Willingness to work • Inter-personal Skills: • Willingness to cooperate • Honesty • Fairness • Willingness to help • Team spirit	• Coordination skills • Organisational skills • Combination skills • Persuasion skills • Decision-making skills • The ability to assume responsibility • Leadership skills

While specilised skills/competence relates mainly to technical skills the other three relate to behavioural or soft skills and are mainly inter- and inter-personal skills. Methodical competence/skills delivers flexibility, e.g., problem-solving, adaptability and analytical techniques. Social and participatory competence are seen on the cornerstones for teamworking, focusing on communication and intetr-personal skills along side leadership and decision-making abilities. Taking into account the Bunk's this framework, for soft skills definition is the inter-personal and intra-personal skills required to be effective in the workplace. This encompasses the following:

"Soft skills" are the inter-personal and intra-personal skills required to be effective in the workplace.

Inter-prsonal skills include – ability to work in a team, communication, influencing skills, leadership and coaching, mentoring skills.

Intra-personal skills include – self-management, orientation to learning, creating, innovation, flexibility, motivation, problem-solving etc.

Today, high perfo~ance practices become organisational norm. The workforce requires the necessary education and training foundation to contribute effectively. With work structure changing, traditional command and control methods are being replaced by flatter, horizontal, structure, teams are being empowered to make decisions; employees required higher skill levels and there is greater partnership between employees and management. Many thinkers describe this transformation in the workplace not only in terms of new organisational structure but also describe the necessary skills required of employees. Therefore, soft skills are becoming increasingly important, both to cope with the level of change and to work with a more participatory management style. The ability to work in a team, get along with the people to communicate effectively and to cope with conflict and work pressure are essential skills in the modem workplace. In an increasingly global, technological economy, it is not enough to be academically strong, people must also be able to work comfortable and cooperatively with people from different cultures, solve problem creatively, think in multi-disciplinary way. The soft skills set are the ticket to economic upward mobility in the new economy.

To conclude some people are good at doing a particular task while others, no matter how hard they are never able to perform it as well. It is because both skills and abilities affect an individual performance. Their acquisition, application and development demands individual attention. Learning skills help to assess' skill level and to identify areas where improvement can be made. Learning skills needed for effective performance future can help to distinguish between the known and unknown, so reducing uncertainty. The process of learning skills provides the opportunity to demonstrate the skills of managing uncertainty and dealing constructively with ambiguity at workplace.

If we accept the fact then human skill development is important. One may ask what kind of expertise an individual need to be effective in his ability to have an impact on the behaviour of other people. We feel an individual, irrespective of his role play, needs three level of skills or expertise.

THREE LEVELS OF SKILLS

- **Understanding past behaviour** – Why people behave as they do. If you are going to get things done through people, you have to know why other people engage in behaviour that is characteristic of them. So understanding past behaviour is the first area you need to examine. What motivate people? What produces the pattern of behaviour that is characteristic of individuals or groups? We say a person is schizophrenic or is paranoid or is a taskmaster and so on. All these classification for communicating to others why individual or group is behaving in certain ways. This obviously needs understanding of past behaviour.
- **Predicting future behaviour** – Although understanding past behaviour is important for developing effective human skills, it is not enough by itself. If you are supervising other people, it is essential that you understand why they did what they did yesterday, but perhaps even more important is being able to predict how they are going to behave today, tomorrow and so on. Under similar or as well as changing environmental conditions. Therefore, the second level of expertise or skill you need in predicting future behaviour.
- **Directing, changing and controlling behaviour** – If you are going to be effective in your role, you need to do more than just understand and predict behaviour. You need to develop skills in directing, changing and controlling behaviour. You must also accept the responsibility for influencing the behaviour of others in accomplishing tasks and reaching goals.

These skills determine whether your (leadership) attempts will be successful or unsuccessful, effective or ineffective. Understanding what motivates people; predicting how they will behave in response to your leadership attempts and directing their behaviour are all necessary skills for effective leadership. Understanding and predicting may not require actions involving other people as these two skills are passive in nature. But the key to obtaining results in directing, changing and controlling the efforts of people in the achievement of institutional goals are important. That is where you as a leader translate thoughts, intentions and actions into end results.

Please remember a hammer won't always do all the job. For every job there is an appropriate tool. Hammer is great in pounding nails. To build effectively you need a variety of tools or skills and the knowledge of what they are designed to accomplish. It is unrealistic to think that single skill is all that is needed to manage effectively. Many social or soft skills have been developed over the years and you should know what to expect from them. You need to understand and be able to use different skills when learning and managing people. Psychologist defines learning as a change in behaviour – being able to do something different from what you were able to do before. When you actually want to learn something, you have to try on or practice, that which you want to learn to make it part of your relevant behaviour. If you practice 'These skills', the more you attempt to get relevant feedback, the more you can predict that the probability of success will increase.

Finally, people are difficult to predict. All that these skills (narrated in this book) can give you ways to increase your behavioural batting average. In other words skills are part of behavioural sciences are probability sciences, there are not any principles of management. Through this book, we will attempt to help you better understand the different skills. We believe that these social, soft skills or tools of social technology will assist you, in variety of situations to sharpen you diagnostic capacity to develop appropriate change strategies while dealing with variety of people. No one person can manage all systems, administrative, economical, technological, decision-making, informational and social systems and sub-systems alone. It takes several to perform the process adequately several people perform roles which seem to be in conflict but really are complementary. There should be some individuals who possesses the entrepreneurial and integrating qualities and skills which can guide a unified organization to new directions. There should be administrators who can translate these new actions into operative systems which should produce results. And there should be performers who can put the systems into action and set an example for efficient operations. Hence, social skills are called ingredients for effective human systems in the organization. Your overall effectiveness depends upon understanding, predicting influencing and controlling the behaviours of other people at workplace.

PEOPLE AT WORK

Today, attitudes, knowledge, experience and social skills have also been influenced by technology. The mass media have shaped our values, beliefs and attitudes and influenced social norms about the ways individuals should act and interact with each other and with the organization. Individual who spend the days interacting with computers, video, television screen sometimes fail to develop the social skills needed effectively with others. Television and the internet have made information and learning resources widely available to the people, but the virtual experience of television and World Wide Web is usually a poor substitute for the personal experience of witnessing or participating in an activity or event. Clearly technology is a two-edged sword. While it provides the means to leverage and extend the capabilities of human in a variety of ways, it can also undermine and devalue knowledge and experience and erode values, beliefs and social skills. The key for leader seeking to leverage their people's skill is to understand the potential and the limitations of technology and to clearly define the objectives and expectations before social changes are made in the organization.

Each individual brings to the workplace a rich and varied collection of skills and capabilities ranging from knowledge gained through formal education to everyday workplace experiences. In describing the individual as a bundle of resources and capabilities, we have narrated variety of skills with their key attributes, each embodied in and inseparable from individuals. Although, it is sometimes useful to consider these skills separately, in fact these skills are tightly woven and highly inter-dependent. Not all of these skills, abilities and capabilities are of equal importance in work environment and the relative importance of each depends, to a considerable extent, on the nature and requirements of the task to be accomplished. Nor can they all be managed or developed in the same manner.

Some are more often task-specific. These can be usually enhanced and redirected through education training and practice. The other tend to reflect more general characteristics, developed over long periods of time both in the workplace and in other settings. These skills broadly influence the person's judgement, decision-making skills, attitude and social behaviour, regardless of the specific requirements of the job. It must be kept in mind that the opportunities for leveraging skills and the approaches that will be most effective, depend on which sets of individual skills and capabilities the organization or leader seeks to address.

NATURE OF TODAY'S WORKPLACE

The instability in workplace and enormous competitive demands on businesses large or small will result in extraordinary pressure for maximum performance. A cult of performance excellence will engulf most businesses. The new and expanded role for employees will exert enormous pressures on employees and companies alike to invest in continuous learning to create a more flexible workplace, and provide employees with the skills necessary to take advantage of rapidly changing technology and prepare employees for new jobs inside and outside. Organizations and employees will have to seek out training opportunities to supplement their existing skills and to learn new skills.

Much more than basic literacy and functional literacy people will need to know how to solve problems, think creatively, influence people and work effectively in teams. Employee development, setting specific goals for training and development and education will become an important part of the performance process. Each employee can expect to have one or more objectives for improving existing skills or developing new skills of values to the workplace. Why education or learning of new skills are so important now? Obviously, one of the reasons is the change in workplace practices. Particularly, the move to turnover more operational and problem-solving responsibilities to employees.

Such changes are not driven by desire. In fact, these changes have been driven by competitive necessity. Given that we have to ask employees to take on more responsibility and if employees do not come to their jobs with the necessary education or skill to perform jobs at workplace, they will have to be educated by employer.

Toady in Developed Nation's, Big Business and Industrial Corporations are masters not of land and material resources, but of ideas and technologies and therefore, it is said that today wealth comes not to the rules of slave labour but to the liberators of human creativity, not to the conquerors of land but to the emancipators of mind. For most of the twentieth century the primary tools for the creation of wealth were physical: land, natural resources, human labour and machines. The worth of company was determined by its measures of tangible resources. In recent years, the companies are built on the foundation of intellectual capital with little tangible investment (i.e., information technology and service industries). Today, the most valuable commodity is knowledge and pulsating flow of ideas exchanging, interacting and expanding. To participate in the game, all will have to possess the requisite skills. In one of the research studies, carried out by American Society of Training and Development (ASTD) researchers assumed that most employers would list primarily technical skills, but they said it proved to be wrong assumption. What employers wanted and said that "They needed most desperately were workers with a solid basic education plus relationship skills, skills in self-management, learning to learn, competence (reading, writing, computation), communication, personal management, adaptability, group effectiveness and influence".

Many new work experiments are carried out at workplace to boost productivity, efficiency, cost-cutting, quality management, inter-personal relations, customer-service, etc. Employees constantly have to learn new skills and or refresh their skills when they are asked to perform a job. The demands for training and retraining in such environment are enormous. We need to encourage individuals as well as organization to develop more such applications, to those people who wish to acquire the skills necessary for them to play successful role in the workplace.

Hence, slogan for tomorrow may be "hire for attitude, train for skills". This essentially emphasis the employee's general knowledge, experience, social skills, values, beliefs and attitudes the individual attributes to be necessary to demonstrate at workplace.

It is not enough to hire superior talent and expect the skills and capabilities of these employees to remain current and competitive throughout the duration of their employment. Technology changes so fast that we estimate 20% of employee's knowledge become obsolete every year. Training in requisite skills is an obligation. The return of training may be hard to calculate, but most experts believe it is real and essential. If you want to have high growth and high quality, then training is a big part of the equation. In every organization human resources plays a big role. The involvement of people is frequently most critical at the points of exchange, decision, flexibility. Hence, the critical role play of human resources must be understood thoroughly: If information exchange is required, does the individual have ready excess to what he needs? If a decision is required, does the individual have the skills, experience, information and guidance he needs to make choices quickly? If flexibility is required, does the individual understand the options available and the consequences of each and have appropriate guidance with regard to organizational policy and preferred practice? The requirement of each situation should be evaluated in terms of the skills and capabilities of the employees. What individual skills and capabilities are brought to bear in the situation? Which are more important? Do employees have the right mix of skills to function most effectively in the situation? Can individual skills be developed or strengthened through education and training? Does the organization need to look for a different mix of skills in its selection and recruitment processes? The sequence of questions outlined above will identify and prioritize a list of potential skills for improving performance by more effectively employing understanding and practicing different skills at workplace required by employees.

SOCIAL SKILLS AT A GLANCE

Interacting with environment, managing the job, developing the team or organization, working with people, influencing others and knowing self are the skills mostly required at workplace. The process of defining skills as outlined in this book provides an opportunity to demonstrate the skill management necessity and dealing constructively with ambiguity, if any. If you do not know where you are going, how are you going to get there? and how will you know when you have arrived? Skills narrated in this book will guide you the right road map, with desired milestones of skill destination.

- **Assertive skills** – Real assertiveness does not happen overnight. Assertiveness is the ability to express yourself and your right without violating the right of others. It is appropriately direct, open and honest communication which is self-enhancing and expressive.
- **The influencing skills** – It entails handling emotions effectively in other people. These people are skilful at sending emotional signals, which makes them powerful communicators, able to sway an audience. People with this skill are skilled at winning people, wield effective tactics for persuasion. Fine tune presentations to appeal to the listeners.
- **Team-building skills** – The ability to make everyone on a team love what they are doing together is at the heart of team-building and team-leadership. People with these skills draw all members into active and enthusiastic participation. Build into active and enthusiastic participation. Build team identity and protect the team and its reputation.
- **Presentation skills** – Your ability to speak well. You may have a terrific idea but who will know if you can't articulate it.
- **Persuasion skills** – Your persuasive talent at motivating others to follow your idea. No idea, however great, ever gets anywhere until it is adopted.
- **Counselling skills** – To counsel means to help, to advice. It is an ability to give and receive feedback and help better understanding of the problems, aspirations, style of work, etc., an opportunity to share ones own problems and issues and offer structure and reassurance to help an individual achieve to the objectives.
- **Listening skills** – Listening does not just meaning shutting up while someone else speaks – though that is a start. But listening – real listening – takes more work than that. It is more than the physical process of hearing. It also takes intellectual and emotional efforts.

- **Transactional skills** – It is one of the human skill may help us judge people's behaviour at workplace. It is a way of understanding behaviour. It is a system of feeling accompanied by a related set of behaviour patterns, in child, adult and parent ego state. Although we cannot directly observe these ego states, we can observe behaviour and from this infer which of the three ego state is operating at particular moment.
- **Time management skills** – Self-management is the bricks and mortar for the strong foundation of time management. Self-management really makes a difference in human interaction and relationship and is naturally flow from a truly independent character. So time management is actually self-management. The secret of managing your time is to work not harder but smarter. Hence, the only solution is to manage it sensibly.
- **Teamwork skills** – Putting people together gives people opportunities to develop, to overcome weaknesses in thinking and increase their competence as individual through working within team. There is no substitute for human beings making a mutual commitment to try to work together more effectively.
- **Coaching skills** – The greatest coach is those who know how to motivate others to succeed, stay focused, believe in themselves and overcome disappointment. Coach inspire others to aim higher, work harder and enjoying doing it. Your role as coach will help you to take your people from where they are (limited) to where they have never been before (unlimited).
- **Team-leader's skills** – It is easy to get players. Getting them to play together that is the hardest part. The leader must be clear on the skills required for his successful role. He must learn how to lead and build team to maximize team-work. To work together and to put teams plan into action requires specific skills in the leader.
- **Johari window** – Johari window is used to depict personality and behaviour. According to this framework of johari window, there are some attitudes or behaviours engaged by people that they themselves know about. This is called known-to-self areas and unknown to self, known to others and unknown to others. These are the situations occur in every organization where people interact and develop relationship with each other and accordingly form their behaviour patterns and set it for practice with different people.
- **Communication skills** – Refers to the individual's ability to listen to, communicate, and share information and ideas with others. For centuries technology has been at work to leverage and extend our ability to communicate, printing press, telephone, cellphone, TV, internet have all extended the scope and reach of our ability to share and communicate our ideas with others. However, these technological advances have had little impact on our willingness or ability to listen attentively to others.

So, to repeat it is not a single ingredient that makes a person skilful. The real skilful person has multiple skills, behaviour and attitudes that are, to some extent, dependent on one another. Skills or knowledge is not based on IQ, genetic, social position, wealth, or luck. Instead it can be learned. In this book, you will learn to maximize each element of your skill. For cultivating within yourself the qualities that will make you standout and make others take notice. You can choose to practice, absorb, and master these beavioural skills. Anyone is capable of doing so. You need not remain who you are. You can greatly improve your personal profile and be all you have always wanted to be: assured, commanding, stimulating and energetic. You can be a catalyst, not one of the cattle.

This book is an attempt to offer a set of requisites skills, studied, collected and complied through research, experience and training undertaken by the author. Following potential skills, it is hoped will help individuals to fine tune, wield effective tactics for persuasion and presentation of self at workplace and also will help organization to educate their employees in specific areas of skill.

CHAPTER

2

Changing Workplace Basics

FOR ORGANIZATIONS

Every civilization has its own ideology – a kit of powerful culture, assumptions that structures its view of reality and justifies its operations. "Pay-me-well", "Treat-me-well" and "Use-me-well" organizational culture assumptions of human resources has its standing of that time ideologies and they justified their management of people relevant to that time. The scientific management, has focused upon the basic physical activities involved in production and is typified by time and method study, while human relations movement, is more concerned with the grand organizational problems. Contemporary development in management and organizational theory draws more on the behavioural sciences. Its approach draws more on emotional intelligence, social intelligence and social ecology of the organization. In this new economy, far reaching business changes have been experienced, where knowledge is considered most vital. So people are crucial to every work operation. All corporate strengths are dependent on people. The organization is built on an effective business philosophy, vision and mission not merely on organizational systems. It is believed that it is only human resources take the organization at desired competence. It encourages people to learn to produce the result they desire and nurture creative and innovative patterns of collective sharing and learning. This ever-learning, ever-evolving, ever-innovative, ever-competitive organization of tomorrow will wrest advantages by marrying the development of every single employee to organizational performance by creating and implementing the new people management. Creating new people management means recruiting people with appropriate knowledge, skills; creating a corporate culture for individual excellence and providing training and developing their assigned roles by appraising and rewarding them for meeting corporate goals.

Organization succeeds largely because its culture offers employee a stable social setting in which they get hearing and draws support to cope with and build the other social relations in their lives. Tradition, climate and values that set a pattern of activities, opinions, and actions instill their pattern in their employees by their examples and pass it down to succeeding generation employees. With this base of values, management begins to look carefully at its approaches to managing people. Company culture is a total of the inherited ideas, beliefs, values and knowledge which constitute the standard that shared bases of social action. These sets of share values affect organizational behaviour at work. Organizational culture thus plays a critical role in socializing its employees in the social systems of the organization. Therefore, organization brings not mere changes in how people be managed but also bring changes in their attitudes, learning, skill development and personality traits.

Learning begins when an employee makes the kind of contact with people and things. This kind of contacts with people within the organization, start with Back-to-Basics approach. Their process of learning starts from observation to problem-solving, involves a set of activities, which is termed as 'learning cycle'. What has been learned then must be incorporated into work activities at workplace behaviour, attitude, opinion values. This gradually represents collective culture and attitude; termed as organizational behaviour. Engaged in knowledge, skill and self-development – as an individual and as an organization we are transforming not only learning environment, but also our organization. Collective learning involves both anticipation and participation. Through 'anticipation', individuals or organization consider trends of learning and make plans. Through 'anticipatory learning' the future may enter into our worklife as a friend. 'Participation' involves more than the formal sharing of decisions; it is an attitude characterized by cooperation, dialogue and empathy. Without participation, anticipation becomes futile; and participation without anticipation can be misguided. Anticipation encourages solidarity in time, participation creates solidarity in workplace. The informed organization is a learning institute and one of its principal purposes is the expansion of knowledge, skill, core competencies not for it but for those employees working with the organization. Knowledge has now become the real capital of the developing economy. Such collective learning must start with a question, a problem to be solved, a challenge to be met collectively. Ideas or theories can never be enough; they have to be tested in reality. The wheel of learning cannot be left to chance or to CEO relaxing in a reclining armchair.

Why these changes occurring in the workplace? Because they have to occur. Faced with the Liberalization, Privatization and Globalization (LPG) it become evident that customer demands better quality, service, product and innovations at workplace by employees. Business leaders have to run their companies in a global boundaries marketplace. As a result, increasingly, the focus is turning to the contribution of people as the ultimate key to the success of an enterprise. With this focus, changes in corporate philosophy, policies and practices are aiming at enhancing the ability of employees to perform, participate and share in the operation. The new style of motivating people has replaced the old style of carrot and stick approach to motivation. Today's organizations are guiding their manager's new styles of motivating employees. Those are like: Empower people through involvement. Assume that employees can and will do extraordinary things of organizational barriers to performance are removed. Be frank and open about the company's business strategies and direction and make sure everyone understands company is trying to accomplish. Trust employees to do the right things. Assume that given enough and right information and self-control, employee will act in the best interest of the company and presumably in their own best interest. Create a unique culture and indoctrinate employee from the start of that culture. Make sure everyone knows how to behave consistent with the company's cultural norms. If someone does not in concert with the values, express your disappointment and encourage him to change or leave. The results of such organizational atmosphere, where employees are cared, challenged, urged and expected to be creative, to think individually, and to take risks to make significant contributions. For the demands of new workplace, this like organization is right fit. On the other hand, new workplace will demand more from every employee more than before. It will also give more responsibility, autonomy, self-control to employees. Obviously, in such changing values of new workplace, individual will have to redefine his personal management for self-development to match the organizational requirements.

It is therefore, management's challenge is to structure, link and blend human and other organizational resources into unique capabilities that maximize individual productivity and organizational performance.

FOR INDIVIDUALS

If we wanted to change the situation, we first have to change ourselves. And to change ourselves effectively, we have to change our perception, assumption about things or persons. We have to rechange our personality and character ethics in a positive way. The character ethics taught us basic principles of effective living and we can only experience truc success and enduring happiness as we learn and integrate these principles into our basic character. Personality ethics have two paths: one of human and public relationships techniques and other is positive mental attitude. Your attitude will determine your altitude. Smiling wins more friends than frowning. Success becomes more a function of personality of public image, attitudes, behaviour, skills that lubricate the process of human interaction. Into the hands of every individual has given a marvelous power for good or evil – the silent, unconscious, unseen influence of his life. This is simply the constant radiation of what man really is, not what he pretends to be. We all know that map is not the territory. It is simply an explanation of certain aspects of the territory. Each of us has many maps in our heads which are divided into two categories: map of the way things are, or realities and map of the way things should be. We interpret everything we experience. We simply assume that the way we see things in the way they really are and our attitudes and behaviours grow out of these assumptions. These assumptions are called our perceptions. Though you see the same object, your perceptions are different than me; you look it in a different angle than me.

Same is the case with our understanding of people at workplace. Different things we see differently as per our perceptions. When with all differences we work together to manage our human resources to get desired result or sometimes get bad results. To reach an agreement on such matters deal with win-win situations and solutions. Enhance your trust in others to build up strong relationships. Relationship is like bank account. We make deposit in bank to build up reserve from which we can make withdrawal when we need it. If withdrawals are overdrawn, the bank cautions us to take care of our reserve and advised us "You can't withdraw unless you deposit further". An emotional bank account is a metaphor that describes the amount of trust that is build up in a relationship. If you make deposits into an emotional bank account with others through courtesy, kindness, honesty and commitment, you will build up a reserve of positive human relations at work. You will feel safe with other human beings in the organization. This is what true personal management is.

Getting hired and surviving in the new workplace will require more and different skills from employees than ever before. No longer will it be sufficient to be good in a narrowly defined technical speciality. No longer will the path to advancement be assumed by carrying favour with influential bosses. The new workplace will be more democratic. Key to success will be acceptance by one's peer. And to gain such acceptance, employees will have to demonstrate their various social skills like leadership, team-building, problem-solving and communication skills etc. The most important thing in a new workplace, employee will have to bring to, his solid basic education and the willingness and ability to keep learning new skills.

Skill at work whether social, soft, personal skills are called social skills, people skills or human skills. Many a times these are used interchangeably denoting the same meaning. To avoid confusion; I termed them all as social skills. It is surveyed that 80% of the man management problems are related due to lack of social skills at work. Inter-personal relations, group relations, departmental relations, superior-subordinate relations, leaders-followers relations and lastly manager-managed relations are related to social skills demonstrated at workplace. And only 20% problems are related to technical skills or other databased techniques used at workplace. Social skills, the foundation skills can consistently make or break improvements. Over the years, it is found that social skills are best built on a foundation of these basic principles:

- Focus on the work process, issues and behaviour, not on person.
- Maintain the self-confidence and self-esteem of others.
- Maintain strong partnerships with your internal and external customers and suppliers.
- Take initiative to improve work processes, partnership and related process skills.
- Lead by example.

Skill acquisition, application and developments are more than just knowing what skills looks like. Skills are developed primarily through practice and feedback. These skills are fundamental to all categories of people and more critical to supervisory and managerial levels. Putting an untrained person on the job to work with trained persons shall be unreceptive, unsupportive or inconsistent to the environment, shall waste everyone's time. Even worse, it may demotivate and frustrate individuals in the group. Therefore skill development is necessary. Personal skills like ability to communicate effectively, planning, negotiating, conflict resolution, building relationships etc. are skills must be possessed by an individuals before entering into work situation. Understanding of these and such skills is grounded on these **Basic Principles:**

- **Work efficiently:** Use all available resources to get the job done. Know the expected results of each new task, assemble necessary materials before starting a task, accept change and help new procedure work smoothly.
- **Communicate clearly:** Help others especially the quiet ones speak up, provide facts and ideas, help keep meeting focused on the topic and purpose, ask others for their reaction to the information given.
- **Provide positive mutual support:** Let others know when they have done good job, make people feel good about their work, show interest in the ideas and opinions of others, share ideas with others.
- **Seek and accept help when needed:** Ask for help as soon as he or she need it, allow others to help get the job done better, keep others informed of what is going on, let others know about problems and conflicts early.
- **Constructively channel emotions:** Keep control of own anger and disappointment, avoid letting own emotion get in the way of teaching results on the job, deal with negative situations in a positive way.

These are some of the basic principles of skills required for personal management and self-developments. What are the key social skills for self-development at workplace, we have incorporated in the succeeding chapters of this book.

KNOWLEDGE, KNOWLEDGE WORKER AND "KNOWLEDGED WORKS"

Human Resources: From Past to Present:

Hamel and Prahalad in their book "**The Core Competence of the Corporation**" described that "The machine age was a physical world. It consists of things. Companies made and distributed things (physical products), management allocated things (capital budget), management measured things (the balance sheet), management invested in things (plant and equipment). In machine, age, people were ancillary, things were central. In information age, things are ancillary, knowledge in central. A company's value derives not from things, but from knowledge, know-how, intellectual assets, competencies – all of it embodied in people." New ideas and new approaches are also changing the world of work. It is no longer business is just a game of market power, financial muscle, economies of scales. Now the locus of wealth creation has shifted from capital intensive industries to information, service industries. Moreover, the powerful sources of growth and wealth creation are found in innovation, quality-driven industries where the key to competitive advantage rely on the effective management of human resources.

Peter Drucker concludes that "Future economic growth can no longer be based on expanding the workforce or increasing consumer demand. Rather, it can come only from a very sharp and continuing increase in the productivity of the one resource in which the developed countries still has a competitive edge: knowledge work and knowledge workers." Change does not happen at once. It takes time for new ideas and new approaches to diffuse through industry or a society and reach a critical mass, but once the advantage become apparent, the older order topples and is swiftly replaced by the new. The new economies of the world become closely inter-wined and the effect of technology become felt in the every corner of the world, the rules of the game will be for ever changed. Traditional approaches simply don't apply.

KNOWLEDGE

First of all, as an economic asset, knowledge is a unique kind of resource, is that it is not consumed in use but grows more valuable and more productive as it is shared and reused.

Second, knowledge comes in different forms: "Explicit knowledge" – knowledge can be articulated in formal language including mathematical expression, specification manuals, etc. "Tacit knowledge" – is embodied in individual experience and involves such factors as personal beliefs, perspective and values. Explicit knowledge can be easily replicated and widely distributed. But tacit knowledge is personal, shared only with the consent and participation of individual who possess it.

Third, knowledge has number of distinct characteristics and social and political connotations that influence and often inhibit its creation, sharing and distribution with organization. New knowledge is continually being created through complex processes of social interaction that links the tacit knowledge embodied in individuals and the explicit knowledge resources that the organization possesses.

Creation of knowledge and how it is applied, shared and preserved for future use has significant implication for organizational effectiveness. Organizational knowledge and information resources contain three broad categories: **Intellectual property** – documentation, legal protected information, i.e., patents, trademarks and proprietary processes. **Explicit knowledge** – technical and financial data, engineering drawing, libraries, sales cataloguger, customer lists, advertising copies and so on stored in files, databases and other forms. Finally, **management process** and industry know-how is embodied in organizational routines, policies, procedures and practices, operational manual, etc. Other resources are physical and financial resources and structural resources. Thus, sustainable competitive advantage depends on interactions and inter-dependence among these resources. Management challenge is to structure, link and blend human and other organizational resources into unique capabilities that maximize individual productivity and organizational performance. The objective of these resources blending must necessarily be the ongoing development and leveraging of the knowledge, skills and know-how of organization's human resources. A growing number of management researchers have come to view the organization as a collection of resources and capabilities. It is useful to extend this perspective to the individual level and consider separate elements that contribute to the unique capabilities, knowledge, skill and experience of the individual employee. There are about eight categories or elements of human resources; motor or technical skills, information gathering skills, information processing skills, communication skills, experience, knowledge, social skills, value, beliefs and attitudes. These elements are highly inter-dependent. Secondly, individuals relate to organizations as employee, team-members, manager, and shareholders. The relationship of an individual to his assigned responsibilities may vary from individual to individual likewise their skills application varies, depending on how individual skills and capabilities are matching with the requirements of the task. The linkage between various skills and various responsibilities carrying individuals and performing at workplace, collectively make up one or more of the larger, organizational processes. To the extent that different kinds of knowledge, skills, experience can be shared and considerable synergies may often be realized through collaborative efforts. This creates significant and sustainable advantage for the company. Today's economy is increasingly driven by knowledge, the returns to the effective management of human and intellectual capital will be greater than those available from the more efficient of management of physical and financial asset. Human resources and their knowledge are going beyond productivity to create winning strategies.

"KNOWLEDGED WORKS".

It is therefore, imperative that the organizations ability to access and leverage the skills and capabilities of its employees by encouraging individuals and organizational learning and facilitating the sharing and application of their collective knowledge, expertise and skill must also be developed and strengthened. We must develop new way to help business, focusing on building not just our financial capital, but our human resources. Organization must also focus on developing a culture, commitment creating an infrastructure that supports and reinforces individual's capabilities and collaborative efforts. The three components of organization architecture: hardware organization's structure and its formal processes; the people-their skills, personality and character; and the software – the informal network and practices linking people together and help them to work effectively.

KNOWLEDGE WORKER

Human resource is generally understood to consist of the individual's capabilities, skills, knowledge and experience of company's employees, as they are relevant to the tasks at hand, as well as the capacity to add to this reservoir of knowledge, skills and experience through individual learning. Since our definition of human resources focused primarily on capabilities, skills, knowledge and experience all of them embodied in and inseparable from the individual. And in order to address the opportunities for effective leverages of an organization's human resources, it is important to understand those skills and capabilities fully. It is useful to extend this perspective to the individual level and consider the elements of skills that contribute to the unique capabilities, knowledge of individual employee. In our book we have identified 28 skills, generally required of human resources. Each individual brings to the workplace a rich and varied collections of skills and capabilities ranging from knowledge gained through formal education to everyday personal experience. In many cases an individual's ability to perform task's skill can be improved or redirected through education, training and practice. An individual's values, beliefs and attitudes, knowledge, experience and social skills are usually less task specific, deeply embedded and more difficult to change through education, training and practice. The opportunities for leverage and the approaches that will be most effective will depend, to a considerable extent, on which skills and capabilities are to be addressed. Task performance depends, to a considerable extent, on how well individual skills and capabilities are matched with the requirement of the task. If requirements exceed the skills, performance will fall short and the organization will suffer a loss of effectiveness. If the individual's skill exceeds the task requirements, task performance may be satisfactory, but the utilization of organization's human resources will be inefficient. Values, attitudes and commitment to the task and the organization are also critically important. Hence, in such changing work environment manager must learn how to retain people. Their tasks and other work processes that leverage the individual and collective skills and capabilities of the workforce in ways that create significant and sustainable competitive advantages for the company. At individual level, opportunities must be recaptured by the manager to leverage human resources by complementing individual employee skills and capabilities with complementary resources by designing tasks to make the best use of employee's skills, matching employee skills to the requirements of the job, multiplying and extending individual capabilities and skills through effective application of technology, enhancing individual knowledge, skills and capabilities by encouraging and facilitating individual learning and providing opportunities for training, skill development and practice.

The management of knowledge and knowledge worker demands knowledged works (organization). People have always been important to organizations through ages. But today along with task specific skills and knowledge it is critical to have knowledge of social skills. In order to complete in business, today's organization must have employees with right skills and capabilities and the right kinds of values and attitudes. Their skills and attitudes must be continually developed, strengthened and reinforced and each employee motivated and his efforts focused on individual and thereby organizational learning. You don't get a second chance to make a good first impression. This embodies the importance of orienting employees to social skills along with their technical skills. Social skills orientation will help to provide for assessing whether an employee have the attributes that are critical for succeeding in his particular career endeavour. The successful development of human resources requires the active involvement of leaders at all levels of the organization. It can't be successful if it is just viewed as a human resources function. People throughout the organization must become involved in leadership processes and play greater roles in building organizations strategies and tactics. Put in another way, to learn and adapt the organizational needs "eyes, ears and brains" throughout the company. One person (CEO) or a small group of individuals (managers) can no longer think and learn for the entire entity.

Much of the research into motivational factors, old and new, indicates that interesting challenging work and feedback are likely to stimulate an individual and to have positive effects on their inclination to work. Encouraging and helping individuals to develop their skills and capabilities and ensuring that work can be related to the organization's purpose, can help them in relation to the organization's future, defines what is expected from individuals and makes it clear what skill will be required for certain level of achievement.

Hence, it is important not to lose sight of the fact that, while personal growth and development are very important, work-related development has to be the prime consideration for the organization. Most organizations are now facing pressure, either from within or outside to change. The desire for change may exist, but making it real is another matter. Therefore, deliberate actions/ efforts must be taken for the organizational learning. Individual effective learning needs partnership of individual and organization. An individual is unlikely to invest in learning without the support and encouragement of their immediate manager. Continuous and collective learning will become order of the day to create a more flexible workforce. Provide employees with the skills necessary to take advantages of rapidly changing technology, and prepare employees for new jobs inside and outside the company. In the workplace of tomorrow will require much skill from all of us. We can't look to others for our salvation to provide with the skills we require. We must in the final analysis, do it ourselves.

IMPORTANCE OF HUMAN CAPITAL

The way in which organizations employ and treat their employees have been affected not only by the changes to the economy, but also by developments in technology. Increased sophistication and complex technology require brain rather than brawn. The pace of developments and advances in technology and machine applications demand that employees remain up to date; they can't rely on old knowledge and skills to learn new ways of working. In some cases this requires employee to learn new skills, so they come to recognize their increased contribution and value to their organization. They expect different forms of reward, treatment and opportunities. Physical prowess is no longer the marketable commodity, the knowledge; skills, experience acquired and the ability to learn are in demand. These skills once were and will continue to be the talents needed. The contributions of all its employees combine to build up the skill and knowledge base of an organization. This base is as intangible and as valuable as a brand name. As financial and other resources are audited, human skills can be identified so that the total value of the organization's skill bank can be assessed. Knowledge of the organization's total skill bank helps achieve recognition of its own distinctive competence. And maintenance of employee's skills continue to increase and help top potential, that may actually outstrip predicted level of organizational performance.

In this changing business world, harnessing the human capital – the accumulated skills, experience, wisdom and capabilities of all the people employed in the organization is fundamental to success. This may seems obvious after all, why pay for the most expensive resources in terms of results than any other, without using it to the full? However, at a time when skills are more complex and transferable, traditional loyalty is reducing and the significance and value of knowledge is rising, there is a premium and reward focus on managing human capital.

To create real value, organization must better leverage their human capital by helping develop larger numbers of their employees into 'better-educated' employees; who will then able to create more high-value-added products and services at extremely low cost. Many organizations simply by understanding that knowledge equals profits, rather than ignoring the relationships, they are acting on the critical interactions among technology, smarter employees and return on investment (RoI).

They invest extensively in employee retraining programmes and reap the short- and long-term benefits increased productivity. Investing in human capital produces better business returns, it provides cost saving and efficiencies, maximizes the use of available resources and addresses specific performance and productivity issues. To succeed, it can help if:

1. Investment in human capital is measured in cash clearly highlighting the benefits of actions and the peril of inaction;
2. The personal knowledge of employees across the organized action is assessed this gives management benchmark for understanding its human capital strengths and weaknesses;
3. Relevant and appropriate performance development programmes in skills, education and training areas are selected. These should directly linked to productivity and work improvement needs and strategy of the business – what skills are needed to progress towards the desired destination?
4. A human capital measurement system is applied so that the best return on investment is achieved in the short and long-terms.

Unless organizations invest in people to reverse the dangerous trend of discontinuing the value of human capital, both technology and management systems will fail as they become more complex and require more people who can think for themselves and adapt information. By investing in their most critical intangible – human capital, organization will rise to the challenges of technology and globalization and speed up the process of building a knowledge economy in their own communities and across the world.

Acquiring new information, skills, knowledge by employees and trying it out by applying it and reaching personal understanding really motivate people to learn. The social aspect of learning is vital for most people. A relationship needs to exist between a good teacher and learner (organization and its employees).

LEARNING ORGANIZATION AND INDIVIDUAL

When organization learns, employees therein also learn. Employees work within system, which is beyond their control. It is organizational's responsibility to change/improve the system.

Surprisingly, many organizations do not encourage the growth of their employees. This results in vast untapped resources. Employees enter in employment as bright, well educated, high energy people, full of desire to make difference. But the time they turn – thirty years the few are on fast track and rest put in their time to do what matters to them. They lose their commitment, the sense of mission and the excitement when they started their career. Organizations get down little of their energy and almost none of their spirit. This is the general experience of people in the organization. Painful though it may be for employees and organization, it is simply a sign of poor turnover of organization's economy.

Non-learning of new things originates in basic ways of our thinking, interacting and policy-making and its practicing. People when placed together in the same system however they are different in skill, knowledge, attitude, behaviour tend to produce similar result and that becomes the organizational culture. It is therefore, necessary to re-examine our learning disabilities more clearly. A true and different insight in the way you begin to see the system causes its own behaviour.

Many organizations learn poorly and make people there in poor learners. The way they designed, structured and managed, the way people jobs are defined and most importantly the way they have been taught to think and interact with each other, customer-supplier's relations create fundamental learning disabilities. These disabilities operate despite the best efforts of committed people often the harden; they try to solve problems, the worse the result – organizational break down. Despite individual brilliance and innovative products, they are unable to pull their diverse functions and talents into productive whole. It is therefore, essential to re-discover about the collective culture of managers and managed and discover new ideas about how to abandon old ideas and how to tap people's commitment, potential and capacity to learn at every level in the organization.

Perhaps the most salient reason for building learning organization is that to understand the capabilities, abilities and skills of the organization as well as people therein.

Learning does not mean acquiring more information, but expanding the ability to produce the results truly wants in our worklife. Learning organization facilitates the learning of all itself for continuous organizational improvement. Learning organization is a place where people are continually discovering how they create their reality and how they can change it. Learning organization is a place where people continually expand their capacity to create more results they truly desire, where new and expansive patterns of thinking are nurtured, where collective aspiration is set free and people are continually learning how to learn together. Organization learns only through individuals. Without their learning no organizational learning occurs. In many aspect of business, the active force is people; they have their will, their mind and their way of thinking. If they are not sufficiently motivated to challenge the goals of growth, if not, simply there will not be growth, in productivity, quality, customer service and technological development. Tapping the potential of people organization requires new understanding, will-power and action of the heart and sincere desire to serve business world.

Shoshana Zuboff, Associate Professor at Harvard Business School has rightly observed that "Manufacturing activity has its roots in the work of skilled craftman, who may not have been intellectual but was certainly knowledgeable. It was the knowledge that occurs to the sentiments body in the course of its activity; knowledge inscribed in the labouring body in hands, fingertips, wrist, nose, eyes, ear, skin, muscles, shoulders, arms and legs – as surely as it was inscribed in the brain. It was knowledge filled with intimate detail and ambiance – the colour and consistency of metal as it was thrust into blazing fire, the smooth finish of clay as it gave up its moisture few of those who have such knowledge were able to explain, rationalize or articulate it. Such skills were learnt through observation, initiation and action rather than being taught, reflected upon or verbalized."

In other words, learning was immediately reactive, responsive and interactive rather than distantly analytical or conceptual. With the advent of mechanized mass production, in today's automated operational context, such craft based activity is successfully translated into skill-base activity. We therefore find and seeing a long way of getting learns the process of skills through ages. Relationships will need to be fashioned or refashioned as part of the dynamism of social processes, like inquiry and dialogue that mediate learning. Such relationships are more intricate because their character derives from the specifics of the situation that are always both pragmatic – what it takes to get work done best and psychological, what people need to sustain their motivation and commitment.

The caring relationship, then intrinsic to learning. Feeling and action becomes a pre-condition for learning. Need to create learning organization in which self-knowledge, self-realization and the progressive individuation of our organizations become our own hallmark. In such learning organizations, we shall ultimately find, quality will be born out of nothing less than a holographic form of integration between the different learning fields. The informatted, organization is a learning institution and one of its principal purposes is the expansion of knowledge – not knowledge for its own sake, but knowledge that comes to reside at the core of what it means to be productive. Learning is not something that requires time out from being engaged in productive activity; learning is the heart of productive activity; learning is the new form of labour.

As the organization learns, so it develops a feel for its people and product, both inside and outside, by dint of willing exposure. To the extent that it learns across the grain, physical reactions are accompanied by social responses; instead of being lean and mean the organization becomes warm and welcoming, of both people and things. The hard and aggressive qualities, acquired in the active struggle for survival are counterbalanced by soft and receptive qualities, acquired in the process of bonding together, as both a community of people and a craftman's guild. The twenty-first century will become the era of the learning organization. Such a learning organization will need to accommodate thoughts, feelings and actions.

CHAPTER 3

Education, Learning and Skills

"A happy cow gives more milk" is a truism but on reality there is much more takes place for high performance. Gimmicks to boost morale can't solve the problems of performance. It is known that unless learning is equal to or greater the rate of change, an organism will become extinct. The acquisition of skills is a must if we have to stay competitive in this changing world. The acquisition of skills cannot rely on evolution alone. If learning cannot be speeded up, the rate of change shall be slowed down.

Education alone can't make learning process complete. Education may equip you for life by providing foundation knowledge and understanding, but essentially, when you are educated, you are given knowledge of subjects, ideas and concepts and are taught how to use them. Secondly, education is concerned with the transmission and understanding of concepts and ideas. This more usually happens formally in a specially designated place and generally, controlled by a person/teacher who has the agenda and then guides and aids the understanding of a person who is receiving the education. On the other hand learning is different.

Learning can often does take place in actual or simulated work settings. The process tend to be more concerned with doing a job and applying, understanding and knowledge to the performance of specific tasks. Often the desired outcome of learning is the acquisition or improvement of skills. Skills can help manager and managed to understand what is expected of them.

Individuals in the organization play key job roles such as operations, finance, accounts, information, logistics, maintenance, hospitality, people management and so on. They are identified as being functionaries in their particular roles. These roles tend to reflect the approaches used to define with the tasks. The technique use to analyze the outcomes of competent performance does not necessarily explore the skills needed to achieve those outcomes. Alternatively, a conceptual framework of the whole which includes skill can help manager and managed to understand which is expected. Hence, it is more useful to create a conceptual framework (job role) into which the skills can be fitted. Occupational standards such as Key Performance Indicators (KPIs), key Results Areas (KRAs), Job Description (JD), Job Specification (JS), etc., provide them job framework, while working in the organization individual manages his job, interact with environment, work with other employees, know himself and his people and guide, direct, enable, recognize, develop and counsel them applying values, ethics, discipline, prejudices, opinion, using personal power and abilities. All these functional subactivities require specific skills to handle the job situations. And the key to learning skills is the ability to question.

When we are expected to accept the world as given, acquiring or retaining the ability to challenge the presented version of reality and assumptions it contains, is not easy. When dealing with people, the chances of there being only one way to treat, manage or develop them are slim. You need to use different strokes to different folks – strategy, while dealing with your superiors, subordinates, peers and fellow-employees. Once there is a sense of direction and idea of what is to be achieved, it is possible to workout what needs to be done to get there. Understanding one's constructs and behaviour pattern is a critical step in working out what action is most appropriate to deal with the situation. Such challenges in work situations demand upgradation, new skill acquisitions in your skill-kit of attitude, behaviour, opinion, assumption. It is the requirement of modern industrial society. Active learning by both individual and organization is the prerequisites for survival. The pace and degree of individual change put pressure on everyone learn and develop skills. If learning new skills and reacquire given skills fail to occur and an unrealistic set of assumptions, preassumptions are left unchallenged, all managers and managed will be burnt out. It is, therefore, essential for individual to learn new skills or sharpen the existing, for improving desired performance at work.

People in the organization with right 'traits' are crucial if a business hopes to obtain the quality in worklife, product and service and in turn customer satisfaction. The 'traits' (skills) needed in people may vary depending on the nature of business and the job. Hence, training and motivation are essential for helping employees understand their roles. An employee must have relevant background to prepare for the job; only in this manner is there hope of long-term success. Again, how do you measure training effect? You do not measure intangibles, but you will see, you can at least measure the outcomes of performance at work. When management assumes that good workmanship is a reality in the organization, they assess employees varying job needs, requirements and starts need-base training. The key to assessment is to understand what skills you want? Assess it and then act upon for getting the results. Management must decide. What human traits they wish to emphasis and upgrade.

Organization must nurture their employees, teach them how to? and allow them to solve problems, find ways to measure their efforts and provide them skill-based training. Training has become a vital part of our lives, helping each of us grow, professionally and as human beings. It is management responsibility to teach all people the basic understanding of how an organization works. Better informed and trained employees make more productive and committed teams. 'Rule of the game' must be made known to them. The result, each employee contributes to the profit of the company. **Employees are intelligent** and it is management's objective to tap their intelligence to become productive. **Employees have an innate** ability to comprehend and understand the meaning of business. **Employees have an ability** to adopt to new situation and to reason intelligently. Employees can grasp ideas and relations and then exercise dispassionate reasoning. How these traits are groom, upgrade, discover and apply at work situation for positive results is management's obligation.

Our buying of technology and technical skills may make sudden and radical changes in the method of business working. But they will not have fertile yield unless social skills of human resources are recognized, reexamined and rewarded. We must develop our social skills to balance the technical and social moves by effecting purposeful social change in the methods of organizational living. If our social skills that our ability to secure and develop cooperation among various people in the organization has advanced step-by-step with technical skills there will not be any organizational break down. Human resources are the nuts and bolts of social technology which operates at workplace.

Some organizations have a strong sense of appreciation for people. They are people-oriented. They take care of their people because it is their people that must take care of their internal and external customers. All the organizations realize that to get any return on investment, will require commitment not only of management but also commitment of people ther in. Individual and organization 'skills conditioning' is all important and careful planning helps us maintain a sense of mutual perspective, purpose and ordered priorities. Remember that our personal integrity or self-mastery is the basis of our success with others. Positive behaviour, action and attitude reinforce our good intention and resolutions.

Many employees, managers, leaders in position of authority may be competent, skilful and knowledgeable, act in an immature way borrowing strength from the position. By doing so, they build weakness at work. **They build weakness in themselves** – by pressure, coercion and taking external help. **They build weakness in other people** – other learns to act, react in terms of fear. **They build weakness in relationship** – strain relations, a little more defensive in approach. People who have the habit of borrowing strength will eventually lose influence with those they want to impress. To overcome weakness, one must examine implications of personal growth.

1. **Growth is a natural process** – you reap as you sow.
2. **We all are different** – in physical, social, emotional and intellectual areas.
3. **Comparisons are dangerous** – it breeds insecurity obstructs positive thinking.
4. **There is no short-cut** – if I am less intellectual and desire to move high intellectual level, I must go through knowledge increasing process. Pretending result in loss of respect including one's own.

5. **To improve we must start where we are** – not from where we should be or where someone else. It takes more patience, understanding courage to increase capacity through hard efforts and discipline to improve. It can't be quick-fix or made to order formula, such self - introspection gives us an accurate understanding of our weaknesses and the power to overcome them. Learning of new skills and upgradation of existing, show way and set forth the motivating spirit to present, serve better and better day after day.

WHY AND WHICH SKILLS ARE IMPORTANT?

Organization spends considerable energy developing non-human resources – the equipments, tools, processes and methods needed to job done. But not enough efforts have been spent on the resource that drives all other that is people. The emphasis on human skills was considered important in the past, but it is of primary importance today. One of the great entrepreneurs, John-D Rock feller stated "I will pay more for the ability to deal with people than any other ability under the sun." These words of Rock feller are often echoed today. It is therefore rated that ability is more vital than intelligence, education, knowledge and job skills. For influencing others there are three general skills necessary.

Diagnosing – The ability to understand the situation you are trying to influence.

Adopting – The ability to adopt your behaviour and other resources you have available to meet the contingencies, and

Communicating – The ability to communicate in the way that easily understand and accept.

The principle qualification of our achiever is the possession of functional knowledge of his field may it be of engineering, accounting or people management. Being productive and having technical skills do not necessarily enable an individual to produce desired results while working with people. He must have social skills too. Management of people is the management of human beings with their activities, interactions, sentiments, attitudes, aptitudes, behaviour, skills and their knowledge. To keep healthy human relations, congruence and harmony between organizational objectives and individual expectation is of vital importance to manager, because those traits are mutually dependent upon each other to produce desired results.

It is generally agreed that there are at least three skills necessary for carrying out the processes of management; technical, human and conceptual.

(a) **Technical Skills** are the abilities to use knowledge methods, techniques and equipments for the performance of specific tasks acquired from experience, education and training.

(b) **Human Skills** are the abilities and judgement in working with and through people including an understanding of motivation, morale and an application of effective role.

(c) **Conceptual Skills** are the abilities to understand the complexities of the overall organization and where one's own operation fits into the organization. It is not only enough to have a good mind; the main thing is to use it well is also necessary.

"To dull mind all nature is leaden. To the illuminated mind the whole world burns and sparkles with lights." (Ralph Waldo Emerson). Skill craftsmanship is always appreciated at all level and all the time.

Most of the management, manager and managed seem to have a kind of tunnel vision. They understand the jobs, but they never get the big picture and that is risky for business, service, personal and organizational growth.

WHAT ARE THE SKILLS?

- Skills are aspects of human behaviour that are learnt and improved with practice.
- Skills used at work need not be learnt through formal education, as they are individual's personal abilities as applied to participation tasks.
- Skills are learnt through observation, initiation and action rather being taught, reflected upon or verbalized.
- Genetic factors are combined with social conditioning and the experiences gained during persons formative years have a profound effect on personality and establish the foundations of an individual character.
- Skill learning is reactive, responsive and inactive rather than distantly, analytical or conceptual.

The skills are grouped into five broad domains;

- Interacting with the environment.
- Managing the job.
- Developing the organization.
- Working with others, and
- Knowing self.

Why some people are good at doing a particular task while others, no matter how hard they are never able to perform it as well. Public speaking requires skills of delivery and communication and an ability to project oneself with a degree of self-confidence. The former may be learnt and improved with practice, but without the latter the speech will never be really good. Both skills and abilities affect an individual performance, but their acquisition, application and development demands attention. Personal growth is an important element of the development process and of course, personality factors have a major impact on individual performance, therefore influencing personality factors may be a necessary part of helping individual's development.

LEARNING, ACQUISITION, APPLICATION AND DEVELOPMENT OF SKILLS

Skills are of course necessary for people to be able to successfully perform their work. This is a basis for further development of additional capabilities. In addition to the basic skills, people are expected to participate in other job activities such as improving communication, inter-personal, team-building skills. If we look more closely within creative endeavour, it is possible to find certain aspects that are easily identifiable and can be learnt. It is true that the exceptional actor, artist, athlete and designer bring a unique talent that is difficult to emulate but the reality is that the pure talent may compromise only 10% of the total. It is almost solely a question of wanting so very much to do it well. With the possibility of duplicating 90% of any process, it is possible to achieve very good results. You will find that there are consistent, teachable and learnable key points within any skills. Identify them and learn how to communicate them effectively to others and you will be able to develop exceptional skills in you or in your people.

We have gone into some details about Skill, Acquisition, Application and Development (SAAP) so that it does help your quest to learn from this book how to develop your skill to be truly exceptional? People learn gradually overtime, in small chunks, by doing, practicing and being coached and learning small pieces of the skill process step-by-step. With this foundation we are suggesting that many different individuals with different types of skills have lot to learn. From each skill then only they can master the specific skill and/or variety of skills. Before you begin any journey, it is helpful to understand both where you currently and where you intend to go. We begin with a process that is essentially same as that used for problem solving. There are important questions to explore, and then you must develop an understanding of what the journey's end will look like. If you don't do these things, how will you know if you are on the correct path? The chapter – self-learning, with its sub-chapters – skill acquisition, skill application and skill development. We have given you some of the how and whys your skill development. But it is up to you to make self-development in your area of responsibility.

SELF-LEARNING – NATURE AND SCOPE

As you grow and develop, you have chance to evolve and involve in the total learning fields where responsive, experimental learning takes place for the development of your skills and knowledge. Here, most specifically, learning requirements are spelled out for self-development in the context of your role in the organization. The learning field inventory will help you discover what kind of learner you are?

(1) REACTIVE LEARNERS –

He is the action man for whom action and learning are inextricably linked with opportunities to do things. The learning you undergo will require plenty of physical action upon which to base your reflections, and physical landmarks to reflect your progress. Reactive learners are the first off the mark and last to see where they are going? They are:

- They are go-getter but, they leap before they look.
- They make things happen but, they lack patience.
- They get straight to the point but, they are intolerant of ambiguity.
- They cope with crises but, they need crises to stimulate them.

(2) RESPONSIVE LEARNERS –

He is a man for whom people, social groups and learning is inextricably linked. The learning they undergo finally will require a close involvement with people and things from which to draw their learning and with social landmarks to reflect their progress. They are people-oriented people. Responsive learners are attracted by down to earth people and things, and put off by airy-fairy concepts and ideas. They are:

- They are helpful to others but, they are dependent on others.
- They are practical and realistic but, they lack imagination.
- They work well in a group but, they can't stand isolation.
- They create a good atmosphere but, they are oversensitive to feedback.

(3) DELIBERATIVE LEARNERS –

He is emotionally turned on-off person, for whom realism and relevance hold pride of place so that management education and personal development link up. The learning these people undergo will finally need to be both varied and mentally stimulating with ideas generated and changes made being the landmarks to reflect their progress. They are change makers. Deliberative learners are systematic and methodical, on the one hand, but can be pedantic and over cautious on the other. They are:

- They are logical, vertical thinker but, they are unable to think laterally.
- They are rational and objective but, they can't tolerate uncertainly.
- They are good of asking probing but, they are intolerant of feeling.
- They are disciplined in approach but, they are full of should, ought and must.

(4) ENERGIZED LEARNERS –

They are fully committed to improving their own performance but often at the expense of others. The learning they undergo will need to be both personally dramatic and organizationally relevant, with commercial landmarks to reflect their progress. They are enterprising people.

- They take initiative but, they are single track mind.
- They motivate others to learn but, they dominate others.

- They resolve crises but, they are oblivious to feelings.
- They respond to opportunities but, they manipulate people/situation.

(5) EXPERIMENTAL LEARNERS –

They are the bright, spark learner for whom management education must be mentally stimulating. The learning they develop will need to be formally accredited and practically realistic, with both theoretical and applied knowledge forming landmarks for their progress. They are analytical people. They are always willing to have ego, but seldom able to stick with things all the way.

- They are flexible and open minded but, they like change for their own sake.
- They are happy to try something new but, they get bored with implementation.
- They like being exposed to differences but, they provoke unnecessary controversy.
- They optimistically accommodate change but, they lack staying power.

(6) HARMONIZED LEARNERS –

They are deeply reflective persons, for whom management in particular and life as a whole are inextricably interlinked. The learning they undergo will need to be both significant and worthwhile to them and organization with fundamental insights and development forming the landmarks for their progress. They are developmental people. Harmonized learners are good at emotionally and intellectually recognizing potential, but are often less adept at actively harnessing it.

- They develop others but, they fail to exploit potential.
- They recognize potential but, they are woolly thinkers.
- They enhance synergy but, they ignore everyday reality.

(7) THE INSPIRED LEARNERS –

They are highly creative persons, for whom management education and creative action must be the same. The learning they undergo will need to involve original ideas and activities with creative breakthrough constituting the landmarks of their progress. They are innovative people. Inspired learners reach for the sky but might be living in cloud cuckoo land.

- Their approach is innovative but, they are day dreamers.
- They have original ideas but, they pursue originality for self.
- They are able to inspire others but, they can suppress opposition.
- They create potential but, they fail to recognize potential.

You may be one of the above learners. In realizing your social self, you will first seek out a familiar circle to which you belong. Your own development can't be separated from that of particular groups to which you have become attached. You learn by associating yourself with progressively broader-based circle of people you grow by building your own communities. In short, as an individual, you have to go through following seven different paths of self-development available to you, although these paths are not clear-cut but they can serve as useful indicators;

1. The learning you undergo will require plenty of physical action upon which to base your reflections and physical landmarks to reflect your progress. (Path of action)
2. The learning you undergo finally will require a close involvement with people and things from which to draw your learning and with social landmarks to reflect your progress. (The social path)
3. The learning you undergo will finally need to be both varied and mentally stimulating with ideas generated and changes made being the landmarks to reflect your progress. (The path of change)
4. The learning you undergo will need to be both personally dramatic and organizationally relevant, with commercial landmarks to reflect your progress. (The path of enterprise)
5. The learning you develop will need to be formally accredited and practically realistic, with both theorctical and applied knowledge forming the landmarks for your progress. (The path of promotion)
6. The learning you undergo will need to be both significant and worthwhile to you and the organization, with fundamental insights and development forming the landmarks for your progress. (The development path)
7. The learning you undergo will need to involve original ideas and activities, with creative breakthrough constituting the landmarks of your progress. (The creative path)

SELF-DEVELOPMENT AND MATURATION

Youth, when you are in twenties, is a time for experimentation and for daring – whether physical, social, commercial or intellectual in nature. It is the age of enterprise and experimentation.

As you enter young adulthood, you need to become more organized in your activities and relationships. It is at this stage, in your thirties, that your path becomes clearly visible. This is the time for consolidation and organization.

In mid-life, if you are successfully pass through the proverbial crisis you need to tap either to hidden powers within yourself. This requires you to reflect on the wider meaning of life and work. As you open out to yourself and to others in your forties, you enter the age of renewal and conscious development.

In the evening of your life, believe it or not, you can be at your most creative. For maturity, in your fifties and beyond is the time to actualize yourself and business vision. It is the age of 'individuation' and of personal and organizational maturation (transformation).

In conclusion, the learning activities you select from the point of view of your own self-development will depend on the self you wish to realize and the stage you have reached in your life cycle. Development is not inevitable. But if you know the sort of direction it takes you are most likely to develop yourself. Although there are at least seven different kind of learning paths, all have to follow the natural law of development. As you develop along any one path. You explore, consolidate, renew and deepen your involvement with people and things. You thereby learn in quantum leaps.

SKILL ACQUISITION

For intellectual learning, the classroom is an appropriate setting and simply reading about or hearing a concept once can be enough to master it. Computer programming can be taught effectively in this mode, removed from give and take of life on the job. For behaviour change, on the other hand, life itself is the true arena for learning and this takes practice over an extended period of time. Cultivating skill learning ability requires an understanding of the fundamentals of behaviour and attitude change. Acquisition of technical skill through training people on the job and off the job is easy but it is much harder to train people to be flexible, to have integrity, be conscientious, or be skilled inter-personally. Without social sensitivity, social skills acquisition will be frustrated almost at birth.

Skill acquisition is more of a journey than destination, learning to process rather than a subject of instant recall. Skill acquisition is a creative undertaking in its own right.

1. REACT – The call to adventure –

When learning ceases to be an adventure it loses its powerful primordial appeals. The call to adventure represents the first and physical step towards skill acquisition. Moreover, such 'call' only arises when learner keeps himself on physical alert, listening to the office grapevine, looking out for people and seeing for himself who is doing what. In short, the individual reacts to all situations and learn the situations. Such sensual exposure is only the start of learning. Without social sensitivity skill acquisition is impossible to call to adventure.

2. RESPOND – Making social connections –

Learning can never take place in isolation from a supportive teacher or a protective mentor. Without a social context into which learning can be placed it becomes depersonalized and sterile. If you fail to respond people, your journey will be vain; you will remain insular and insulated. You attempt to acquire delegation skills, for example will be divorced from the very people to and far whom such delegation is required. Nevertheless, such social responsiveness is not enough. You need to engage in a road of trials.

3. ADAPT – Learning from experience –

The road of trials involves process of trial-and-error, whereby learners adopt to situations in which they find themselves and then learn from their experiences. Thus, period of mental alertness and of intellectual discovery is so much a part of growing. Thus any task you tackle, therefore, should lend itself to such exploration and adaptation before you commit yourself to a particular line of thought or action. As a result, for e.g., you need to seek out and adapt to different social situations before working out your own approach to social skills. Such experimentally based training will involve a combination of travel, books, short courses and work-related experiences. However, such intellectually based exploration is not enough. You will also need to expose yourself to psychologically laden risk.

4. EXPOSE – Yourself to emotional risk –

Whenever ideas you pick up intellectually you need to have the courage to put for them and yourself to the test. In the process you may become different person, disassembled and reassembled as a result of the emotional wrangles you have undergone. In fact, in order to significantly enhance your skills in a area which has previously been weak, such a risk taking process is unavoidable. For e.g., in developing your presentation skills, should stage-speech be alien to you. You will not only have to be mutually alert, but will also have to risk exposure. If you keep at it purposefully and conquer fears, then you face the next learning task of fitting the skill into your job role or organization.

5. ANALYZE – The skill, systematically –

As your newly acquired skill becomes physically, socially and mentally integrated within yourself, so the need arises to relate it to your job and to your organization. This ability to conceptualize, to analyze the parts and to relate the parts to the whole as well as to relate theory to practice and practice to theory, serves to integrate your skill. Analysis is enhanced when you investigate the different elements contained within a skill, subskills and the way in which particular subskill such as listening relates to whole skill. Such as 'facilitating', for e.g., listening ability in theory becomes integrated in practice when you are habitually called upon to exercise such skill, as part of your overall role.

6. DEVELOP INSIGHT – Penetrating to the source –

You may have integrated skill within yourself, and your organization without gaining any fundamental insight into its meaning and significance. For e.g., you may have developed problem-solving skills without much appreciation of their timing and context, particularly within different cultural settings. Such understanding requires depth of individual, organizational and societal insight. The insight is developed through a capacity to listen, a power to observe, and willingness to be humbled and an ability and inclination to link with like with unlike, actual with potential, both in yourself and through others. It involves seeing meaning and context in all things. However, even such power of insight does not necessarily lead to you into the realms of pure imagination, the ultimate in skill acquisition.

7. IMAGINE – Enhancing your originality –

True originality in the process of learning skill, is only displayed when you develop the capacity to imagine yourself exercising that skill in your own unique way. By means of imaging you marry up your uniqueness as an individual with the particular skill at hand. In the final analysis, through the acquisition of skill, integrated learning is only a means to an end, the application of skill, extroverted innovation.

In final say, our emotional intelligence determines our potential for learning the practical skills that are based on these five elements: self-awareness, motivation, self-regulation, empathy and adeptness in relationships. Our emotional potential how much of that potential we have translated into on-the-job capabilities. For e.g., being good at serving customers is an emotional competence based on empathy. The skill base empathy that translate individual performance into superior customer service. Therefore half the skills you need are technical. But the other half is in the softer domain – social skills.

Each organization has its own social ecology and the most adaptive skill for employees will differ accordingly.

In this new age economy, with its emphasis on flexibility, teams and strong customer orientation, the sharpening of social skills are becoming increasingly essential for excellence in every job and every part of the world of work.

SKILL APPLICATION

The organization does not look at technical skills because they are specific to each organization and vary broadly according to products and services people produce there. But skills like inter-personal, human or people skills are at the very centre of your inner product-ring. These skill areas and the role they play in work improvement process is of utmost important for development of self and your organization. The goal of skill acquisition, development and its application is to change behaviour and related actions, tasks at work as envisaged by you or other people in your work environment.

The full application of any skill requires innovation, in its creative and active entirety, in the same way that the complete process of skill acquisition requires learning, in its most complete sense. Such innovation range from envisioning what you want to create, through the exercise of a particular skill, to the detailed implementation warranted. The questions you need to address at each point, in the course of applying the skill you have been acquiring.

If your skills are put to best use, you need to master competences too. How do you keep yourself to change better? The answer to this is: there is crucial difference between declarative knowledge, knowing a concept and its technical details, and procedural knowledge, being able to put those concepts and details into action. Knowing does not equal doing, its application at the right moment is very important for success. Intellectual understanding of any skill may good, but it is not sufficient in itself to result in behaviour change. Knowing and applying skill demonstrate the change in behaviour and to get results as per above, you have to create your vision and so on.

CREATING YOUR VISION –

- What is your farreaching mission in applying the skill?
- How is its application going to change the world around you?
- How will it change your life, work and vocation?

RECOGNIZING NEED –

- What organizational; potential will you be realizing?
- How is technology and society evolving so as to fit in with the application of your emergent skill?
- What underlying need will you serve?
- What linkages arise between one skill and another in fulfilling that need?

DEFINING THE SKILL –

- What definable skill are you applying?
- What subskill components need to be applied?
- How does the application of the subskills fit with the skill as a whole and the skill as a whole with other skills?

COMMITTING YOURSELF –

- What is in it for you personally in applying the skill?
- What competitive advantage will you gain, internally and externally?
- Who will champion your skilled cause?
- How will you be selling your newly skilled self?

EXPLORING ALTERNATIVES –

- What are you aiming for, in applying your skills?
- What alternative approaches have you adopted?
- What feedback process have you introduced, for comparing actual with the desired results of exercising your skill?
- How have you built exploration into the organizational fabric?

INVOLVING PEOPLE –

- How do you affect shared values, whereby people will cooperate with you in your application of a particular skill?
- How do you ensure that whatever skill you apply is accessible to the people with whom you work?
- How do you keep people enthusiastic?

IMPLEMENTING THE SKILLS –

- How do you keep your people's energy level from waiting, in relation to the skill being implemented?
- How do you impose a sense of urgency?
- How do you maintain a bias for action?

The skills are generally best developed mastered overtime and through application in the workplace and sometimes with ongoing mentoring from someone skilled in practice.

SKILL DEVELOPMENT FROM LEARNER TO MASTER

Skill development is more than just knowing what skills looks like. Skills are developed primarily through practice and feedback. The goal of skill training is to equip an individual with suitable tools, techniques and skills to show them how they can contribute to and support in improvement of in concern field. The goal of skill training is also to change behaviour. Behaviour change precedes rather than follow attitude or style change. Behaviour change induces attitude change. If we get an individual to do something – to experiment, to try it, to learn about their native competence, to increase their self-esteem and self-control, well, then, the desired attitude change will follow. It is change in behaviour lead to a change in attitude. To change one's behaviour, it is first necessary to change his attitude. There is some validity to this, but mostly it is the other way around, if we first change people's behaviour, that will change their attitude. If an individual wants to grow to master skill in any area, he must learn to change his present style, behaviour and attitude to get fit into desired 'case of skilled character'.

How skills are developed, in terms of the 'cast of skilled character' and then processed, implemented and presented through skills and subskills set are considered as approaches to skill development or learning styles. These approaches correspond, more or less to learning style of individual. For e.g., development-oriented individual will aspire towards 'artistry' skill wise; the analytical orientation individual will be more of a pragmatist; and innovative orientation individual might aim, to achieve absolute mastery. Let us go into details of "cast of skill characters" one-by-one.

MASTER

The master learner is a more familiar figure in the classical music tradition. However, in organization or business, noted men/women have become masters in such areas of salesmanship, negotiation and even managing people. Such mastery involves not only a depth and breadth of experience, but also a combination of self-discipline and self-knowledge relating to skill in question. Moreover, such mastery operators are invariably unique in their approach to delegating, influencing and team-building or whatever the particular skill happens to be. Finally, they have the capacity to inspire others through their own skilled example.

ARTIST

The artist learners do not possess the degree of originality of the master. They have not completely transcended their own personal limitations through their skill. However, to the extent that their skilled management has become a true art form they are able to interweave personal style and impersonal skill beautifully. As a result, their approach is a highly distinctive blend without being a totally original product. As negotiators, they see potential for mutual gain when everyone else remains bogged down in adversarial relationships. As a problem-solvers they see wide-ranging opportunities where others see circumscribing constraints. Finally, they have the capacity to arouse the potential of others because of their combined insight and sensitivity.

PRAGMATIST

Pragmatic learners acquire skills, step-by-step, following the example of authoritative others, reading one or more of the extensive range of books and attend a suitable methodical course of instruction. Such pragmatists can't separate the acquisition of skill from its implementation, the two being for them inextricably intertwined. They are not interested in acquiring any originality in their skills but rather in doing something that works, efficiently and effectively.

OPPORTUNIST

Opportunist learners acquire skills on the hop, as and when they are required. As course or a book on, say, influencing skills will only be considered relevant in the heat of the moment. However, unlike the pragmatist who will respect a suitably accredited or authoritative individual, the opportunist will only respect he who delivers the goods.

SCIENTIST

Their learning cycle includes active experimentation (test), concrete experience (audit), reflective observation (survey) and abstract conceptualization (hypothesis). The acquisition and implementation of a skill therefore requires the individual to complete the learning cycle, continually, whatever in relation to team-building, salesmanship skill development therefore becomes a primarily intellectual process.

CRAFT PERSON

Learner craft persons pick-up skills on-the-job, under the guidance of master craftsman, with whom they can identify emotionally rather than intellectually. In other words they respect skilled operators – whether as a coach or problem-solver, a leader or a negotiator because they can identify emotionally with them. Because master and learner share the same respect for the craft tradition, they feel they belong to one another.

ACTOR

Actor learners are the people who develop skills by physically mimicking skilled people around them. As actors, in this imitative sense they are close observers of the skilled coach, the expert salesman, or the astute problem-solver, but only from outside. In other words, they mimic managerial behaviour to a greater extent than managerial thought or feeling. To that extent such "actors" are the direct opposite of the learner as artists. Organizations do have such cast of skilled characters on their roll.

In a nut shell, whether you aim to develop organizing or directing skills or facilitating or influencing abilities, you may approach above 'cast of skill characters' of master or an actor, a pragmatist or an artist.

CHAPTER 4

Skills and Their Primary Attributes

It is well demonstrated that human abilities make up the greater part of the ingredients for excellence at work. Whether you work in a large or small organization of any type, you are evaluated in terms of your abilities, competencies and skills though you may not know it thoroughly. If you are fresher and applying for a job, you are likely to be scrutinized through this lens, though no one tell you so explicitly. Whatever your job, understanding how to cultivate and develop skills is essential for success in your career. Today management people are looking at your personal traits – character, personality, attitude, social and human skills as prime qualities that make and keep you employable.

Our level of skill, ability and competency is not fixed genetically nor does it develop only in early childhood. These are to be learnt and it continues to develop as we grow through life and learn from our experiences and our skills in it keeps growing as age grows. We learned most, all we know from and with each other. That takes social intelligence (social relationship) not just cognitive ability. Many people have trouble because they don't understand how you become part of a human situation, part of relationship. It is easy to focus on cognitive ability and ignore social intelligence. But, it is when you bring those together, there you can create magic. Many a times it is observed that supers, intellect and technical talents alone do not make people great performer. It is the social skill which lubricates the mechanisms of positive relationship network at workplace. Intellectual understanding is a threshold process, necessary for learning, but not sufficient for lasting improvement. Deep change requires the retooling of ingrained habits of thoughts, feeling and behaviour.

There is a crucial difference between declarative knowledge, knowing a concept and its technical details, and procedural knowledge, being able to put those concepts and details into action. Knowing does not equal doing, whether in playing the piano, or managing a team. Intellectual understanding of a skill or competence may be necessary but it is not sufficient in itself to result in behaviour change. Skills can be seen as coordinated bundle of habits, what we think, feel, assume and do to get a job done. When such habits, feelings, assumptions are dysfunctional; replacing it with a more effective one requires enough learning, understanding and practice to make it better and acceptable.

The set of skills/competencies, well suited to develop personal abilities are listed here for your study and examination. These skills are helpful in developing your personality at work. You can master these skills for successful career planning, if they rightly learnt and practised. As Daniel Goleman in his book "working with emotional intelligence", has rightly pointed out that there are some elements of emotional intelligence that are so basic as to constitute "meta-abilities", which are essential for most other competencies. These basics include self-awareness, self-regulation, motivation, empathy and social skills. These primary capabilities are essential for supporting the emotional competencies that flow from them. For instance, a manager who tries to shift his leadership style may also need to improve in self-awareness in order to make the other change. Following are such of the skills that are essential to build your abilities at work.

SKILLS-KIT

(1) Emotional Awareness

(Recognizing one's Emotions and their Effects.)

The recognition of how our emotions affect our performance, and the ability to use our values to guide decision-making. People with this skill:

- Know which emotions they are feeling and why.
- Realize the links between their feelings and what they think, do, and say.
- Recognize how their feelings affect their performance.
- Have a guiding awareness of their values and goals.

Such awareness is our guide in fine-tuning on the job performance of every kind. Managing our untruly feeling, keeping ourselves motivated, tuning in with accuracy to the feelings of those around us, and developing good work-related social skills including those essential for leadership and teamwork. It is a focusing ability, knowing the internal meters and subtle signals that tell you what you are feeling and using them as an ongoing guide to how you are doing. A person excelling in this skill is aware of his emotions at any given moment often recognizing how those emotions feel physically. He can articulate those feelings, as well as demonstrate social appropriateness in expressing them.

(2) Accurate Self-assessment

(Knowing one's Inner resources, Abilities and Limits.)

A candid sense of our personal strength and limits, a clear vision of where we need to improve, and the ability to learn from experience. People with this skill:

- Aware of their strengths and weaknesses.
- Reflects learning from experience.
- Open to candid feedback, new perspective, continuous learning and self-development.
- Able to show a sense of humour and perspective about themselves.

Before you can lead others, before you can help others, you have to discover yourself. If you want creativity to take place, if you want the kind of performance that leads to truly exceptional results, you have to be willing to embark on a journey that leads to an alignment between an individual's personal value and aspirations and the values and aspirations of the company. Accuracy in self-assessment is a hallmark of superior performance. It is not that star performers have no limits on their abilities, but they are aware of their limits and so they know where they need to improve or they know to work with someone else who has a strength they lack. Superior performer intentionally seek out feedback; they want to hear how others perceive them, realizing that this is valuable information. They may be part of the reason people who are self-aware are also better performers. Presumably their self-awareness and self-assessment help them in a process of continuous improvement. Knowing their strengths and weaknesses and approaching their work accordingly is the skill they possess.

(3) Self-confidence

(A strong sense of one's Self-worth and capabilities.)

The courage that comes from certainty about our capabilities, values and goals. **People with this skill:**

- Present themselves with self-assurance have 'presence'.
- Can voice views that are unpopular and go out on a limb for what is right.
- Are decisive, able to make sound decisions, despite, uncertainties and pressures.

Self-confidence gives us the requisite self-assurance for plunging ahead or stepping in as a leader. Self-confidence can reveal itself in a strong self-presentation, a projection of presence: people with self-confidence typically see themselves as efficacious, able to take on challenges and to master new jobs or skills. They believe themselves to be catalysts, movers and initiators and feel that their abilities start up favourably in comparison to others. Self-confidence gives the strength to make a tough decision or follow a course of action one believes in despite opposition, disagreement or even explicit disapproval from those in authority.

(4) Self-control

(Keeping disruptive emotions and impulses in check.)

Managing disruptive emotions and impulsive effectively is a skill. People with this skill:

- Manage their impulsive feelings and distressing emotions well.
- Stay composed, positive and unflappable even in trying moments.
- Think clearly and stay focused under pressure.

People with this skill are optimistic, action-oriented people. If something goes wrong in their lives; they immediately start to think about how to make it better. This skill is in a sense largely invisible. Self-control manifests largely in the absence of more obvious emotional fireworks. Signs include being unfazed under stress or handling a hostile person without lashing out in return. Hence, the ultimate act of personal responsibility at work may be in taking control of our own state of mind. Moods exert a powerful pull on thought, memory and perception. When we are angry, we more readily remember incidents that support our ire, anger, irritability. Resisting this despotic quality of moods in essential to our ability to work productively.

(5) Trustworthiness and Conscientiousness

(Maintaining integrity and taking responsibility for personal performance.)

Credibility stems from integrity, stars know that trustworthiness at work translate into letting people know one's values and principles, intentions and feelings and acting in ways that are reliably consistent with them. They are forthright about their own mistakes, confronts others about their lapses. **People with this skill:**

For Trustworthiness

- Act ethically and are above reproach.
- Build trust through their reliability and authenticity.
- Admit their own mistakes and confront unethical actions in others.
- Take tough principled stands even if they are unpopular.

For Conscientiousness

- Meet commitments and keep promises.
- Hold themselves accountable for meeting their objectives.
- Are organized and careful in their work.

Integrity acting openly, honestly and consistently set outstanding performers in jobs of every kind. People with integrity are frank. They are clear-cut in their thinking and doing. So being trustworthy is all the more important. You will be more successful if you stay in alignment with your personal values.

Conscientiousness is a taproot of success in any field. The everyday signs of conscientiousness are being punctual, careful in doing work, self-disciplined and scrupulous in attending to responsibilities are hallmarks of the model citizen, the people who keep things running as they should. They follow the rules, help out, and are concerned about the people they work with.

(6) Innovation and Adaptability

Being open to novel ideas and approaches and being flexible in responding to change. People with this skill:

For Innovation:

- Seek out fresh ideas from a wide variety of sources.
- Entertain original solutions to problems.
- Generate new ideas.
- Take fresh perspectives and risks in their thinking.

For Adaptability:

- Smoothly handle multiple demands shifting priorities and rapid changes.
- Adapt their responses and tactics to fit fluid circumstances.
- Are flexible in how they see events.

Creativity on the job revolves around applying new ideas to achieve results. People who have this skill can quickly identify key issues and simplify problems that seem overwhelmingly complex. The emotional foundation of the innovator at work is taking pleasure in originality. Risk taking and the drive to pursue innovative ideas are the fuel that stokes the entrepreneurial spirit of such people.

(7) Achievement Drive

(Striving to improve or meet a standard of excellence.)

People with this skill:

- Are result-oriented with a high drive to meet their objectives and standards.
- Set challenging goals and take calculated risks.
- Pursue information to reduce uncertainty and find way to do better.
- Learn how to improve their performance.

Such people talk about and take more calculated risks; they urge and support enterprising innovations and set challenging goals to achieve, and they throw their support behind others entrepreneurial ideas. The need to achieve is the single strongest competence that sets apart these people from average people. They are driven by the need to achieve, seek ways to track their success.

(8) Commitment

(Aligning with the goals of a group/organization.)

People with this skill are:

- Readily make sacrifices to meet larger organizational goals.
- Find a sense of purpose in the larger mission.
- Use the group's core values in making decisions and clarifying choices.
- Actively seek out opportunities to fulfil the group's mission.

The essence of commitment is making our goal and those of the organization one and the same. For them commitment is an emotional issue. They feel a strong attachment to their group's goals when they resonate strongly with their own. They value and embrace an organization mission are willing not just to make an all-out effort on its behalf; but to make personal sacrifices when needed.

Self-awareness is a building block of commitment. People who know their own guiding values or purpose will have clear, even vivid sense about whether there is a 'fit' with an organization. When they feel match, their commitment is spontaneous and strong. Their organizational commitment grows from such emotional bonding.

(9) Initiative and Optimism

(Displaying productivity and persistence.)

People with this skill:

For Initiative:

- Are ready to size opportunities.
- Pursue goals beyond what is required or expected of them.
- Cut through red-tape and bend the rules when necessary to get the job done.
- Mobilize others through unusual enterprising efforts.

For Optimism:

- Persist in seeking goals despite obstacles and setbacks.
- Operate from hope of success rather than fear of failure.
- See setbacks as due to manageable circumstances rather than a personal flaw.

These people often take anticipatory action to avoid problems before they happen or taking advantage of opportunities before they are visible to anyone else. Possessing this farsightedness may mean taking steps when no one else sees the need to. These people act before being forced to by external events. While initiative is generally laudable, it needs to be balanced with social awareness in order to avoid unintended negative consequences.

Optimism can more readily make a realistic assessment of a setback and admit how they contribute to it. The nearness of optimism is hope knowing the steps needed to get to a goal and having the energy to pursue those steps. It is a primal motivating force for optimism. In some jobs, where stress is high and frustrations common a rosy look may get better results. Hopefulness is crucial when anyone undertakes a tough task. Positive expectations may be especially beneficial in the toughest jobs, where high optimism may be a pragmatic job category.

(10) Understanding others

(Sensing others feelings and perspectives and taking an active interest in their concerns.)

People with this skill:

- Are attentive to emotional clues and listen well.
- Show sensitivity and understand others perspectives.
- Help out based on understanding other people's needs and feelings.

Empathy is essential as an emotional guidance system, piloting us in getting along at work. Beyond mere survival, empathy is critical for superior performance wherever the job focus is on people. Understanding some ones point of view or perspective knowing why they feel as they do – does not inevitably mean embracing it. Particularly in business dealings understanding how someone feels need not lead to giving in but to more skilful negotiation and management. As a result, tough decisions may generate less resentment and lasting it well. People with this competence are trusting people who believe that people are basically good, tend to be more highly attuned to feelings.

A finely tuned ear is at the heart of empathy. Listing well is essential for workplace success. Listening well and deeply means going beyond what is said by asking questions, restating in ones words what you hear to be sure you understand. This is 'active' listening. A mark of having truly heard someone is to respond appropriately, even if that means making some change in what you do. Empathetic people cared about other people, their needs and concerns. This is especially true if the empathy go hand-in-hand with the sense that the other people could be trusted.

(11) Developing others

(Sensing others developmental needs and bolstering their abilities.)

People with this skill:

- Acknowledge and reward people's strengths and accomplishment.

- Offer useful feedback and identify people's needs for further growth.
- Mentor, give timely coaching and offer assignments that challenge and foster a person's skills.

The simple bit of advice exemplifies coaching, which lies at the heart of developing others. The heart of coaching and developing is the act of counselling. And the effectiveness of counselling hinges on empathy and the ability to focus on our own feelings and shared them. Strong coaching and mentoring help employees perform better, enhances loyalty and job satisfaction. An open trusting relationship is the foundation of success in on the job coaching. The best coaches show a genuine personal interest in those they guide and have empathy for and an understanding of their people. Coaches who show respect, trustworthiness and empathy are the best coaches.

(12) Service orientation

(Anticipating, recognizing and meeting customer's needs.)

People with this skill:

- Understand customers need and match them to services or products.
- Seek ways to increase customer's satisfaction and loyalty.
- Gladly offer appropriate assistance.
- Grasp a customer's perspective acting as a trusted advisor.

The key to service orientation success lies in the customer-services. First of all to make feel good and make everyone comfortable. Superlative service entails being a trusted advisor. This kind of trust based relationship grows overtime. To shine at service we need to monitor the satisfaction of customers, not waiting to hear complaints but freely offering information on that might be helpful without self-interest motivating to gesture. This lays the groundwork for trusting relationships. As advocated by P. Drucker, the purpose of business is not to make sale, but to make and keep a customer.

(13) Leveraging Diversity

(Cultivating opportunities through different kinds of people.)

People with this skill:

- Respect and relate well to people from varied backgrounds.
- Understand diverse world views and are sensitive to group differences.
- See diversity as opportunity, creating an environment where diverse people can thrive.
- Challenge bias and intolerance.

Success through others who are different from yourself, there is strength of difference, and this makes the ability to leverage diversity an increasingly crucial competence. Variety of people working in organization of every kind demands a greater awareness of the subtle distortion that stereotypes and bias bring to working relationship. You being able to read people accurately, without distortions of emotionally laden stereotypes, set superior performers apart from average. Beyond zero tolerance for intolerance, the ability to leverage diversity revolves around three skills; getting along well with people who are different; appreciating the unique ways others may operate; and seizing whatever business opportunity these unique approaches might offer. When leaders of organizations value the insights brought to work by people of diverse background; it can lead to organizational learning that boost competitiveness. Learn, and change and so do better by leveraging diversity.

(14) Political Awareness

(Reading social and political currents.)

People with this skill:

- Accurately read key power relationship.
- Detect crucial social networks.
- Understand the forces that shape views and actions of clients, customers or competitors.
- Accurately read organizational and external realities.

The ability to read political realities is vital to the behind the scene networking and coalition building that allows someone to wield influence no matter what their professional role. Mediocre performer lacks such social acumen and so betrays a distressingly low level of political savvy. Skill at reading the currents that influence the real decision-makers depends on the ability to empathies on an organizational level, not just inter-personal one. People who maintain rich personal networks in an organization typically are savvy about what is going on, and this social intelligence extends to understanding the larger realities that affect the organization.

(15) The Art of Influence

(Wielding effective tactics for persuasion.)

The art of influence entails handling emotions effectively in other people. Star performers are artful communicators, able to sway an audience. The emotional exchange constitutes an invisible inter-personal economy. Part of every human interaction, but it is usually too subtle to notice. Emotions are attention grabbers; operating as warnings, invitations, alarms, and the like these are powerful messages, conveying critical information without necessarily putting that data into words. Emotions are a hyper efficient mode of communication. Emotion is the sum total of the exchanges of feeling among us. In subtle ways, we all make each other feel a bit better or work as part of any contact we have. Social skill is essential in handling another person's emotion artfully, underlie several competencies.

These include: influence-wielding effective tactics of persuasion; communication-sending clear and convincing messages; conflict management-negotiating and resolving disagreements; leadership-inspiring and guiding; change catalyst-initiating, promoting or managing change.

Empathy is crucial for wielding influence. The first step in influence is building rapport. Charm and social polish in themselves do not add up to competence at influence. True influence exhibits in the true competence in harmonizing with the collective goal. In the world of work, no matter the business at hand, emotional element plays a crucial role. Emotional competence requires being able to pilot through the emotional under currents always at play rather than being pulled under by people.

(16) Communication

(Listening openly and sending convincing messages.)

People with this skill:

- Are effective in give and take, registering emotional cues in attuning their message.
- Deal with difficult issues straightforwardly.
- Listen well, seek mutual understanding and welcome sharing of information fully.
- Foster open communication and stay receptive to bad news as well as good.

Being an adapt communicator is the keystone of all social skills. Communication competence strongly distinguishes star performers from average or poor ones. Listening well the key to empathy is also crucial to competence in communicating. Listening skills – asking astute questions, being open-minded and understanding, seeking suggestions are the skills of effective communicator.

(17) Conflict management

(Negotiating and resolving disagreements.)

People with this skill:

- Handle difficult people and tense situations with diplomacy and tact.
- Spot potential conflict brings disagreements into the open and helps de-escalate.
- Encourage debate and open discussion.
- Orchestrate win-win solutions.

One talent of those skill of conflict resolution is spotting trouble as it is brewing and taking steps to calm those involved. The arts of listening and empathizing are crucial for handling conflict management. The ability to read the feelings of the opposition during a negotiation is critical to success. Those who have mastered the art of the deal realize the emotionally charge nature of any negotiation. The best negotiators can sense which points matter most to the other party and gracefully concede there, while pressing for concessions in points that do not carry such emotional weight and that takes empathy. Skill at negotiation obviously matters for excellence in professions like law and diplomacy. Conflict resolution requires that each side be able to understand not just the others point of view, but their needs and fears. This empathy, makes each side better able to influence the other to their benefit, by being responsive to the others needs. In other words, to find ways in which both parties win.

(18) Leadership

(Inspiring and guiding individuals and groups.)

People with this skill:

- Articulate and arouse enthusiasm for a shared vision and mission.
- Step forward to lead as needed, regardless of position.
- Guide the performance of others while holding them accountable.
- Lead by example.

In general emotional charisma depends on three factors: feeling strong emotions, being able to express those emotions forcefully, and being an emotional sender rather than a receiver. Highly expressive people communicate through their facial expression, their voice, their gestures, and their whole body. This ability allows them to move, inspire and captivate others. The ability to convey emotion convincingly, from the heart requires that a leader be sincere about the message being delivered; truly believing the emotional message is what separates the charismatic leader from the self-serving one. To be a charismatic messenger, the leader must act from authentic belief. Leadership entails exciting imagination and inspiring them to move in a desired direction. It takes more than simple power to motivate and lead. The superior leaders managed to balance a people-oriented personal style with a decisive command role. They did not hesitate to take charge, to be purposeful, assertive and business like. The most effective leaders are more positive and outgoing, more emotionally expressive and dramatic, warmer and more sociable, more democratic, more cooperative, more likable and 'fun to be with', more appreciative and trustful and even gentler than those who were merely average.

(19) Change catalyst

(Initiating or managing change.)

People with this skill:

- Recognize the need for change and remove barriers.
- Challenge the *status quo* to acknowledge the need for change.
- Champion the change and enlist others in its pursuit.
- Model the change expected of others.

Beyond technical expertise, the change catalyst needs other skills like high level of self-confidence, effective leadership, influence, commitment, initiative and optimism. When you work with a company to help them transform their business, the personal abilities of the leader of their team count immensely.

You need someone who takes this change as a mission, not just a job.

Transformational leaders go beyond management and as usual such leaders are able to rouse people through the sheer power of their own enthusiasm. Such leaders don't order or direct; they inspire others. And they are committed to nurturing relationships with those they lead. The successful leaders are rated by people who worked for them as highly charismatic and flexible. They seemed to spread their own sense of confidence and competence, and they inspired people to be more imaginative, adaptive and innovative. Leadership of this kind, then is an emotional craft they develop through skills and competence.

(20) Building Bonds

(Nurturing instrumental relationship.)

People with this skill:

- Evaluate and maintain extensive informal networks.
- Seek out relationships that are mutually beneficial.
- Build rapport and keep others in the loop.
- Make and maintain personal friendships among works and associate.

One of the virtues of building relationships is the reservoir of goodwill and trust that arises. Highly effective people are adept at cultivating such relationships. These human links are the routes through which people come to be known for their abilities and skills. Rapport building is central to developing strong, useful relationship. Rapport hinges on empathy and typically emerges naturally in the course of casual conversation about family, sport, children, and the stuff of life. Finally, the building of a close work relationship means establishing an alliance, a relationship that can be counted on. The people we get along with trust, feel simpatheic with, are the strongest links in social relationship networks. Web like connectivity is the secret of success in many organizations where people spend their career in a single organization with high-intensity relationships. Networks of personal contacts are the kind of personal capital.

(21) Collaboration and Cooperation

(Working with others toward shared goals.)

People with this skill:

- Balance a focus on task with attention to relationships.
- Collaborate, sharing plans, information and resources.
- Promote a friendly cooperative climate.
- Spot and nurture opportunities for collaboration.

Building collaborative and fruitful relationships begins with healthy relationship at work. Our relationship with coworkers have a parallel emotional component, something akin to the pleasures, jealousies, etc. This inter-dependence ties together in a way that can become highly charged. If superior and subordinate do well emotionally, if they form a relationship of trust, rapport, understanding and inspired effort, their performance will shine at work. But if things go emotionally awry, the relationship can become a nightmare and their performance shall be a series of minor or major disasters at work.

(22) Team Capabilities

(Creating group synergy in pursuing collective goals.)

People with this skill:

- Model team qualities like respect, helpfulness and cooperation.
- Draw all members into active and enthusiastic participation.
- Build team identity, **esprit de crops** and commitment.
- Protect the group and its reputation, share credit.

People in teams tend to share common understandings. They are competitive and even **handed** in matching members to the best role for their talents. They have strong anticipative need, they like people for their own sake, which makes them more harmonious, better able to handle conflicts and offer mutual support. They share a commitment to the group goal. The best team leaders are able to get everyone to buy into a common sense of mission, goals and agenda. The ability to articulate a compelling vision that senses as the guiding force for the group may be the single most important contribution of a good team leader. The competencies of star teams are: empathy or interpersonal understanding, cooperation and unified effort, open communication, setting explicit norms and expectations and confronting underperforming team-members, a drive to improve, so that the team paid attention to performance feedback and sought to learn to do better; self-awareness in the form of evaluating their strengths and weakness as a team, initiative and taking a proactive stance toward solving problems, self-confidence as a team, flexibility in how they went about their collective tasks, building bonds to other teams. Such competencies/skills let teams work better on problem-solving, decision-making, negotiation and agreement with others. The organizations of all kinds have come to the realization that the success of peoples talent can be orchestrated in a team that cut across traditional boundaries for improving business processes, products and troubleshooting.

Learning, practicing and presenting these skills at work make you champion of the masses. It is important to realize that there are no great people. There are just ordinary people with great ideas and great courage to learn. We must have the great courage to change our philosophy, our beliefs, assumptions, perceptions, attitude and behaviour. We have to retool our ways of communicating our beliefs in ourselves, people and organizations.

The primary reason, therefore, some people are great champions because they have bon-dip commitment and passion for learning new things and practicing it and thus create their own 'personality brand image' as great persons. Their developments in knowledge, conduct personality are all the creation of coherent mental constructs to represent the surrounding environment has resulted from the interplay between the challenge of complexity and the urge to master it. They reduce complexity first by attempting to simplify realty and then absorb complexity by differentiating restructuring and improving their means to cope with it. They followed innovative learning path. Through such learning they developed the capacity to face new situation of growing complexity of modern world.

Innovative learning involves both anticipation and participation. Participation involves more than the formal sharing of decision, suggestions, guidelines, it is an attitude characterized by cooperation, dialogue and empathy. It means not keeping communications open but also constantly testing your operating rules and values against those of others. Without participation, anticipation becomes futile, and participation without anticipation can be misguided. Cultivating understanding in isolation can lead to reliance on self-defeating, quickly obsolescent and ignoring the context of others, usually run danger of narrow-mindedness and false sense of security. Whereas anticipation encourages solidarity in time, participation creates solidarity.

Therefore, your relationships will need to be fashioned and refashioned as a part of the dynamism of social processes like inquiry and dialogue that mediate learning. Such relationships are more intricate because their character derives from specifies of the situation that are always both pragmatic and psychological. Pragmatic takes to get work done best and psychological, what people need to sustain their motivation and commitment. The caring relationship, the interviewing of thought, feeling and action becomes a precondition for learning. This type of mental make up will help change mediocre man into star performer.

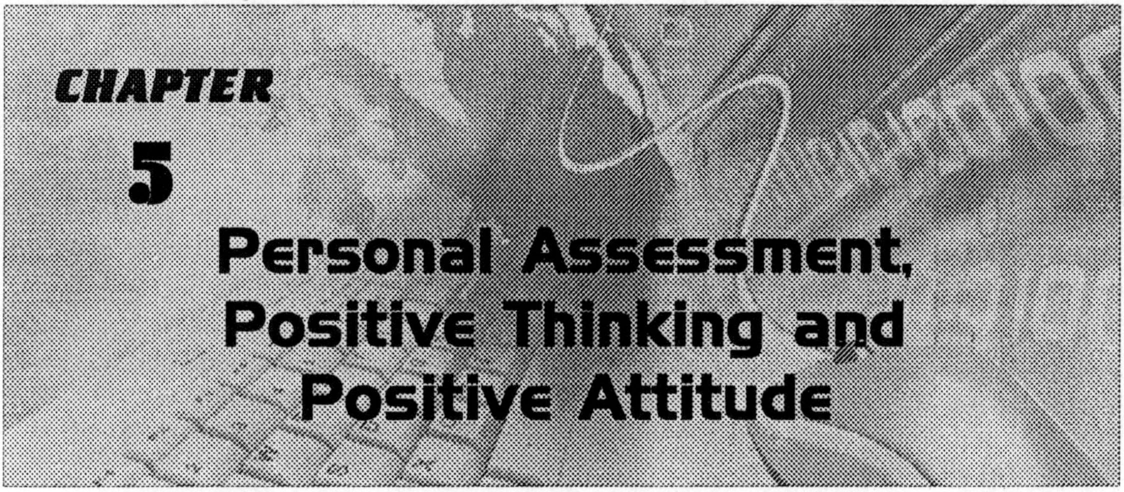

CHAPTER 5

Personal Assessment, Positive Thinking and Positive Attitude

In today's changing and revolutionized world of work, employees, executives and professionals are in dilemma as they build their professional career. They are sometimes lured by 100% salary jump, training abroad, fast promotions. But the end result is generally discouraging. It is because we, as individuals never go seriously into our personal assessment. As a result, we choose wrong road and destiny. "It is therefore necessary and also helpful to assess yourself before taking any assignment in the organizations."

❖ Know where you want to go

Job opportunities and risks are numerous in career advancement, what is important is that each of us make a considered decision of where one wants to reach ultimately. Think yourself and then act.

❖ Define success in your terms

It is critical for individual to define what their parameters of success are. One can't say a hermit sitting in isolated hill of Himalaya is unsuccessful. One can't say professor in a university does not live in the real world because he gives his life to teach thousands of pupils and is content to live in a small house, without car, in a corner of the campus. One can't say a manager in Indian company getting less salary than his colleague in multinational company living abroad is not successful. Today's life is full of peer pressure and trapping of success is defined by others. Looking at your skills, what you want to contribute and what is important to you in life means taking ownership for your life and defining success in your term is absolutely your choice.

❖ Be willing to learn and adapt to new ways

Continually reinvent/rediscover yourself and adapt to situations and circumstances as they happen. With the myriad organizations now operating in the corporate environment with diverse culture, values, beliefs and working styles. Once having made a choice to work with an organization to get closer to your own goal, be sure that you have built the capability to innovate and learn. This is critical because changes are rapid and there is no time to first dip your toes in the water to learn to swim, it is not just important, it is critical for survival.

❖ Think contribution – not just tasks and activities

"Making a difference" is the name of the game. There are thousands job positions in the job market each day. What set you apart? What are you willing to contribute, what legacy or lasting contribution do you want to make is rest with you. It require us to align ourselves with the organization we work with, not the organization work for. Your employability and ongoing marketability is based on what you can truly give, getting in return the fruits of success as you have defined.

❖ Be result driven

Have a touch of the practical. Not everything should be speculation, you must also act. The wisest are easiest to deceive. They may know extraordinary things, but they know nothing of lives ordinary necessities. So let the wise have a touch of the practical. Know how to get things done. It may not be the highest things in life, but it is most necessary.

❖ Continuously develop your self as resource

Learning and adapting to new ways of functioning is the unfailing work to develop yourself as a resource in terms of your skill and capabilities. The efficiency bar is being raised daily and unless we learn new skills and battle with our own inadequacies, you will never be able to reach to your full potential. There is a constant tussle between specialization and generalization. Important is do we have new skills that are required in the marketplace and what are you doing to develop these skills. Your future employability is entirely in your hand.

❖ Build your network and be known for what you do

In competitive environment, it is important not just to do but also to communicate what you have done and what you are capable of. Build your own network in the organization and outside. Build your reputation and keep it. Let people know how you are developing yourself as a resource and keep working on it without letting yourself rest on past laurels.

The secret of self-correction is simply to gain a normal view and that is always slanted on the positive side of thinking. You will radiate courage and magnetism; regain confidence by simple process of positive thinking and self-conditioning.

You can radically improve your life and opportunities by doing one small thing – having the courage to be yourself. It may seem that you are the one who always has to make the allowances and changes to accommodate others. So, never mind, as boss of your own life, you can do it, you can make all the changes necessary, you can grow and develop and solve your own problems. You have a wide choice of courses of action plan open to you. Keep trying them out in different circumstances. Practice, and make it a habit of life. Most people would agree that you get more from life when you think positively than when you think negatively. That is why human behaviour is sometimes so baffling. Make a decision now! Choose positive thinking and be happier with your life.

POSITIVE THINKING

Following successful results, you will see if you have positive thinking power.

- Always picture success no matter how badly things seem to be going at the moment.
- Whenever a negative thought concerning your personal power comes to mind, deliberately voice a positive thought to cancel it out.
- Do not build-up obstacles in your imagination depreciate every obstacle. Minimize them. Difficulties must be studied and efficiently dealt with to be eliminated.
- Do not be awestruck by other people and try to copy them. Nobody can be you as efficiently as you can.
- Make a true estimate of your own ability. Do not become egoistical but develop whole some self-respect. Believe in your own God related powers.
- Believe in you and receive power from invisible source of power.

Thus priaritise, picturise and actualize. Priaritise means make a daily system of creative and positive things of the side. Picturise is a basic factor in human psychology is the realizable wish. The man who assumes success tends to have success. Actualize that which you have priaritised and picturised and actualized according to the pattern of your basic realizable wish. You will feel full of realization. One of the deepest drives of human nature is the desire, to be appreciated. The longing to be linked, to be held in esteem, to be a sought after person is fundamental in human being.

Again, getting people to like you, you must have a set of positive manners:

- Be comfortable person so there is no strain on you.
- Acquire the quality of relaxed easy-goingness so that things do not ruffle you.
- Don't be egostical. Guard against the impression that you know it all. Be natural and normally humble.
- Cultivate the quality of being interesting so that people will be with you and get something of stimulating values from their association with you.

- ❖ Study to get scratchy element out of your personality.
- ❖ Drain off your grievances. Sincerely attempt to heal honesty. Every misunderstanding you have will disappear.
- ❖ Never miss an opportunity to say a word of congratulations upon anyone's achievement or express sympathy in sorrow or disappointment.
- ❖ Give strength to people and they will give you affection to you.
- ❖ The power of positive thinking is practical technique of successful living that works at work.

Your thinking, manners and attitude and philosophy of life will show in your job as a service-giver and so a positive, constructive, creative approach is always important in your private life too.

POSITIVE ATTITUDE AND WORK CULTURE

Attitude is nothing but a settle way of thinking and feeling about person, process, action and other things.

An employee is exposed to several situations, experiences in his worklife, as a result, he develops certain attitude which exerts powerful influence on his behaviour and this directly affects his understanding, perception and judgement.

Perception is the intake of information; received from the environment, the background of the persons, past experiences, expectations and interests.

Why do people form attitude?

- ➢ Attitude allows them to express their fundamental values of judgement, feelings and thinking about people, company policies, etc.
- ➢ Help them adjust to their environment by providing a certain amount of predictability.
- ➢ Protect their self-esteem by making it possible for them to avoid unpleasant truth about themselves.
- ➢ Help them understand the world around them by organizing and simplifying a very complex input from their environment.
- ➢ Make it easier for them to get along with people who have a similar attitude.

How attitudes are formed?

Attitudes are formed by family influence, cultural background and influence by society, neighbours, colleagues and superiors.

We form and develop our attitude either from direct experience or from other people.

- The influence of culture plays dominant role in the formation of development of attitude in person.
- Inter-personal relations are developed when two people are attitudinally similar and have an opportunity to interact, they psychologically reward each other.

ATTITUDE – POSITIVE OR NEGATIVE

- A person with high level of job satisfaction holds positive attitudes toward the job. A dissatisfied person with his job holds negative attitude.
- Individuals who express high involvement in their jobs are likely to be more productive and less likely to be dissatisfied, frustrated.
- This depends on working conditions, relations with others, growth prospects, salary and benefits.
- Positive attitude would mean that the employee would highly committed to the organization and would perform well. Attitude and productivity or efficiency is thus connected to each other.

Some examples:

- Once one M.D. of a shoe factory deputed two of his marketing managers to Africa to identify market potential for their shoe product.
- One manager sent back a fax stating that nobody here wears shoes, there is absolutely no market for our product. (Negative)

The other manager sent a fax stating that nobody wears shoes, market potential. therefore, is abundant. Let us get start before our competitors come here. (Positive)

They are having divergent conclusions of the same market because of differences in attitude and market perceptions by them.

- First, a **Dy. Manager** tells his subordinate that they are below average performers.
- Second, a **Manager** tells them they are average performers.
- Third, **AGM** kept on repeating to them that they are really above average and intelligent.

When we go for uniform results of production review, we found that the same subordinates achieved highest productivity.

The above types of attitude of each one are based on their thinking of their subordinates in different way:

❖ Employee's attitude, motivation, his joy from work rests with the person to whom he directly reports. Thus, your immediate boss is the critical factor in the whole process of developing your attitude at work – positive or negative.

Fit between person's talent and his task is the best way to motivate people for positive work culture.

The positive thinking gets positive results. The negative thinking, expectations get negative results.

Attitude is a power factor in patient's healing process. For e.g., a group of people from a department had a headache. A famous doctor gave them a capsule ensuring them of the fast relief. It was found that majority people felt better even though the capsule was a dummy one.

See how positive thinking gets positive results. Positive attitudes improve positive thinking at work.

If you continuously tell yourself that you are good at work, you will automatically expand your capabilities, abilities, etc.

Attitudes and habits tend to go together. Change one and you automatically change the other.

If you want to be a winner, you have got to change attitude – think – positive.

❖ Winners do not do different things. They do things differently.

❖ One of the biggest stumbling blocks to our given attitude is not the company culture, nor lack of career growth opportunities, but the major obstacle is "WE".

You have to decide whether you are a 'winner' or a 'loser'.

People with positive attitude have certain personality traits that are easy to recognize. They are caring, confident and patient and humble. They have high expectations of themselves and others. They anticipate positive change.

➢ Having positive outlook we increase productivity.

➢ Foster team spirit and teamwork.

➢ Solve problem.

➢ Improve quality.

➢ Make congenial atmosphere.

➢ Foster better relationships with employees, customers, etc.

Hence, your attitude is more important than your attitude. Attitude decides your Altitude.

We can't tailor-make the situation of life but we can tailor-make the attitude to fit them before they arise. We can alter our lives by altering our attitude.

How can we change our attitudes?

- Think of improvement in personal life, habits, behaviour, mannerisms, etc.
- Relations with neighbours, colleagues, superiors.
- In work methods procedures and practices in interaction – personal, departmental, etc.

In order to bring attitudinal changes in individual, it is better to analyze his function and then adapt to right method. The method would vary depending on the individual and the attitude requiring change.

- Willingness and sustain environment that better the performance of people. (Performance management and reward system)
- Structure the organization to permit effective and innovative ideas of people to rise above the demands of day-to-day working. (Work involvement and empowerment)
- Clearly define a strategic focus for people to develop their innovative efforts realistically in ways that will pay-off in person or of rated responsibility, efficiency and productivity. (Defining Key Result Areas (KRAs) and job descriptions, role and goal management)
- Assist in implementing the good ideas of people. (recognition, appreciation and success stories)

If efforts are properly channelised to institutionalize above, the results in attitudinal change among people will result in effectiveness of the organization.

Positive attitude of people and organization are the foundation stones of POSITIVE WORK CULTURE.

Positive work culture can be built on:

- Teamwork – togetherness.
- Proper use of resources for effective performance.
- Waste control, cost, time, money, energy, etc.
- Doing right things, the right time.
- Careful scheduling of activities.
- Set time limit for tasks at hand.
- Delegate when feasible.

Persons who perform efficiently and effectively on the job help establish positive work culture in them in their department and in their organization.

Positive management or manager never blames circumstances, conditions for their behaviour. Their behaviour is a product of their own conscious choice based on values, rather than a product of their conditions. Proactive leaders are value driven and if their value is to produce good, quality work, it is not a function of whether the weather is conducive to it or not. Proactive leaders though sometimes influence by external environment, but their response to the situation is always value base. Proactive leader's productivity is a part of their organizational culture. Sometime, they may be dormant but they are there. They provide their people clear, undistorted reflection of their social mirror – image in society. I am what I am today because of the choice I made yesterday. No one can hurt me without my consent is the basic directive principle of positive and assertive leader in proactive management culture.

CHAPTER 6

Understanding People — MBTI-Skills

We all are different. There is no other person in the world exactly like me or you. Our attitudes, behaviours and styles are different from one to another person. Also, we have so many approaches to look at persons or things. The answer to this is rooted in the fact that each of us has a preferred way of relating to others. It is called our 'Personality Style" or behavioural style. Understanding those styles is an important skill, which boost to our chances of success in any filed. The truth is more of us don't try hard to understand others. So, we ignore them or deal with them as little as possible, often to our detriment. But when we fail to understand others, we create tension and discomfort, otherwise is known as personality conflicts. You can reduce or eliminate those conflicts by learning to understand behavioural style, including your own people and who are emotionally adept, who know and manage their own feelings well, and who read and deal effectively with other peoples feeling have an advantage is all of life arenas. Further they are more likely to be content and effective in their lives, mastering the habits of mind that foster their own productivity. Thus, you will lessen tension and it will likely help build your career, foster better relations, maximize your strength. In general make successful, life; if you learn to identify attributes of these skills or styles. You will go long way toward becoming more skilful person.

From centuries, people have been fascinated with each others differences. But a breakthrough came in 1920, when Carl Jung wrote his book "*Psychological Types*" in which he described four behavioural styles; the inuitor, the thinker, the feeler and the sensor. Jung believed that each of us carries all four attributes but we tend to rely on one or two over the others. Jung's contribution later on is known as the Myers – Briggs Type Inventory (MBTI). Any individual who takes up MBTI will have a common composite "type" personalities; inuitor, thinker, feeler and sensor.

WHY THE MBTI?

Not only is the MBTI itself one of the most widely used thoroughly researched psychometric instruments, but the four dimensions of preference make sense to people from all backgrounds and all cultures. The differences in thinking style that Jung arrived at after years of clinical practice and personal reflection appear to the fundamental. The MBTI identifies differences between people, but it does so in an entirely non-judgemental way. Each type is as valuable to a team as each other type; individual differences are seen as resources to the team and people are encouraged to look for complementary strengths. It is human nature to categorize and the MBTI replaces unconstructive categorization into 'right' and 'wrong', 'clever' and 'stupid', 'good' and 'bad' with constructive categorization. One reason for the development of the MBTI was to resolve conflicts. It is useful instrument to help teams in conflict often the conflict is between different thinking types: for example, the intuitives are proponents of a change, the sensing thinkers are responding with healthy scepticism. The MBTI enables the conflict to be identifed whilst blame is entirely avoided. It also encourages the Opposing side to focus on how they can work together and use these differences rather than on how they can convert each other to their own way of thinking. Central to the theory behind the MBTI is the idea that while everyone has their natural preferences in thinking style we can all develop behaviours and hence capability in the non-preferred styles. So, individuals and teams are encouraged to do something about their weakness.

The MBTI looks at four aspects of human thinking: Extroversion/ Introversion, Sensing/ Intuition, Thinking/Feeling and Judging/Perceiving. Now let us see each of one's aspects of thinking and style.

1. EXTROVERSION/INTROVERSION (E/I)

(a) **Extroverted Preference** – Does an individual draw most of his information and energy from the outside world of events, people activities? **Then extroverted thinkers** typically communicate more spontaneously, enjoy, are energized by contacts with people, interruption, lot of activity and are relatively easy to read. They will tend to speak or act first, think later and develop their thinking while communicating. Extroverts no surprises talk more; they are outgoing, fast paced. They are both empathetic, energetic talker. Their second major sign is that these people say and how they say it: their words and the pace and priority of these words is important to observe. These types of people are aggressive, result-oriented people for accomplishing tasks is very important you can expect them to speak quickly, strongly. They tend to listen less and talk more, usually making strong statement rather than asking questions. Their way to move the discussion firmly ahead of toward and their most prized goals: solutions, progress, winning. If such a person you meet is assertive and talkative, he is extrovert, (i.e., director). You can determine that almost instantly. When you listen to his words like output, competition, success. Such persons can project a more relaxed image in pacing themselves. Become more often open, patient listeners. Give verbal compliment; act less hastily, more cautiously.

(b) **Introvert Preference** – Does an individual draw most of his information and energy from inner world of ideas, impressions, reflections and emotions. **The Introvert thinkers** typically communicate in a considered way, need space and time to develop their ideas, find too much contact, or too many interruptions draining and are like ice-bergs, much of their thinking and indeed of themselves is below the surface. They will tend to think first and sometimes never even communicate their thoughts to others; and they develop their thinking before communicating. In contrast to extrovert, these people are quiet and softspoken; they are probably thinkers or relaters. These two types more naturally introverted, are not so quick to assert themselves or reveal what they are really thinking. The introvert is also outgoing verbal person. But he is more sociable, playful and fun. They are inclined towards people than tasks. In fact, introverts are usually down right chatty but their words will have different rings from those of extrovert. The introvert, who is seldom authoritarian, will be more likely to include other people in the conversation and be more vague about results. The introvert will talk more about people and ideas and include words like feelings, impression, team and concept. Introvert cries out for more recognition and excitement. They need approval and want to become your friend. Introverts think out loud and love brain-storm, to engage in verbal give and take. Introvert can control time and emotions and try to be more objective. Follow-up on promises, tasks, focus on the job at hand.

2. SENSING/INTUITION - (S/I)

(a) **Sensing Reference** – Does an individual pay more attention to present realities which can be ascertained through the five senses. **Sensing Thinkers** are typically very realistic and draw attention to evidence and facts, prefer reasoning to be clarified step-by-step and respect system and action that have been proven. They can be suspicious of new ideas, particularly if they are not convinced by reasoning behind them.

(b) **Inituitive Preference** – Does an individual pay most attention to future possibilities and link which are intuited. **Intuitive Thinkers** operate at broad-brush, big picture level and are much more comfortable with concepts than with details. They are often creative and their thinking tends to proceed in leaps and bounds.

You can see that there will often be conflict and break down in the communication between sensing and intuitive thinkers. At worst sensing thinkers find intuitive to be creative delinquent with no appreciation of the real world. Intuitive consider sensing thinkers to be hide bound and procedure ridden, stick-in-the-mud.

3. THINKING/FEELING – (T/F)

(a) **Thinking Preference** – Does an individual's base decisions on logic and objective analysis. **Thinking Thinkers** are detached when it comes to making decisions. They can take themselves and their own feeling out of the analysis, at their most extreme; they can operate almost as thinking machines, very hard headed and oblivious of the human side. They tend to be asking, rather than people focused and they can hurt people's feelings without meaning to. Thinkers are not interested in information in friendly attention, as they are always having information about the things. Caution by nature, thinkers want to reduce risk. They will turn off to a person who seems to be too direct or too enthusiastic. Thinkers distrust hype in any form, when you approach thinkers, remember that they want data, not chit chat. They are thoughtful and will prepare and make survey your presentation matches their organized thoughtful approach. And thinkers like to be right, so allow them time for deliberation and analysis to find out the best or correct answer you must not rush a thinker. Thinker can openly show concern and appreciation of others. Make timely decisions. Use policies as guidelines, not laws and collaborate by seeking common ground.

(b) **Feeling Preference** – Does an individual base decision on personal values and feelings. **Feeling Thinkers** respond naturally and instinctively to the human, emotional side. They can find it difficult to be detached and they often value harmony above logic. At their best, they can warm, charismatic and draw others deep commitment. At their worst, they can be swayed by the personal and be inaccessible to reasoned arguments. These people want to trust you before making any relationship. They are rarely in hurry and likely will be turned off by pushy, aggressive to a person. They respond well, sincere, friendly to those who listen and are sensitive to their needs. They say no occasionally. Take some risks. Avoid undue modesty, accept logical changes.

4. JUDGING/PERCEIVING – (J/P)

This dimension has an overriding influence on the way the other dimensions are expressed. It is concerned with whether an individual prefers structure, organization and closure.

(a) **Judging Thinkers** – are typically decisive and systematic. They prefer to settle issues and move on to next things; they dislike open-ended debate. They appreciate structure and stability and at times of change will seek to establish a degree order as soon as possible.

(b) **Perceiving Preference** – It is concerned with fluidly, ambiguity and openness. **Perceiving Thinkers** enjoy the process of gathering information for self, even if it not clear where it will lead. They are inclined to postpone decision out of a sense that more information may come along which will influence how the decisions should be made. They are flexible and opportunistic. They tend to thrive on the uncertainty of change.

Judging thinkers tend to make perceiving thinkers feel claustrohobic, perceiving thinkers tend to irritate or even frighten judging thinkers.

Having seen these four aspects of human thinking, guess what a balance aspect of human thinking is. The focus is on the notion that people have different characteristic style of thinking, problem-solving, interacting and behaving; or to put it another way, certain activities that are good; others are not: For example; one person may enjoy planning, organizing, judging, another may excel

at thinking up ingenious solutions, yet another person may be renowned for an ability to challenge assumptions and expose flaws. The balance approach aspect will include at least an individual who has a strength in each of the necessary activities and will not include too many of a particular type.

CHAPTER 7

FIRO – B – Understanding Inter-personal Relations Skills

The only efficient way to tackle any improvement or complex problems is through teamwork, which allows individual to grow. The use of the team approach to improvement has the advantage over allowing individual to work separately. Problems are exposed to diversity of knowledge, skills, experience and are solved more efficiently by team than individual. The team approach is more satisfying to team-members and boost moral and ownership through participation. When team is put together individuals therein pass through the stages of;

- Forming (awareness)
- Storming (conflicts)
- Norming (cooperation)
- Performing (productivity)

and they develop team with these understanding. It makes possible to team leader to address the need of the task, the role of individual in team, the brainstorming on issues and find out solution acceptable to all. Through these processes, knowledge, understanding and awareness of inter-personal relationship is understood and valued.

FIRO – B (Fundamental Inter-personal Relationship Orientation Behaviour) is an instrument, a kind of psycho-social skill for helping individuals understanding and values each other for their differences as well as similarities. It also forms the basis for thinking of culture change based on inclusion, control and openness of individual types.

For any individual or team to succeed, need to be facilitated through the stages of:-

- Becoming aware
- Needing to accept
- Needing to adopt
- Needing to adapt, and
- Needing to act

And then think about achieving successful working of team or individuals. The FIRO-B is fundamental psychological instrument which can be used to give valuable insight into the needs individual brings to their relationships with other people. The instrument assesses needs for inclusion, control and openness and thereby a framework for understanding the dynamics of inter-personal relationships. It helps individuals to be more aware of how they relate to others and to become more flexible in their behaviour. Consequently it enables people to build more productive teams through better working relationships. The FIRO-B first used by Schultz in this book. Three Dimensional Theory of personal behaviour (1958) and described three dimensions in the form of the decisions we make in our relationships regarding whether we want to be:

- In or out – Inclusion
- Up or down – Control
- Close or distant – Openness.

Thus, the FIRO-B estimates our unique level of needs for each of these dimensions of inter-personal interaction. Again these dimensions are divided into expressed behavior – the behaviour we feel most comfortable exhibiting towards other people and the behaviour we wants from others – **wanted behaviour**

	Inclusion	**Control**	**Openness**
Expressed Behaviour	Expressed Inclusion	Express control	Express Openness
Wanted Behaviour	Wanted Inclusion	Wanted Control	Wanted Openness

The expressed aspect of each dimension indicates the level of behaviour the individual is most comfortable with others.

Expressed Behaviour

- **Inclusion** – Makes efforts to include other people in his activities, tries to belong to or join groups and to be with people as much as possible.
- **Control** – Tries to extent control and influence over people and tell them what to do.
- **Openness** – Makes efforts to become close to people, expresses friendly, open feelings, tries to be personal and even intimate.

The wanted beahviour

The wanted behaviour of each dimension indicates the behaviour the individual prefers others to adopt towards him.

- **Inclusion** – Wants other people to include him in their activities, to be invited to belong to or join groups even if no efforts is made by the individual to be included.
- **Control** – Wants others to control and influence him and he told what to do.
- **Openness** – Wants others to become close to him and express friendly, open, even affectionate feelings.

Understanding what drives this behaviour can help individuals to further develop understanding of themselves and others. FIRO-B skill for measuring feelings, self-concept can deepen the awareness of what lies behind our behaviour with respect to inclusion, control and openness. Overall relationship between feeling and self-concept skills is as given:

Behaviour related to:	**Feeling related to:**
Inclusion	Significance
Control	Competence
Openness	Likeability

Issue around control behaviour then may arise because of underlying feeling about competence. Similarly, underlying feelings concerning significance may lead to certain inclusion beahviour. FIRO-B in the workplace – the inclusion, control and openness dimensions can help groups of people to understand how their individual and joint behaviour develops as teams are formed and effectively display:

- Clear objectives and agreed performance goals
- Openness and confrontation
- Support and trust
- Cooperation and conflict
- Good decision-making
- Appropriate leadership
- Sound inter-group relationships
- Individual development opportunities

These attributes are not particularly new but are very applicable and useful in the management of team and its individuals for work improvement. However, for the benefit of team and individuals within, it need to become **aware** of the theory FIRO-B. They need to **accept** the principles as valid, **adopt** them for themselves in order to **adapt** their behaviour accordingly. This will lead to individual and team's **action**.

In conclusion, the FIROB looks at social behaviour and needs. It is not a true psychometric, because an individuals profile tends to vary quite a lot overtime. However, as a snapshot insight into social needs and expectations in a group of people, it can be quite revealing.

What shows, for each of the three dimensions of inclusion, control and openness are both the extent to which an individual behaves towards others so as to satisfy their needs on that dimension – expressed behaviour and the extent to which an individual is looking for his own needs to be satisfied – wanted behaviour.

Use of the FIROB

This sort of questions which FIROB addresses about a team or individuals are:

- How much 'social glue' is there in the team? Will it be a very close-knit, sociable team or rather more distant team.
- Will there be struggles for control and responsibility? Will there be a clear natural leader? What proportion of the team wants to be reassured and supported? What proportion wants to go their own way?
- How much open feedback will there be? Will the feedback meet everyone's needs?
- Are there some fundamental social needs (such as for closeness or distance, for control or freedom) which are likely to get in the way of effective application to tasks?

Why use the FIROB

- The emotional needs on which the FIROB focuses tend to exert a profound influence even if you try to ignore them. The FIROB creates a language for putting these needs on the table; acknowledging their potential impact and planning to contain their destructive influence.
- The FIROB can be used as snapshot and certainly meant to be thought-provoking rather than definitive.
- The teams profile can be drawn up in a very appealing visual way, which highlights differences between individuals, clusters and likely alliances and overall team style-inclusion, control and affection.

CHAPTER 8

Johari Window

This conceptual framework is developed by Luft and Ingham is called Johari Window. Johari window is used to depict personality and behaviour. According to this framework of johari window, there are some attitudes or behaviours engaged by people that they themselves know about. This is called **known-to-self area** includes their knowledge of the way they are coming across the impact they are having with other people they are trying to influence. At the same time, part of their personality is **unknown to self** that is in some areas they are unaware of how they are coming across to other people. It may be that other people have not given them feedback or it may be that a person has not been alert enough to pick-up some of the verbal or non-verbal feedback that actually exists at work place. We also look at people's personality that includes behaviours and attitudes **known to others** in a persons setting, as well as areas **unknown to others**. It is termed as known to others and unknown to others. I put the framework this way:

Johari Window

Known to self	Unknown to self	
A - Public	B – Blind	Known to Others
C - Private	D - Unknown	Unknown to Others

There are some parts of the person's behaviour and style which are known to him and some parts which are unknown to him.

A – Called **Public Arena** is known to all at workplace. For e.g., information like name, education, age, physical appearance, familiar organizational affiliation, etc.

B – The arena that is unknown to self but is known to others is referred to as the **Blind Arena**. It is unknown to you either because others have been unwilling to share feedback or communicate to you. This contains those aspects of a person's behaviour and style about which others know but the person does not.

C – The arena that is known to self but unknown to others is referred to as **Private Arena**, since it is only known to the self. It may be private because the person is unwilling to share or disclose this to others at workplace.

D – The last arena, unknown to self and unknown to others, is called the **Unknown or Dark Arena**. There are a certain portion of a person's behaviour and personality that is above the surface. But much of the iceberg exist beneath the surface and unless we will really never have any sight into its consistency. And yet much of that part of a person's personality referred to as unknown may be having a relevant in which a person engages when trying to influence the behaviour of others.

There are two processes that affect the shape of johari window are called feedback and disclosure. For e.g., treating people at workplace with respect lead to a relationship in which they feel free to share and talk. The more relative feedback that takes place at workplace, the more public arena of a person begins to extend into and displace the blind arena. The other process that affects the shape of johari window is disclosure. This is the extent to which a person is willing to share with others at the workplace happenings about themselves. Disclosure is important and helpful at workplace as long as it is relevant to operation of the workplace. In the process of disclosure, the more and more workplace relevant information that a person disclose about the way people think or behave, the more public arena opens into private arena. These are the situations occur in every organization where people interact and develop relationship with each other and accordingly form their behaviour pattern and set it for practice with different people.

CHAPTER 9

Transactional Analysis

While the amount of technical and conceptual skills needed at workplace varies from level-to-level in organizational ladders, the common denominator that appears, to be crucial at all level is human skills. According to American Management Association's survey, it is agreed that the most important single skill of a person is the ability to get along with people is more vital than intelligence, knowledge and job skills. Ability and judgement in working with and through people including an understanding of behaviour and its application, people demonstrate at works is of prime importance. At work, it is true that we can't always anticipate the reaction of people to our acts or deeds. How can we better predict the kind of response to our action may evoke from people? Transactional analysis is one of the human skills may help us judge people behaviour at workplace. It is a way of understanding behaviour. It is based on the belief that we can learn from studying more closely the way our decision and communications are based on our thoughts and feelings. Under transactional analysis ego-states are described phenomenologically as coherent system of feelings, and operationally as a coherent behaviour patterns. In more practical terms, it is a system of feeling accompanied by a related set of behaviour patterns. Each individual seems to have available a limited repertoire of such ego-state, which are not roles but psychological realities. Colloquially their exhibitions are called Parent, Adult and Child.

Transactional analysis is a method of analyzing and understanding behaviour. Why people behave as they do? To diagnose this we have to judge three sources within human personality that stimulate, monitor and control behaviour. According to Eric Berne, "Transactional Analysis" the personality of a person is the collection of behaviour patterns developed overtime that people begin to recognize as that person. These behaviour patterns are evoked in different degrees from three ego-states; parent, adult and child. These ego-states have nothing to do with chronological age, and are only related to psychological age. As Berne states, "Although we cannot directly observe these ego-states, we can observe behaviour and from this infer which of the three ego-states is operating at that moment".

(1) The Parent Ego-state

It is our evaluative part of state that evokes value laden behaviour. This value laden behaviour is not necessarily real value behaviour. It is learned behaviour through past experiences. In this ego-state there are two kinds of parent ego-states: **Nurturing Parent and Critical Parent.**

(a) **The nurturing parent** is that part of a person that is understanding and caring about other people. Behaviour coming from nurturing parent may set limits on and provide direction for people's behaviour; it will not put people down and make them feel not okay as individuals.

(b) **The critical parent** makes people feel that they are not just, their behaviours are not okay. Thus, critical parent behaviour attacks people's personalities as well as their behaviour. When people are in critical parent ego-state, they are very evaluative and judgemental. They are always ready to respond with a "should" or "ought" to almost anything people tell them. People with heavy critical parent ego-state "should" on other people as well as "should" on themselves.

(2) The Adult Ego-state

This state evokes behaviour that could be described simply as logical, reasonable, rational and unemotional. Behaviour from the adult ego-state is characterized by problem-solving analysis and rational decision-making. People operating from the adult ego-state are taking the emotional content of their child ego-state and the value laden content of their parent ego-state and checking them out in the reality of the external world. These people are examining alternatives, probabilities and values prior to engaging in behaviour.

(3) The Child Ego-state

It is associated with behaviour that appears when a person is responding emotionally. A person's child contains the natural impulses and attitudes learned from childhood experiences. There are two kinds of child ego-states; **Happy Child and Destructive Child**.

(a) People behaving from their happy child are doing things because they want to, but their behaviour is not disruptive to others or destructive to the environment.

(b) People in destructive child are also doing things because they feel like it, but their behaviour is either disruptive to others or destructive to themselves or their environment.

Whether a person's behaviour is coming from the happy child or the destructive child depends on the transaction or feedback from others. There are again two kinds of destructive ego-states; **Rebellious child and Complaint child.**

(a) When people are in rebellious child ego-state, they are not going to listen to anyone who tells them what to do. They either rebel openly by giving negative or rebel subtly by forgetting, being confused or putting off doing something. Person's behaving from rebellious child will not do anything an authority figure asks them to do even if it makes sense.

(b) Another destructive child ego-state is complaint child. When people are in this ego-state, they do what others want. Complying with the wishes of others is okay if the person really wants to or if it makes sense to do it. However, complaint child can hurt the development of people who comply unquestionably all the time, even when it makes no sense with them. These people tend to remain dependent instead of becoming independent. When this occurs, complaint child becomes a form of destructive child.

Behaviour coming from child ego-state is often almost a stimulus response relationship. Something happens and the person responds almost immediately, what happens is not processed intellectually. It almost goes in one ear, picks up speed, and goes out the other ear. With adult ego-state behaviour, when something happens, there is not an immediate response. A response follows only conscious evaluation and thought.

All people behave from these three ego-states at different time at workplace. A healthy person has a personality that maintains a balance among all the three. While a balance among all three ego-states seems to be most healthy, some people seem dominated at times by one or two ego-states.

(a) Most specifically **Child-dominated people** who are mainly coming from destructive child ego-state do not engage in much rational problem-solving. They learned in their early years that they could get things by screaming, hollering and being emotional. Instead of solving their own problems, these people want them, want their managers or some other person to tell them what to do, where to do it and how to do it or what is right, what is wrong and what is good and what is bad.

(b) **Parent-dominated people**, who are mainly coming from critical parent, also do not engage is much rational problem-solving because they already know what is right and what is wrong. These people characterized with the comment "look! Don't confuse me with the facts. I have already made up my mind". It really does not matter how much real information anyone brings to these people. They have already with 'it is good, it is bad' set of words.

(c) Even **adult-dominated people** can be troublesome, because they can be very boring people with whom to work. They are often workaholics. They don't seem to act like other people. They are never able to let down their hair and have fun. Thus, a balance between the three ego-states makes for a healthy person.

Depending on these three ego-states, in the process of growing up, people make basic assumptions about their self-worth, as well as about other people at workplace. These assumptions about oneself and another person are called life position. Life positions tend to be more permanent than ego-states. These assumptions are described in the terms of "okay ness". **Four possible relationships results from these life positions are:**

1. I am not ok, you are not ok – Neither person has value at workplace.
2. I am not ok, you are ok – You have value but I don't have value.
3. I am ok, you are not ok – I have value but you don't have value.
4. I am ok, you are ok – We both have value.

1. These people tend to feel bad about them and see the whole environment as miserable. People with this life position don't trust other people and have no confidence in themselves.
2. People with this life position often feel that others are more capable and generally have fewer problems than they themselves do. This is the most common life position for people who have a high deference for authority. They see their world as don't have any control or much power, but those people in power seem to have all the power, rewards.
3. People who feel they are ok often come from their critical parent ego-state. They often regard other people as sources of criticism. They feel that if they are not exactly perfect, people will be excessively critical to them. They want to break away or rebel from some authority figure and become more independent, but they are either not sure how to go about this or they have had unpleasant experience in attempting it in the part. With this life position, listening often tends to stop even when someone is still trying to communicate with this person. People with I am ok, you are not ok life position, while acting are self-confident and under control. Their way they play out "not ok" feelings often is expressed in the need for power and control.
4. This is healthy life position. People with these feelings express confidence in themselves as well as trust and confidence in other people in the environment. The behaviour lends to come from their nurturing parent, adult and happy child ego-states.

This transactional analysis enables people to identify patterns of transactions between themselves and others. Ultimately help us determine ego-state is most heavily influencing our behaviour and the behaviour of other people with whom they interact. I have tried to review literature on transactional analysis with the intention of integrating sources for understanding and analyzing behaviour of people at work. It is you to haul the skill in transactional analysis. For changing, directing and controlling yours as well as others at work, this skill analysis may help get you on the right road of understanding people.

CHAPTER 10

Assertive Skills

Human beings are driven by social needs, which make them interact and communicate with others, both in their personal as well as professional relationships. In the course of this communication they experience a wide variety of emotions like – anxiety, fear, anger, irritation, suspicion, despair, etc. This happens because the style in which they communicate either robs them of their personal significance or denies the same to the people they interact with. But how do you react when people critics you, shout at you, blame you for something you have not done; keep you waiting; interrupt you; or exploit you? Frequently, people react by either going on the defensive (For e.g., it is not my fault. I was only doing my best) or by attacking back (You can talk. What about the time when you.....)

When we react defensively we are being SUBMISSIVE, when we attack we are AGGRESSIVE. There s however, a third more satisfactory alternative and that is to be ASSERTIVE.

Submissive behaviour is when

We fail to stand up for our rights or do so in such a way that others can easily disregard them; express our thoughts, feelings and beliefs in apologetic, cautious or self-effecting way; fail to express our views or feelings altogether. Submissive mode of behaviour is based on the belief that our own needs and wants will be seen by others to be less important than their own.

Aggressive behaviour is when

We stand up for our own rights in such a way that we violate the rights of another person. Express thoughts, feelings and beliefs in unsuitable and in appropriate ways, even though we may honesty believe those views to be right. Aggression enhances us at the expense of others and can serve to put another person down. It is based on the belief that our opinions are more important than other people's. It is characterized by blaming other people or outside factors, by showing contempt and being hostile, attacking or patronizing.

Assertive behaviour is when

We stand up for our own right in a way that does not violate another person's right. It leads to an honest, open and direct expression of our point of view which, at the same time, shows that we understand the other person's position. Assertive behaviour facilitates equality in relationship with others and about being able to safeguard your interests and sanity without harming others. With conditioning and repeated behaviour one tends to adopt a particular style of behaviour more often and that becomes his predominant style or behaviour.

WHY PEOPLE BEHAVE AGGRESSIVELY, SUBMISSIVELY OR ASSERTIVELY

No one behaves assertively, aggressively or submissively all the time. People vary their behaviour between all three and are more likely to react aggressively or submissively rather than assertively in a conflict situation. This is to do with the level of their self-esteem.

Self-esteem is the evaluation we make and hold about ourselves. It is high or low level at which we rate ourselves. It is our judgement of our worth as a person. It is based on the extent to which we believe ourselves to be competent, likeable and successful. If our self-esteem is low, then we feel anxious when conflict arises. We feel insured and threatened by the situation and the people in it.

It is a basic instinct when we feel threatened either to hit out (aggression) or to turn the defensive (submission). Aggressive behaviour is often successful in getting us what we want. It can give us a sense of power over others and help us to release bad feeling such as anger and frustration, i.e., to let off steam. Submissive behaviour can defuse a conflict very quickly by avoiding it. It helps us escape the anxiety of a confrontation. It also helps us to avoid feeling guilty, about letting someone down or upsetting them. Assertive behaviour is a balance behaviour between submission and aggressive.

NON-ASSERTIVE PEOPLE

People accept the non-assertive behaviour when they possess no control of their lives, they become unsure and unsecured. They do not recognize their strength hence learn to act in inferior ways, because they believe to be inferior. They find it impossible to express emotions like anger. They know to the wishes of others and hold their own desire inside themselves. In psychology this state of unassertiveness is termed as inhibitory personalities.

- Such persons live their lives by the rules and whims of others.
- They do not know who they are, what they feel, what they want.

- From passivity and fear they justify it with excuses "My boss will fire me if I ask for long leave".
- These people suffer the sad and severe consequences of their non-assertiveness: such as lack of personal growth and success; undeveloped relationships; mental anguish; lack of positiveness. Such people have some problems inherited because of non-assertive behaviour.
- They are timid soul – you say 'yes' when want to say 'no'.
- You allow yourself to be pushed around and remain passive in all situations.
- If some one steps on your foot, you say 'I am sorry'!
- You have communication difficulties. You don't make direct request, dishonest in communication, you say 'it is good to see you" I have been thinking about you only since morning, when you would not careless and the other person knows it. You seem to be open and honest but this seeming assertiveness hides a basic lack of honesty.
- Inappropriate communication – you remain unknowledgeable about the realities of social relations, you say what you think is the right thing at the wrong time. For e.g., "your boss tells you of his terrible day with marketing people's meeting and in response, you offer a list of employees demands on salary increase". Though you are open and honest but the presentation was in immature way poses inter-personal difficulties. Because you say wrong thing at the wrong time. Sometimes, your split assertiveness makes you fail in one area and successful in the other, for e.g.:
  - A man can be the epitome of passivity at the work/office and behave like a tyrant at home.
  - He can act assertively at work, in his social relations, with his children and yet be unassertive with his wife.
- You can't make eye-contact or small talk, handle confrontation, start a conversation. (Behaviour deficits)
- You know what you should do and have the skill to accomplish it but your fear of rejection, anger, criticism, tenderness. Inhibit you from carrying out the action. (Blocks)
- You don't understand what you say or do as right. But very often, the other person because of his own needs, feelings, just works. You don't grant independence to other people.
- You don't understand that different kinds of relationships exist with different people. (Wrong concept of social reality.)
- Because you have learned to do things in the wrong way, you may have trouble, doing what you want to do. For e.g., to tell your friend, 'why don't you tell your wife to stop making lunch for us'. Friend replies, 'wife! I make my own lunch'. Your unwanted behaviour is the cause. (Your interfering habits.)

ASSERTIVE PEOPLE

People with excitatory personality do not fear their feelings, frightened neither of closeness nor combat; they act out of strengths. The excitatory man knows who he is, what he wants.

- He is an assertive person. Assertive person state or affirm positively, assuredly. Plainly or strongly his statement.
- He feels free to reveal himself – through words, actions.
- He makes the statement: this is me. This is what I feel, think and want.
- He can communicate with people on all level with – superior, subordinate, colleagues, and strangers. He attempts to make things happen.
- He has an active orientation to life – he goes after he wants.
- He acts in a way he himself respects – he is always strives to make good try so that win, lose or draw. He maintains self-respect. Aware that he can't always win, he accepts his limitations.

Assertiveness means your ability to act in harmony with your self-esteem without hurting others. Being assertive, you will be able to change your attitudes and feelings about yourself and others.

ADVANTAGES OF ASSERTIVENESS

(a) Close working relationships –

Assertion tends to breed assertion, so people work more happily with you than against you. You are then, with their help, more likely to achieve your objectives in a conflict situation.

(b) Greater confidence in yourself –

You develop a strong regard for yourself and a high level of self-esteem, reducing the chance of boastfulness (aggression) and hopelessness (submission)

(c) Greater confidence in others –

You have a healthy recognition of the capabilities and limitations of others as opposed to seeing them as inferior.

(d) Increased self-responsibility –

You take responsibility for you, your wants, opinions, needs, etc., rather than blaming others (aggression) or excusing yourself (submission)

(e) Increased self-control –

You can channel your thoughts and feelings to produce the behaviour you want, rather than being controlled, by outside events or people or inner emotions.

(f) Saving in time and energy –

You can take decisions more swiftly based on your individual merit and save time when handling disputes. A lot of time and energy is wasted or worrying and scheming. If you are not worried about upsetting people (submission) or scheming how not to miss out (aggression) then you can save yourself a lot of stress.

(g) An increased chance of everyone winning –

Assertiveness increases the likelihood that all parties will see their need met their ideas and opinions heard and considered and your abilities put to good use.

Please remember assertiveness is not a cure-all. The ability to discern is very essential while using assertive skills.

CHAPTER 11

Public Speaking and Presentation Skills

The ability to speak confidently is not only one of the major underpinnings of charisma; it is also one of the major marketable skills you can acquire. Organizations continually seek individuals who can sale products, present proposals, report findings and explain ideas effectively. It is therefore, level of public speaking is now needed to get sharpen to reach your message across.

WHAT IS PUBLIC SPEAKING?

It can be in many terms, giving a speech to a large audience in public forum, presenting a proposal to the corporate conference room full of board members, or addressing one other person in a formal environment, such as sales presentation, if your presentation is boring or professional, it can leave you with nothing but a weak round of applause or cause you to lose the sale. Hence, good presentation can provide opportunities for growth, recognition and prestige. Effective public speakers establish themselves as experts to whom others turn for advice. Thus, being able to stand on your feet confidently and express you thoughts clearly and logically is a major building block of public speaking. For building your presentation skills at least three important points to be kept in mind. **One**, you are never too good or too experienced to ignore some of the fundamentals of good speaking. **Two**, you can give an occasional poor speech and still retain your charisma. **Three** and most important, the ability to communicate well to groups or people can make a critical defense in your career. It is professional success and upward mobility is how much you enjoy and how good you are at public speaking. Following statement warms you against the pit falls of public speaking. "When you applaud me at the start that is faith; midway through that is hope. But if you applaud me at the end, that will be charity." So to avoid requiring such charity, you need to build your presentation skills. Secondly, do not one of such speakers "Before they get up, they do not know what they are going to say, when they are speaking, they do not know what they are saying and when they have sat down, they do not know what they have said".

Public speaking is an effective two-way communication demands that you capture both content and intent and learn to speak the language of logic and emotion, we must seek to understand the intent of communication without prejudicing or rejecting the content. We can do this by giving time, being patient, seeking first to understand and openly expressing feelings. To be effective in presenting your point of view, start by demonstrating a clear understanding of the alternative points of view. Articulate them better than their advocates can. Effective presentations begin with pre-assessment. Communication, after all, is not so much of a matter of intellect as it is of trust and acceptance of others, of their ideas and feelings, acceptance of the fact that they are different and that from their point of view they are right.

BUILDING YOUR PRESENTATION SKILLS

Influencing others among small groups of people and influencing a large group will initially involve some form of public speaking. Nowadays, media in general and television in particular have loomed larger in our lives. So self-presentation has become an even more important skill. While making any presentation, three most important things to keep in mind are:

(i) Who you are?

Your personality, relevant knowledge and experience you must engage the whole yourself: voice, eyes, arms, hand and total body language.

(ii) How you say it?

Increase/enlarge your vocal range, create the right atmosphere.

(iii) What you say?

Requires careful selection and ordering everything you say must be relevant. Lot of emphasis on emotional factors is to be placed for public presentation and only secondary a matter of saying the right things in the right way at the right time.

Following are some of the tips to remember while presenting you to group or public.

1 – Prepare your mind and heart before you prepare your presentation – what we say may be less important than how we say it.

2 – Recognize and take time to know what to present, when, where and how and to whom.

3 – Agree on the time limits, rules, expectation and consequences of presentation. It must be agreed upon, understood and enforced.

4 – Speak the language of logic.

5 – Involve people in meaningful debate.

PREPARING THE TALK

Abraham Lincoln once said "If I had eight hours to chop down a tree, I would spend six hours sharpening my axe". What makes one presentation better than next is the amount of time that goes into it before you assume centre stage. Thus, planning the speech involves six basic steps:

- Identifying the purpose of your presentation.
- Knowing your audience.
- Knowing your material.
- Focusing on the big idea.
- Getting and holding the audiences attention.
- Practicing your presentation and visualizing success.

Then comes what is the purpose of speech? The first and foremost critical step in planning your speech is understanding:

- Why am I giving this speech? – Purpose.
- What do I want the audience to know or do at the end?
- How do I want the audience to feel?

The more aware you are of the feelings you want to promote through your speech, the better you will choose your words. Once you know your audience, you are clear about your purpose and you are committed to through preparation. Therefore, you need to structure your presentation so it supports your ideas, but they should all reinforce the primary focus of your ideas and its relevance to the audience. As you develop the details and images for your speech 'with purpose', keep checking back to your one big idea and make sure it all relates directly. As you present your speech, keep in mind 'tell them what you are going to tell them, and tell them what you just told them'. Also let them know what you expect at the end of presentation – question and answer session? Now by this time, you know your aim? and your audience. You have prepared your speech/presentation material and honed the big idea until it is sure to get peoples attention. This is the time now to deliver the speech. There is an old saying among speakers: Have a powerful, captivating, opening and a strong, memorable close – and put them as close together as possible. Grab your listeners with something vitally interesting to them.

DELIVERING SPEECH/PRESENTATION

Before you stand up for delivery overcoming stage fear is most necessary. You can overcome stage fear by approaching the right attitude. The way you feel about yourself, the audience and the subject – as well as how well you have prepared and how hard you have worked on delivery, will have direct impact on you as well as walk towards the stage/podium. With a good attitude and effective preparation, you can convert a paralyzing fear into positive anxiety, which keeps you sharp; make a strong, wholehearted commitment to your audience. Concentrating on them and their needs will help you forget about your self-consciousness. Following are some of the tips for overcoming stage fear:

- Know your material well.
- Then practice your presentation. Do a dry run.
- Make at least few persons in the audience your friends before you speak.
- When speaking look directly at specific individuals in the audience.
- Always check in advance the place where you will be speaking and audio-visual equipment, if any.
- Make sure you are dressed properly.
- Use your own style. Don't try to imitate someone else.
- Remind repeatedly yourself that the reason you are speaking is because you are the expert. Those who are you to speak believe that you have something of value to share.

This way you can learn to manage your stage fear.

Check your body language

Beyond the standard visual aids, there is an important "visual aid" that we are less aware of the non-verbal gestures you include in your presentation. Your body movements, facial expression and gestures reveal much more than the words alone do about emotional state. Body language is one of the most effective tools. Find the gestures that feel natural and reinforce your presentation. Make bold rather than timid gesture and use broad as well as subtle movement. In other words, how you say something is as important as what you say.

Your eyes – Are known as windows to the soul. It has been discovered that speakers who were rated "sincere" looked at their audiences and average of three times longer than speakers who were rated "insincere".

Your face – Delivering your material with an unchanged facial expression is as bad as delivering it in a monotone voice.

Your hands – You also communicate through your hands. When you are proud of what you are saying, you usually show your hands quite openly. When you are not feeling good, you probably put your hands in your pockets or behind your back.

Your arms and legs – Crossed arms acts as a protective guard against an anticipated attacks you convey readiness, when you put your hands on your hips you communicate thoughtfulness, when you put one hand to your chin and rest your elbow in the other hand. In terms of your legs, walking around on the stage communicates that you are comfortable with yourself and you are open with the audience.

Your voice – Dr. Carol Fleming points out that what you sound like indicates your personality, suggests your intelligence level, and reveals a lot about your background. Within few seconds talking on the phone with a stranger. You can learn his gender, approximate age, temperament, his confidence, etc., obviously, when you give speech, there is a lot more that is communicated to your audience. Your vocal qualities like, rhythm, speed, pitch, volume, reflection, clarity, pauses communicate a lot to your audience. You convey your competence, leadership strength with your tone of voice.

CHAPTER 12

Listening Skills

"Nature has given us one tongue, but two ears, that we may hear from others twice as much as we speak." But our mental attitude colours and shapes reality for us and that is why most people do not listen with the intent to understand; they listen with intent to reply. They filter everything through their own way and read their autobiography into people's live. We filled with our rightness, we want to be understood. We never really understand what is going on inside another person. Because we autobiographically, tend to respond in one of four ways:

- We evaluate – we either agree or disagree.
- We probe – we ask questions from our frame of reference.
- We advise – we give counsel based on our own experience.
- We interrupt – we try to figure people out, to explain their motives, their behaviour, based on our own motives and behaviour.

These responses come naturally to us as we are deeply scripted in these responses that we don't even realize when we use them. This is because we seek to be understood than seeking first to understand. By setting aside our own autobiographical responses and really seeking to understand can make your responses emotional. Lot of people just don't listen. Listening takes effort. It is more than just keeping quiet. It means really concentrating on the other person. We don't listen well. We think we already know what someone is going to say. We assume that we have a full understanding right from the start, so we jump in and interrupt, we don't take the time required to hear people out. We don't listen well because we don't know how. We do more listening than speaking, reading or writing. It is not our listening it is just hearing. We only pretend to listen. Listening does not just meaning shutting up while some one else speaks – though that is a start. But listening – real listening – takes more work than that. It is more than the physical process of hearing. It also takes intellectual and emotional efforts.

Four levels of Listening

When another person speaks, we are usually "listening" at one of four levels:

- We may be ignoring another person, not really listening at all.
- We may practice pretending – yes, right, I see.
- We may practice selective listening – hearing only certain part of the conversation.
- We may practice alternative listening, paying attention and focusing energy on the words that are being said. But very few of us ever practice the highest form of listening.

Different profiles of Listeners

We typically listen at one of four levels of attentiveness.

1. **The Non-listener** – Is a person who does not hear the speaker. No real effort is made to hear what the other person saying. Blank stares and nervous mannerisms usually greet your attempt to make a point. He pays attention elsewhere. They are usually considered social bores and know it all and they are typically disliked or merely tolerated.
2. **The Marginal Listener** – He is superficial listener. He hears the sound and words but not meaning and intent. Marginal listeners stay on the surface of the conversation or issue never risking to go deeper. Many marginal listeners, in fact, sometimes look for outside distractions: incoming calls, E-mail, message or computer screen to use as excuse for pulling themselves away from the conversation. If at all they listen they tend to listen only for the bottom instead of the overall message when you have finished your statement, the marginal listener, having missed the nuances the body language and much of the content itself, is likely to say, 'so what is the point'. Marginal listeners are especially dangerous because of the enormous possibility for misunderstanding due to non-listening.
3. **The Technical Listener** – He actively tries to hear what the speaker is saying. So, this is the label most of us would give ourselves if we consider ourselves to be good listeners. More concentration and attention are required at this level. However, technical listeners generally don't make effort to understand the speaker's intent. They are great with sematics, facts and statistics, but poor in terms of sensitivity, empathy and true understanding. In other words, technical listeners believe that they understand the speaker but the speaker does not feel understood.

4. **The Active Listener** – He unquestionably at the most powerful level of listening. Active listening is also the most demanding and tiring because it requires the most mental and emotional effort. The active listener refrains from judging the speakers massage and instead focuses on understanding his point of view. So, the active listener concentrates on the thoughts and feelings of the speaker including what is not being said as well as the actual words. To listen actively means suspending your personal thoughts and feelings. It means giving attention solely to the speaker. It means sending out verbal and non-verbal feedback that feals the speaker you are absorbing what is being said. This is important. If you expect to get the speaker's support, he needs to know they are being heard.

➢ Active listening requires a high degree of alertness and sensibility. The words being spoken by the speaker need to heard, but what they are not saying also needs to be picked up. The speaker may say everything is fine, but have a facial expression and demeanour of extreme unhappiness. His body may be tense and his fingers fiddling nervously. The real skills of being an active listener lie in the listener's ability to help the speaker express what he want to say. The listener can hear the content of what is being said and hear the totality of the message – the emotion as well as words.

Are you good or poor listener

1. When you want to win someone's attention and gain his confidence, listening is just as important as speaking. Good listening draws people to you, poor listening causes them to drift away. Poor listening is an acknowledged problem between superior-subordinate, child and parent, wife and husband and so on. Lack of effective listening leads to loss.
2. Leaderships are practically impossible for the person who can't listen effectively. Mis-communication, mistakes are the by-products of poor listening. People view poor listener as self-centred, disinterested and aloof. Mans inability to communicate is a result of his failure to listen effectively, skilfully and with understanding to another person. Listening better can transform people and relationships by:
   - Making others feel appreciated and valued because you make the effort to share their excitement and ideas.
   - Saving time by reducing mistakes and misunderstandings.
   - Increasing trust, credibility and cooperation.
   - Helping solve problems more quickly.

For some people listening is the most neglected and least understood of all the aspects of communication. And largely, this weak link springs from bad habits. In short, we have not been trained to listen. An untrained listener is likely to understand and retain 50% of a conversation moments after it is finished. After two days, no wonder he seldom agrees about what has been discussed.

But few of us listen as effectively as we should.

Empathic listening

It is with intent to understand. Seeking first to understand, to really understand. Empathic listening gets inside another persons frame of reference. You look out through it, you see the world the way they see the world. You understand their way, you understand how they feel. Empathy is not again sympathy. The essence of empathic listening is not that you agree with someone, it is that you fully, deeply, understand that person, emotionally as well as intellectually. In empathic listening you listen with ears, but you also, and more importantly, listen with your eyes and with your heart. You listen for feeling, for meaning. You listen for behaviour. Empathic listening is powerful because it gives you accurate data to work with. Instead of projecting your own way and assuming thoughts, feelings, motives and interpretation, you are dealing with the reality inside another person's head and heart. You are listening to understand: it is deeply therapeutic and healing because it gives a person psychological air. Listening involves patience, openness and the desire to understand qualities of character. Listening well is essential for any workplace success.

It is surveyed that on listening we spend 55% of total time we spent. Those who do not listen come across as different or uncaring which in turn make others less communicative. Listening is an art. Listening is giving the sense of one is open to listening in the first place. It is open door policy, who appears approachable or goes out of their way to hear what people have to say, embody this competence and people who seem easy to walk to be those who get to hear more. People who trusting others, who believe that people are basically good tend to be more highly attuned to feelings. Hence, listening attentively is perhaps the highest form of respect one person can pay another.

If you are listening be prepared to act on what you hear. Because asking questions raises expectations that something will be done. Listening and not visibly and fairly quick responding is worse than not listening.

Listening is one of keys to build effective inter-personal communication and seek first to understand, and then to be understood is basic principle of building positive inter-personal relations. Your effective interaction will influence other people, provided you understand them, care them. So if you want to be really effective in the habit of inter-personal communication, you can do it with technique alone. You have to build the skills of empathic listening.

Listening skills are important in fostering human relationships with the society, workplace or family. They require a deeper, empathetic quality than those involved in merely 'relating' to others. With the advent of long-term and more intensive relationship between child and parent, student and teacher, superior and subordinate, customer and supplier, manufacture and subcontractor, more intensive skills are increasingly being called for. Listening skills are closely related to powers of observations, body language, communication content, etc.

- Do you deal with people's long range needs or with their immediate needs?
- Do you restrict yourself to superficial relationships?

- Do you really get involved with people?
- Are you self-focused when you interact with others.
- Do you focus entirely on them?
- Do you assume you already know your people's wishes?
- Are you constantly reviewing them?
- Do you treat all people around you the same.
- Do you take account of each of their individual differences?
- Do you expect people to respond to a situation the way do, or not?

In final analysis, good listeners are more likely to be adept at recognizing potential in other people.

You as a salesman, to shine at service, you need to monitor the satisfaction of customers, not waiting to hear complaint but freely offering information that might be helpful without self-interest motivating gestures. This lays the groundwork for a trusting relationship one where the customer or coworker will feel a positive regard and start to see you as a source of reliable and helpful information elevating the relationship above one simply of buyer and seller. That of courses takes empathy. It is said that a finely tuned is at the heart of empathy.

Listening well and deeply means going beyond what is said by asking questions, restating in one's own word what you hear to be sure you understand. This is active listening. A mark of having truly heard someone. Appropriately, to respond in positive manner.

Understanding someone points of view or perspective, knowing why they feel as they do does not inevitably mean embracing it. Particularly, in business dealings, understanding how someone feel need not lead to giving in but be more skillful negotiation and management. As a result, tough decisions may generate less resentment and lasting illwill. Empathy is sensing what people are feeling, being able to take their perspective and cultivating rapport and attunement with people. So, listening with empathy means asking yourself, 'Where is this person's anger coming from'? What can I do that is reasonable and non-condemning? Genuinely listening well is, at heart, an act of love, and as such may help heal the person. Mathew MC-Kay and Martha Davis in their book, "*How to communicate*" say "Listening is a commitment and a compliment. It is a commitment to understanding how other people feel, how they see their world" and it is a compliment because it says to the other persons: "I care about what is happening to you, your life and your experience are important".

Skills of Active Listening

To acquire listening skills and to react the highest level of listening proficiency, you need to develop separate skills:

- **Concentrate** – Focus your attention on the speaker and only on the speaker.

- **Acknowledge** – When you acknowledge the other person, you show your interest and attention.
- **Research and respond** – Gather information about the other person, including his interests and objectives.
- **Exercise emotional control** – Deal with highly charged messages in a thoughtful manner and wait until the entire message is received before reaching.
- **Sense the non-verbal message** – Be aware of what the speaker is saying with his body language and gesture.
- **Structure** – Organize the information as you receive it. This is what you do with the time gap between speaking and hearing speed.
- **Keep eye contact** – It is a sign of attention. When you don't have eye contact with your listener, you may feel like you are talking to a brick wall.
- **Keep verbal responses and vocal participation alive** – Yes, wow, these show interest in what is being said.
- **Acknowledge gesture** – Acknowledging gestures such as smiling, nodding one's head, leaning forward with interest, directly facing the speaker and appropriate facial expressions or body language. All these gestures say, in effect, "I am really interested in what you have to say". Speakers like to see that.
- **Clarify remarks** – This kind of acknowledgement is making clarifying remarks that restate the speakers points, such as "If I understand you correctly, you are saying that ...." or "In other words, the biggest hurdles are........"

Use these skills and techniques and you will show courtesy to the speaker. Equally important, you will enrich yourself by joining in a give and take that increases your understanding.

Improving your listening habits is vital. That is because when I talk; I only know what I know. But when I listen, I not only know what I know, I also know what you know. Thus, listening is power. This creates an active listening attitude. Learning to be an active listener is like learning to be active jogger. It takes effort. You start little by little and work upward. It is as a much a state of mind as a physical activity. Besides, as you work longer and get better, it pays ever-increasing benefits. An active listening attitude can help tremendously in breaking your poor listening habits. Exercising such an attitude means:

- Appreciating that listening is as powerful as speech – what someone says to you is just as critical as what you have to say to them.
- Realizing that listening saves time and effort. These who listen create fewer mistakes, fewer misunderstanding and fewer false starts.

- Understanding that listening to everybody is important and worthwhile. Look for what something you can learn from each and every person you meet.

Your listening skills rarely taught and infrequently practised. Listening is none the less a key to communicating and making others feel special in your presence.

CHAPTER 13

Influencing Skills

Sometimes, people who, despite their good intentions, fail to connect emotionally with other people fall at bottom of influence competence. They mean well, but they lack the means to get their message across. People must be emotionally engaged. Without an accurate reading of how a listener is taking in an idea, that ideas is in danger of falling on deaf, indifferent or even hostile ears. No matter how intellectually brilliant we may be, the brilliance will fail to shine if we are not persuasive. Creating an atmosphere of openness is not a trivial gesture. You have to communicate openly; you open the possibility of getting the best out of people, their energy, creativity and positive behaviour. If you don't, then they just feel like trapped and unhappy. 'Are you telling me only what you want me to hear instead of what I need to know' a kind of feeling people will develop if you are not open in communication.

If you involve people in at least some of the steps in communication, they will behave like missionaries for you. As we give grace to others, we receive more grace ourselves. As we affirm people and show a fundamental belief in their capacity to grow and improve. We build greatness in our personality to influence others. At the most basic level, influence and persuasion hinge on arousing specific emotions in the other person – whether that be respect for our power, passion, enthusiasm for out-doing a competitors or appropriate outrage over some fairness. People adept at influence are able to sense or even anticipate their audiences' reaction to their message and can effectively carry everyone among toward an intended goal. Influencing people know that a simple good argument may not be enough to win people over, they have the ability to sense that kind of other appeals will persuade key decision matters. Critical in these skills is being able to notice when logical arguments are falling flat and when appeals that are more emotional may add impact. The habit of responding to the inner desire to make a difference, to matters and to extend our influence to the people and causes we most value all, begins with a mind-set or attitude, a choice to use the voice of influence.

The great leaders integrating emotional realities into what they see and so instilling strategy with meaning and resonance, they allow their people's emotional intelligence blending with the elements into an inspired vision. Their leadership entails exciting people's imagination and inspiring them to move in a desired direction. It makes more than simple power to motivate, lead and influence. In such leaders mental and emotional identification is more powerful force than involvement. We see this with the followers of Mahatma Gandhi, Nelson Mandela. Perhaps, you, yourself, have so admired someone that you buy deeply into their vision, even though you were not involved in creating that vision. This is identification and it is a very powerful psychological force, sometimes, even more powerful than actual participation. When we refer Greek Philosophy of influence called Ethos, Pathos and Logos, we learn what skills required for influencing people.

Ethos - means trustworthiness.

Pathos – means seek first to understand, and

Logos – then to be understood.

Ethos means your ethical nature, your credibility, amount of trust and confidence others have in your integrity and complency. **Pathos** means empathy. It means that you understand how another person feels, what his needs are, how he sees things and what he is trying to communicate and feel it. **Logos** means logic. It has to do with the power and persuasion of your own presentation, your own thinking. The sequence, of course, is supremely important. To move logos before feel understood is futile; to try to create understanding when there is no faith in your character is likewise futile.

We expect positive influence with people in our personal and professional lives. Our motive may be to win new friends, keep customers, change behaviour or improve relationships. But how to do it? Stephen R. Covey in his book "*Principle Centred Leadership*" has given two basic categories of influence:

- To model by example – others see us.
- To build caring relationship – others feel us.

How others see us –

Retrain from saying the unkind or negative things particularly when you are provoked or fatigued. If you have no such model of restraint to follow, you will likely to take out your frustration on your fellow-workers. We need to find new models, new examples to follow and learn to win over, to get our motive straight to gain perspective and control, and to back away from impulsively speaking or striking out.

- **Exercise patience with others** – In stressful situation over impatience surfaces and we may say things we don't really mean. Sometimes through emotions and attitude rather than words, eloquent messages of criticism, rejection, etc., we then harvest hurt feeling and strained relationships. Patience is the practical expression of faith, hope, wisdom and love. Patience is emotional diligence.
- **Distinguish between the person and the behaviour or performance** - We may disapprove of bad behaviour or poor performance. We first need to communicate and help build a sense of intrinsic worth and self-esteem totally apart from comparisons and judgements. Doing this will powerfully inspire superior effort. The power to distinguish between person and performance and communicate intrinsic worth flows naturally out of our own sense of intrinsic worth.
- **Perform anonymous service** – We gain insight into the worth of others by serving them without expectation of publicity and reward. Selfless service has always been one of the most powerful methods of influence.
- **Choose the proactive response** – Unless we exercise our power to choose wisely, our action will be determined by conditions – our ultimate freedom is the right and power to decide how anybody or anything outside ourselves will affect us – choosing means to accept responsibility for our attitudes and actions, to refuse to blame others or circumstances.
- **Keep the promise you make to others** – Our ability to make and keep promises is one measure of faith in ourselves and of our integrity. Using self-knowledge, we can be very selective about the promises we make. By making and keeping our promises, we win influence with others.
- **Focus on the circles of influence** – We can change our circumstances by a mere change of attitude. Deciding within ourselves how anything or anybody will affect us, we can control our reaction to the problem. When we focus on doing something positive about the things, we can control, we expand our circle of influence.
- **Live the law of love** – We encourage obedience to the laws of life when we live laws of love. People are obedient and tender. Particularly those who act as if they are tough and self-sufficient and if we listen to them, they will us so. We can gain influence with people by showing love, particularly unconditional love, as this gives people a sense of intrinsic worth and security unrelated to conforming behaviour or comparisons with others. We all distrust superior human relations techniques and manipulative success formulas that are separated from sincere love.

How others feel us –

Do understand and care for others – assume the best of others. Assuming good faith produces good fruit. Whenever we assume good faith, born of good motives and inner security, we appeal to the good in others.

- **Seek first – to understand** – Until people feel that you understand them, they will not be open to your influence. So, first seek to understand, then to be understood. When your communication is clear with another person then only you will see each others clear point of view, you will walk the talk positively to influence others.

- **If offended, take the initiative** – If someone offends you unknowingly and continuous to do so, take initiative to clear it up. When taking the initiative do it in good spirit. This preserves the dignity and self-respect of other persons, who then can respond and learn without feeling threatened. Our feelings, opinions and perceptions are not facts. To act on that awareness takes thought control and fosters humility.

- Admit your mistake, apologies, ask for forgiveness.

- **Accept the person and then the situation** – Acceptance is not condoning a weakness or agreeing with an opinion. Rather, it is affirming the intrinsic worth of another by acknowledging that he does not feel or think a particular way. Therefore, the first step in changing or improving another is to accept him as he is. A feeling of acceptance frees a person from the need to defend and help release the natural growth tendency to improve.

- **Be influenced by them first** – We have influence with others to the degree they feel they have influence with us. As the saying goes "I don't care how much you know until I know how much you are" when another person feels you genuinely care about him and that you understand his unique problems and feelings he also feels he has influence you.

CHAPTER 14

Coaching Skills

"All the coaching in the world will fall short if the behaviour you expect is not honoured and recognized"

— S. Bartlett

Everyone can develop the skills, the personal techniques, and the attitude to successfully coach other people. You can learn how to improve your coaching skills and become a person who inspires others to give 100% result. If you want to be a coach what is your attitude about being a coach? Do you really understand the need to be an effective coach? Do you grasp how important it is to be a good coach? These fact findings shape your attitude about being a coach, because people act on what they believe or value. You only succeed when people are communicating, not just from the top down but in complete interchanges. Communication comes from fighting of 'my ego' and listening. Highly successful and innovative leaders have tapped into an unlimited resource – their people and they by learning the secrets of coaching skills made it happen. You as a manager, is it not your role much like that of a coach? Your team-members all have different talents and skill level; they are people with strengths, short coming and personal lives that sometimes affect their ability to perform at work. And regardless of how difficult it may be at times, you as a team leader responsible for winning with that special mix of people for keeping your people inspired, motivated and working together toward team goals. The greatest coach is those who know how to motivate others to succeed, stay focused, believe in themselves and overcome disappointment. Coach inspires others to aim higher, work harder and enjoy doing it. Henry Kissinger once said "Leaders take their people from where they are to where they have never been before". That is what your role as a coach will help you to take your people from where they are (limited) to where they have never been before (unlimited). Therefore, you as a leader and coach must keep in mind three critical facts.

<u>COACH:</u> Three critical facts for you.

(1) Leader's responsibility is getting things done through people. Your job is to work through people who works for you. That is how you will get results from your people. When you do everything yourself, you are just a technician, when you get things done through others, that is when you become a leader or coach.

(2) You need your people more than they need you – because the only way you are going to get result is through them. You can't do every job; only your people can get everything done.

(3) You get paid for what your people do not for what you do. It is true that the people who work for you are helping you get results, then what they are doing, you get paid for. Thus, no other investment will pay higher dividends than an investment in your people. Winning coach use to inspire their people to excel.

The most enlightening fact about leadership is worthless until someone decides to use them, to actually apply this truth in your job setting. And that happens only when leader/coacher believe their potential values, as a result of their actions. So let us consider the values of successful coacher.

Values of Good coach

(1) Clarity – A strong sense of direction and purpose make sure people are communicated clearly, if not people start to fail or do nothing.

(2) Supportiveness – A commitment to stand with and behind team-members. Providing the help people need, giving understanding and encouragement shows that you are standing behind people. It is important to communicate your intention to be supportive.

(3) Confidence building – A personal commitment to build and sustain the self-image of each team-member – reviews with people the keys to successes and praise the commitment to excellence behind every victory. Publish/advertise team accomplishment periodically. It provides performance exposure for team-members within and beyond the team environment.

(4) Mutuality – A true partnership orientation – mutuality means sharing a vision of common goals. To make sure your team goals are mutual, shared by every member; explain your goals in details. Why is this goal for the team? How will it benefit individual members what steps must be taken to achieve the goal? When? What reward can we expect when the goal is achieved? This type of coaching will make that the goal achievement is mutual. Without goals mutuality is impossible.

(5) Perspective – An unflappable focus on the entire business enterprise understanding from inside out "is getting inside a person and seeing things from his perspective" said by George

Kelly. To understand someone from the inside out, you have to ask: How is your new life? Anything I could do to make it easier for you. These kinds of get involved can ultimately reveal who your team-members really are.

(6) **Risk** – The encouragement of effort that reduces punishment for mistakes and encourages learning in all things – risk is letting team-member know it is ok to fail. The only way you can grow it by taking risks. Failure is not terminal, as long as everyone learns from it. Establish a clear, unthreatening way to deal with errors, a way that starts with the individual.

(7) **Patience** – A view of time and performance that equitably balances learning and business demands – as a coach, you should know that time and patience are the keys to preventing from simply reacting. A coach can and should avoid kneejerk responses to unexpected situations. Evaluate the situation objectively; identify alternative solutions; get respected opinions and input; implement your chosen response and assess result and alter your approach as needed. The best coach don't react, they act. They use patience to their advantage.

(8) **Involvement** – A genuine commitment to allow team members to control their work-involvement means caring for someone enough to attempt to understand his experiences. It is finding out what is going on with your people. It is being interested enough to find out the significant facts about family background, hardship, ambition, drive as well as what type of person the employee is: shy, outgoing, easy to please, suspicious, etc.

(9) **Confidentability** – An ability to protect the information of team business – confidentability results when people demonstrate the rare ability to keep quiet. It takes discipline to stop yourself and not give away confidence. The moment you betray a confidence, trust is lost. And once you lose an employees trust, it is almost impossible to get it back.

(10) **Respect** – A commitment to value and see the treasure within your people. Respect involves coach/manages perceived attitude toward the individual he leads. You may respect your people highly, but if they don't perceive that value ...... if this contradicted by your failure to share goals, your willingness to become involved, your inability to exercise patience, you communicate disrespect. How far do you think a team can go together if its members feel the coach disdains them? If you answered 'nowhere', you are right!

Successful coach passes above values and skills plus character and personality traits that make them effective. You must learn to incorporate these values to get yourself as skilful coach. "Good coach is not necessarily a winner but a person who is a good teacher .... Who does not abuse his players, who gets the most from the players and who works within the framework of the rules." (Dan Devine)

Skills of High Performing Coach

Knowing what must be done is the essential first step toward doing it. Success is not established by how high we climb as coach, but by how many people we take with us to climb. Coach is often unaware of the impact his values have on other people's lives. The truth is, everyday you imprint your values upon your team-members. Hence ask yourself this: what kind of values and attitudes do I communicate to the team I lead? An attitude of supportiveness, confidence, commitment, mutuality, patience and involvement? To answer these questions, it is often helpful to identify where your attitudes come from. Your parents, teachers, friends, siblings, spouse, boss, subordinate were probably, who helped you become who you are today. They probably inspired you taught or corrected you. They were also the people who taught you understood cause and effect, imparted desire for knowledge, helped and corrected you when need be. They were the people touched your inner chords and helped you develop your skills. Remember those people who especially inspired, taught and corrected you, and the attitudes they had that you admired. Are these attitudes you communicate to others daily. Your personality traits of today are the by-products of their positive attitudes they demonstrated while you were a child, young and adult. They challenged you to go "above and beyond". Obviously, no coach has ever had the perfect team. The difference between the success and failure of any team is how well the coach understands its members and motivates them. To make this happen, a coach must possess following skills:

(1) People reflect their views of life

Please understand there are people who have negative, pessimistic, grumbling and complaining attitudes. You can predict exactly how they view their life negatively. If people are happy and see problems as challenges, you can pretty well count on that people having a positive outlook of life. Hence, you need to understand the philosophies/attitudes the people work for you. You as a coach never understand what makes people tick unless you spend time with them. You have to get close enough to understand the person's attitude or action. Helping people develop positive perspective is essential, but be honest in your methods.

(2) Individuality should be valued and explored:

People have capabilities and creative minds. When you tailor this tool to your specific needs, go for their talent inventory. Working together will naturally reveal more about the talents and potentials of your entire team. People who excel in their performance ideally be involved in planning, scheduling etc. Those who are creative be involved in concept development. In short, let your people express their individuality with the project framework. You will find your people morale will increase dramatically.

(3) Lack of motivation often reflects discouragement

Some people are not motivated; it is because they are discouraged, not because they are lazy or stupid. Find out why they are discouraged. If you identify that, then be creative in your encouragement. The motivation you were missing can suddenly begin to surface. Apply RAP to find out your peoples problems and perspectives. Review the past, analyze the present and plan the future. With this approach, you and your people can focus on a review the past performance contrasted with present performance and then look together to an improved future. As a coach this will help you keeping track of where and what progress is made by the team.

(4) Consequences determine performance

If some people are constantly performed unsatisfactorily, examine the consequences of their behaviour. The consequences negative or positive, must fit the behaviour in order to change it and they must be implemented and consistently.

(5) People treated responsibly take responsibility

People in team who are viewed as responsible for their actions tend to take responsibility. When someone gives you responsibility, you tend to rise to the level of trust. As you give them responsibility they will rise to it. They will develop pride, self-respect and loyalty.

Role of a coach

You as a coach of the people what will you do before, during and after the project you have undertaken. Critical to your ability to function effectively in the coaching role, are your willingness and ability to become involved with your people/team and develop trust, confidentce, honesty, and support to team people. Encourage free communication and reward performance clarifies expectation and verifies understanding. Motivate and inspire them and provide the challenge to look beyond the tasks at hand to new horizons. Tell your people the truth, even if it hurts. Many coaches believe that the game is won or lost before the actual competition. Ideas work best when you do. Hence, you do and practice your coach role this way:

(1) Communicate your involvement with people

Coach involvement in team activities are perceived by its members as "caring". Tom Peter's MBWA, teaches simply being with the members of your team means getting out from, asking them question about people, project. How are people doing can you help. Is there something you can do to improve a process? Management By Walking Around (MBWA) involves you with your team. The more you involve, they feel they involved with your goals. Once you start getting involved with the people, you will find the next step to filling the coaching role comes very naturally.

(2) Develop trust among people

Every team-member should be convinced you are the right coach for the team........ even if your decisions are not always popular: without trust a team may win occasionally, but when the pressure is on when performance really counts victories without trust become less the rule and more the exception. Trust is built on confidentiality, honesty, support and reward. Encourage for communication freedom. When your team trust you with personal or professional news and expect you to hear them with objectivity, understanding and compassion, you are a coach who will be able to count on the extra mile from your people.

(3) Clarify expectation and verify understanding

Best working team does not guarantee success unless the plan is communicated and understood by its members. Victories can't happen without clear, purposeful direction from coach and consistent team-members comprehension. Therefore, it is necessary to communicate in terms, team-members can understand. (Policy, procedure and practice to follow.)

(4) Verify teams understanding

When you put up your plan to team, clarify your expectations by reviewing it to team-members and you verify the teams understanding. You may ask questions to members. Make it sure that freedom exists among team-members. "Is there anything that might still be a little unclear about what I have said?" Such questions can encourage members to search their understanding and verbalize any doubts that may exist especially when the coach asks it in an agreeable voice.

(5) Affirm the team

Once you have established a trusting mutual relationship, you are ready to turn your attention to affirming team-members in their best efforts to improve performance. No team-member works well-for long without a compliment and no coach compliments people if his view of an employee is always negative. Like rewarding employees, affirming or complimenting them on efforts and attitude must be the nature of winning coach.

(6) Motivate and inspire the team

Your job as a coach means helping the people catch a vision for victory in every task. It means energizing them. You must have willingness to be involved with your people, to earn their trust by being real and by respecting their points of view, to keep the lines of communication clear and to affirm their efforts to be the best they can be. As a coach, you will provide challenge to look beyond the tasks at hand to new horizons.

CHAPTER 15

Mentoring Skills

While the catchwords for coaching are 'inspire' and 'motivate' the catchwords for mentoring is 'instruct'. When you mentor, it is your job to teach new skills and that is the only way average performers can grow and begin experiencing improved performance. You as a mentor walks alongside, come alongside the people of your team. You work with them side-by-side, giving instruction and not just verbal instruction. It is hands on instruction. It is doing the task together. Besides, instructing and leading by example, your other task as a mentor is to develop new abilities in the people you work with. You will help develop new skills, help them do things never knew they could do. You will teach person how to be more competent in more areas. Mentoring is a process of development not a practice of shooting from the hip. Therefore, each mentor has to build a plan on these three successful components:

(1) Mutual Trust and Commitment

It comes from spending time together. The more time you spend teaching someone, the more commitment you have to that person and he will have to you. Mentoring is hardwork and it takes time hence commitment is a necessary element.

(2) Patient Leadership

Patience is extremely important in the mentoring process. Once you have established the commitment and trust, you maintain it through patience. And patience will present itself in three basic areas. Employee attentiveness, employee attitude and pressure of usual business.

(3) Emotional Maturity

An effective mentor is able to control his emotions for the sake of effective leaderships. Even when you are sick of hearing the same questions over and over again, you must remain calm and eager to help.

Following three things will make mentor and mentoree comfortable in their interaction and relationship building;

- See the mentoree as a child.
- Schedule mentoring sessions to end with reward.
- Speak with a smile.

These things will exercise great positive effect on your attitude and responses. It will have special relevance as you interact with mentorees.

One of the main reasons for mentoring someone is to instruct him and how you are able to teach and instruct depends on how well you understand how adults learn. If every adult learns exactly the same way, then your job may not be specifically challenging. But the truth is everyone learns differently! The learning process depends on how people accept or receive knowledge. So you as a mentor must understand six basic ways of how people think. It is necessary for you to judge people, the way they think. So that you can motivate them to learn.

THE SIX WAYS PEOPLE THINK

(1) Authority – Driven Thinkers

Such people rarely talk back or question your orders. Those can be commendable characteristics, but remember also that problem can arise in dealing with people who respond to authority with "kneejerk" obedience. They may do whatever you tell them to do, but sometimes they don't do anything unless you tell them. Your task is to recognize where that line of motivation exists within each authority – driven team-members and to help him recognize it.

(2) Deductive Thinkers

When you mentor people whose mind work through deductive reasoning. You must make things logical. These people prefer liner, analytical explanations – point A to point B. You have to go into detail, someone almost defending your own thought processes. These people have to understand each step. When you stop and say 'ok' now you go ahead and do it, they will probably say, "Can you run through that one more time please?" These deductive thinkers will test your patience threshold. You will be tempted to shout, "I told you twice!" why do I have to tell you again? But they are not doing it to upset you. They truly need to understand. Once they do understand a task, they will know it forever.

(3) Sensory Thinkers

These are "hands on" people. Their learning is through sensory experience. They have to see it, hear it, and touch it. They have to go through the full experience. Only then will they own the process with you. To best mentor sensory-oriented people, give them the time they need to explore. Encourage them to touch and feel and they will learn faster.

(4) Emotional Thinkers

Some minds let in information primarily through emotions. These people need to feel good about the work experience, about the process, about their skills, about the task outcome. If they do not, their performance will soon show it.

You can often motivate emotionally responsive team-members by understanding that each human being responds to one of four basic emotional needs.

- **The need for control** – some team-members/mentorees respond poorly to assignment unless they feel in control of their environment. If they are not in control, they grow uncomfortable.
- **The need for attention** – some people won't respond very long to anything if they don't get positive attention from it. Not that they must constantly be in the spotlight, they simply need to know that their contributions are consistently appreciated. They need a clear cause and effect relationship between good performance and favourable reviews.
- **The need for love** – many people must know that the mentor cares about them personally as well as professionally. These people are motivated by knowing that the mentor sees special attributes in their character or abilities. They need to feel that the mentor is grateful for them and for the mentors they are.

(5) Intuitive Thinkers

These people assimilate data by intuition. Intuition is an unconscious process that is neither rational nor emotional.

(6) Scientific Thinkers

These people process information scientifically. To mentor these people means letting them test it, try it, experiment with it.

Allmost all of us are combinations of these six types of people. Hence, you will have to manage your mentorees using different stroke for different folk approach.

SUCCESSFUL MENTORING

When you **tell** an adult learner to do something he will remember 10% of what you say. If you **show** an adult how to do something, he will remember 60%. But if you **do** something with that same adult, he will remember 90% or more. The three phases of mentoring process – observe, participate and conduct can be used to instruct mentorees so they will learn and grow to their potential in the least amount of time. In the mentoring role you will use these three phases whenever you teach your mentorees.

(1) Observe

Mentoree whom you teach observes you doing the job. As he watches you do the job, you should be answering questions. You need to answer these questions, even if they are not asked outright:

- Why is this job important?
- What are the key components of this job?
- What are the cautions?
- What timing issues are important?
- What is in this for me?

Give your mentoree time to learn on these questions and he will give you many reasons to be glad you did.

(2) Participate

How the task can be shared meaningfully. Generally, it is good idea to allow the mentoree to assist in the task while you perform the task. This allows mentoree more freedom to learn and less pressure to get it right the first time. For example, if you were helping your mentoree learn how to paint a wall, his part of the task might be holding the ladder, keeping brushes clean, etc. **How the mentoree understands?** Is the next step in participation? Make sure the mentoree demonstrates understanding of the task, asking him to explain it to you or colleague. **Is there time to learn?** – allow plenty of time for instruction. Don't rush the process; don't make the mentoree feel under pressure to complete the task. Allow time for the training to be done well.

(3) Conduct

Once you have done the task with your mentoree, you as a mentor must resolve before you begin the conducting stage.

- How can the mentoree demonstrate competency?
- What level of competency will be adequate?

- How much inaccuracy will be allowed?
- When will unsupervised work be allowed?

After reviewing these three phases, it may require to develop general guidelines for every task your mentoree might attempt. If you do your job as a mentor well, your mentoree will begin to show the outcome of effective mentoring:

- Awareness of task, environment and culture.
- Appreciation for networking.
- Proactive approach to their tasks.
- Eagerness to learn.
- Positive attitude, etc.

As your mentoree completes this process with you his inclination for efficiency will increase and when you can help that happen, you have just given your mentoree a life-time gift.

Your willingness to invest yourself in the life of another person will be the key that unlocks a treasure of fulfilment and accomplishment for many people.

CHAPTER 16

Team Leaders Skills

"It is easy to get players. Getting them to play together that is the hardest part."

— ***Casey Stengel***

Helping team-members to move beyond knowing why teams and team-work are important and what their roles are doing, adopting and behaviour that will optimize the team's effectiveness, the leader must be clear on the skills required for his successful role play. He must learn how to lead and build team to maximize team-work. Getting a group (team) of diverse people with conflicting interests and varied background to pull together is a big part of what team leadership skills are all about. It takes team leader to get a group to be committed, get team agree to work together and to put teams plan into action requires specific skills in the leader.

Daniel Galeman in his book "*Emotional Intelligence*" said that "much evidence exists that people who are emotionally adept who know and manage their own feelings well and who read and deal effectively with other people's feelings have an advantage in all life arenas. They are more likely to be content and effective in their lives, work sphere, mastering habits of mind that foster their own productivity." If you learn to identify these skills and adapt to them, you will be a charismatic team leader. Your behavioural skills and or styles, all these traits will make you good leader. With these skills, knowledge and personality traits, you can take control of your compatibility with others. You will improve communication and be able to build rapport with other team-members. Further, it will help you understand yourself better.

Many people just are not skilled at the art of persuading. No matter how brilliant your ideas, it will go nowhere unless you get others to go along with it. And the only way you do that is by persuading them by communicating clearly why they really should not to do what you really need done.

Following are some of the fundamental skills of successful team leader:

(1) Adaptability skills

Everybody is easy to please, if you know how? Adjusting your style to the style of others is called adaptability. Highly adaptable people are not prisoner of their own style. They are good at getting in sync with others because they use their brains as they were intended to be used to determine what type of behaviour are most suitable in what situations. Cultivate a style that is adaptable. Give your full attention to the other person and seek to cooperate, not confront. The adaptability skill is the key to build successful relationship with team-members and other people and workplace. Adaptability comes from understanding people's inner need and then working to meet them. Do so. And you will find that your needs will get met, too. You can sharpen this skill of knowing when and how to adapt. You can learn to adapt to all kinds of people and situations. As a result, you can find success and acceptance, you never dreamed of. By dealing with people as they want to be dealt with you heighten the chances of a win-win relationship among team-members.

(2) Persuasive Skills

Persuasion is that all important ability to get others to do what you want them to do, because they want to do it. Persuasion is what is needed to make things happen. There are three keys to persuasion: establish rapport, cultivate behaviour and initiate ideas. To build rapport, you need to cultivate behaviour that will make people trust you and make them feel it is in their best interest to follow your lead. Here, are some ideas for making yourself more persuasive for getting things done.

It is critical than ever to have this skill that heighten your power of persuasion. Being good at persuading skill is a major building block of successful team leader. Persuasion is a four step process consists of explore needs and goals, create and select solution, commit to an action plan and assure success by identifying, monitoring and measuring result. To win over teams trust the emphasis must be on getting people to acknowledge and share a perceived need and then to be willing to collaborate with you of solution. You will be very powerful leader, when you can align your vision with the needs, wants and objectives of other team-members and get their feedback. Keep following crucial tips on persuasion skill building:

- **Do and ask yourself**: What do my team really wants. Shared values with them, recognize people on fulfilment of tasks, give freedom, solve problems collectively, serve team people and create win-win attitude.
- **Shift your focus to others** – Make a conscious effort to think of others wants and needs before your own. Start training your mind not to focus automatically on what separate you from other team-member. Rather than figure out what unites you and how you can build upon that base. Such empathy will become a habit.

- **Be quick to compliment** – Honest compliment shows that you appreciate the person you admire. Regular feedback motivates people as they want and need to know how they are doing on the project. By doing these positive acts and attitudes, you will convince team-members that you care for them.
- **Empower others** – If you put fences around people, you get sheep. Give team-members the room they need skilful team leader send out the messages that he appreciate others abilities in problem-solving. Listen them attentively, encourage experiment; they will feel and will contribute positively for team's success.
- **Try to arouse positive emotions** – Appreciate team-members, put an award ceremony for good work done, light tap on shoulder to emphasis a job well done, try playful gesture, etc., it will encourage people to work unitedly.

(3) Guiding Skills

- **Developing and sharing goals and ideas** – A team vision is crafted and shared among the team-members and the goal are debated and constantly restated as a part of normal work activities. Restating the goals does not imply that they are being changed; it is more a case checking them out, validating them and reaffirming them.
- **Sharing is important** – Understanding requires explanation and time for consideration. To obtain commitment to goals team-members should be allowed to participate in debate. Otherwise, how can they be expected to be committed to something they do not understand and not allowed to discuss?
- **Monitoring progress** – It also essential to make everyone enable to know where they are going so they know when they get there. Monitoring allows the environs to be tested and to obtain feedback so that modifications can be made, if required.
- **Managing the parameters** – If team-members are not reminded of the direction and not given feedback to help them monitor for themselves that are doing the right things, it can be very easy for them to find themselves working very hard to little effect. To avoid this, the leader needs to be positive in the management of the edges.
- **Taking responsibility** – All the team tasks cannot be delegated and some decision that a leader should not avoid. Most tasks can be assigned to other team-members, but some can't move from leader's shoulders. A leader can't duck decision-making nor can delegate the responsibility for developing staff. Whether team-members like it or not, their performance will be judged by the actions and abilities of the members.
- **Collaborating** – Collaboration requires trust and a sense of unity of purpose. It means helping each other in the team to problem-solving. This increases the resources base of experience and enlarges the creative brain power. It is for the leader to establish the climate, demonstrating to his team-members how they collaborate in practice with their peers in team and beyond.

(4) Directing Skills

- **Motivation team-members** – It means encouraging team-members giving them feedback rewarding them. Team-members need to be given tasks that will stretch them and develop their skills without over challenging them. What is being expected from them, what authority they have and what outcome are required must be made clear to them by the team leader. Positive working relationship does not require linking but it does demand mutual respect, honesty and trust.
- **Leading team-members** – Leading does not always have to be done from front. It is better to encourage them from behind, hurrying the slow checking the wanderers and occasionally slowing down the bolters. The occasional nip at the renegade's is the only discipline required. Leading team-members require collective directions with quiet determination and strength of purpose.
- **Instructing, training and coaching** – Information from team-members about the goals is important but the communication needs to be supplemented by demonstration and instructions. Team need to be taught, trained, how to do new tasks and new pattern of behaviour have to be handled. If changes are radical, command need to be issued. But this does not have to be in a dictatorial fashion. Support and coaching from the leader can help the new skills to be learnt and developed through practice.
- **Delegation** – Delegation of tasks can be used to help members work in new ways and develop their skills. By giving them responsibility of new project, providing necessary help to learn how to do it, will increase their motivation level. Delegating without support can leave an individual feeling as though they have had work dumped on them and achieve the opposite of motivating.
- **Managing conflict** – Conflict is not pleasant or easy to manage and the skills of dealing with it constructively are scarce. All too often it seems to be an inevitable part of working life. It can occur among team-members, between members and team leader. Conflict if go away unnoticed, it festers and wait for the opportunity to erupt, often in other guises. Leaders find himself dealing with symptoms unable to get to the root of the conflict. Hence, the chances of resolving it are much greater.
- **Enabling** – Leader is responsible for helping his team-members to do their jobs. This goes beyond telling them what to do and expecting them to get on which it. Enabling means helping members to do their job effectively not doing it for him. It means opening doors and providing support, skill, patience and the ability to trust team-members to get on with it in their way are prerequisites.
- **Listening attentively** – It is more than hearing the words being spoken. Concentrating on what someone says is harder. Try repeating verbalism what someone says to you to test your abilities. Attentive listening is always enriches leader grasping of content of the word meaningfully.

- **Recognizing and developing potential** – If team leader is able to recognize the signs of potential and the indicators of ability, he is able to plan and allocate work load and develop skills by taking calculated risks, thus reducing the chances of failure.
- **Facilitating learning** – Means making things easy and achievable. A leader should not and can't learn members, nor should he remove its inherent challenge. But he can help to make the process of learning as smooth and trouble free as possible. Facilitating skills range from the specific one of the listening and subsequently recognizing potential in people and things to that of team-building in particular and of building alliances in general. Facilitator or team leader must be aware sensitive to the needs for change and development and alert to his team where blockages are likely to be. He must be social entrepreneur, as trader are broker more in terms of personal and team development than the tangible rewards.
- **Counselling** – It is a process used to aid learning by helping individuals to find ways of resolving their own problems. A leader as counsell or uses his skills to assist the identification of the source of the problem and to help the individual decide his own course of action. A leader must decide when it is appropriate to act in this capacity or when it is more appropriate to refer the individual to someone better placed to help. (More details please see under Counselling Skills).
- **Positive encouragement** – If team-members believe that their leader have faith in them, they will be able to meet the challenges most positively. Hence, encouragement is important to help team-members to face difficult situation. Positive encouragement is given by means of monitoring feedback, praise, reward presentation, etc.
- **Nurturing** – Contains a sense of giving nourishment as well as training and encouragement. It implies care and tenderness.

We have identified above major skills with subskill every team leader possess. Each of these skills can be acquired and applied in different ways, irrespective of your role as team leader, manager or coach.

CHAPTER 17 Teamwork Skills

Someone said that the membership of a club (group) is made up of four kinds of bones. They are WISH BONES, who spend their time wishing someone else would do the work. There are JAW BONES, who do all talking but little else. Next comes the KNUCLE BONES, who knock everything that everyone else tried to do. And finally, there are BACK BONES, who get under the load and do the work.

If you simply throw people together and deal with them as a group you may destroy the possibility of team-building. Individuals need both, knowledge in order to commit to a team, and also the opportunity to express their feelings. If the team leader handles these individual's requirements well, he will have the strong foundation for team-building. Putting people together gives people opportunities to develop, to overcome weaknesses in thinking or social cycle and increase their competence as individuals through working within team.

Team-building is a human process involving human feeling, attitudes and actions. It is something that people have to accomplish among themselves. There is no substitute for human beings making a mutual commitment to try to work together more effectively.

SOME DIMENSIONS OF TEAM-BUILDING

Any team has a basic activity and goal. People in team to make decisions about variety of matters: defining goals, developing strategy, giving/taking assignments to persons, allocating resources, cutting, expanding resources for various functions, preparing budgets, setting schedules and deadlines and so on. It is important for a team to understand that the quality and acceptance of team's decisions can have an immense impact on many other people at workplace. Members of a team must together, perform a set of interlocking tasks in order to accomplish an end results, products, service or activity. The evidence is that people who trust one another can work together productively and effectively on a team. In fact, the building of trust should be a key goal for any team. Trust is the glue that keeps team-members together. Most of the research and writing on human factors clearly points out that there are three component forces that seriously affect human performance. The three components are culture, systems and individual.

THREE COMPONENTS OF TEAM-BINDING

Unless team work and collaboration are part of the organization's culture, the organization's systems and the individual's arsenal of skills and knowledge, the organization will probably unable to sustain a process of high involvement and participation at all levels in the organization.

Culture – This component is the most powerful, is often difficult to detect, and it is the most difficult to change culture of any organization which represents the basic shared values and assumptions held by the people. Culture defines what things are right or wrong, what matters are important, how troubleshooting is done and how people are expected to see the whole organization. It is critical to the work team that the shared culture emphasize that teamwork is essential and that people at all levels get into trouble if they do not collaborate with others and respond readily as a member of the total team.

Systems – Functions of the team in the organization are carried out on the basis of agreed-on-methods. These integrated agreements or systems regulate almost all aspects of organizational life. It is critical that the systematic aspects of the organization be in agreement with the broader, shared cultural orientations.

Individuals – Inside the fabric of the culture and systems of the organization are people, with power and influence. Most of these people spend considerable time orienting their people to the demands of the culture and the systems. People are to function effectively and consistently with the most popular aspects of the culture or the systems, they must have appropriate knowledge and skills.

The organizational world today is extremely complex, and it appears that those organizations that can create diverse, creative, effective teams will have the advantage. These organizations will work to keep the culture, systems and individuals consistently congruent.

WHY TEAMS ARE REQUIRED?

(1) Teams are helpful to solve problems. In this context it plays two roles: one is to support individual as they do their work and the other is to solve problems to improve how the work is done together.

(2) People need to feel a sense of belonging and teams help to fulfil this need. It is a formal vehicle to address the workplace problems and find out solutions for the well-being of workplace collectively.

(3) Teams are not only necessary to solve complex problems and effectively implement solutions, but the problem-solving process itself reinforces teamwork. The methodology of solving problems establishes a standard or a goal and a purpose for getting there.

(4) Teams are most effective and efficient than the sum of individuals and that when they are given the skills and systems of problem-solving, the sky is the limit when the team and process come together the balance between creativity and discipline is achieved. By having teams in work processes that rely on facts and consensus, are able to weld the ideas that have a better chance to make an impact and create improvements.

(5) The most important role of terms is in developing team-members, maintaining discipline needed for following standardized work processes and continually improving it.

(6) Without the team functioning systems will collapse and improvement will stop in its tracks. Teaching people to work together cooperatively both within team and across teams to solve problems, with new and improved version is the basic objective of team formation.

(7) Without formal and informal support it is impossible for individuals to develop to their potential in the people value systems. Hence, people supporting formal and informal teams are necessary at workplace. Particularly, mix of formal and informal team-member's practices reflect norms and values about supporting team-members in a physically and psychologically safe environment. The strong belief in objective problem-solving that focuses on improving systems instead of blaming individuals underlies a good deal of work improvements.

(8) To sustain the individuals, team-members and working team in their coordinated efforts to add value, every opportunity to solve work problems, in support with each other helps every one to contribute value-added work. The emphasis of team formation is to encourage participation, keeping with the values and actively supporting the commitment to continuous improvements.

BUILDING BLOCKS FOR TEAM

Workplace is a happy place to be, people enjoy themselves wherever possible. This enjoyment is conducive to goal achievement, nor barrier to it. People get satisfaction from their working lives and to some extent meet their needs and aspirations. Therefore, the wise team leader does not intervene unnecessarily. The leader's presence is felt, but often the team runs itself.

Henry Ford an industrialist once said "coming together is a beginning, keeping together is progress, and working together is success". These characteristics are also seen in team-building. The team may be an organization, division, department, section or any working team. Generally, teams are build on following blocks:

- **Design a Team** – Develop a mission. Team needs purpose. They need to know why they are being set-up and what they must achieve.
- **Clarify Roles, Boundaries and Expectation** – The clearer it is the quicker team people will get going and the fewer the conflicts.
- **Plan to Transfer Responsibility** – Develop a milestone chart to promote the orderly transfer of tasks to the team.
- **Determine Team Structure** – Decide whether the team should be cross functional or a collection of people doing similar tasks.
- **Understand the Purpose of the Team** – Be clear about what to expect from the team.
- **Selecting Team-members** – Develop a profile sheet for each member and position in the team. Select the team leader. Encourage participation understand culture, systems and individuals, give constructive feedback, enjoy promoting people.
- **Starting the Team Meeting** – Explain purpose, indicate goals, its measurement criterion, strategy, for performance improvement, negotiate ground rules of team discipline, confirm agreement to rules, identify skills of members to see how they complement each other, increase delegation of responsibilities, and meet periodically to ensure the momentum does not stop.
- **Measure Critical Success Indicators** – Such as quality, timeliness, cost-effectiveness. Set team rather than individual goals for key indicators. Provide regular feedback on team performance. If performance declines do not look for victims. Involve the team in problem-solving. Find out why performance is dropped and ask for ideas on how to improve.
- **Develop Team Action Plan** – For improvement involve all in the process, develop a list of actions with specific dates for implementation. Ask members to take responsibility.
- **Encourages the Development of a Team** – Allow to develop their own ceremonies for recognition, arrange informal get-together for promoting a sense of belonging.
- **Remove Poor Performer** – Poor performer and negative attitude people spoils the team spirit. They will sap the energy of the team and cause dissension.

Maintaining performance at high level for the benefit of the organization is essential. You can sustain and even improve performance if you look into the above team-building blocks.

CHAPTER 18

Negotiation Skills

Skills at negotiation obviously matters for excellence in majority of professions and businesses. And those who can resolve conflict and head off trouble are the kind of peacemakers vital to any business/profession and organization. Negotiating and resolving disagreement is nothing but conflict management. It is so hard to get people to take the time to be good listeners. It is not just being nice, until you are good you will get enough listeners, until you can sense what the other person is going through, you don't be able to make a reasonable suggestion, to come up with something they will buy. One of the skills at conflict resolution is spotting trouble as it is brewing and making steps to calm those involved. The ability to read feelings of the opponent during negotiation is critical to success.

- Negotiation contracts and contacts are psychological and emotional. It is not just what the words say, but how the parties think and feel about them, that matters.
- The best negotiator can sense which points matter most to the other party and gracefully concede there, while pressing for concessions in points that do not carry such emotional weight.
- Negotiation is an exercise in joint problem-solving, since it belongs to both parties.
- The reason for the negotiation of course, is that each side has its own competing interest and perspective and wants to convince the other to capitulate to its wishes. But the very fact of agreeing to negotiate acknowledges that the problem is shared one and that there may be a mutually satisfying solution available. In this sense negotiation is a cooperative venture, not just a competitive one. Herbert Kelman, psychologist points out that "the process

of negotiation itself restores cooperation between conflicting parties; solving their problems together transform their relationship".

- Negotiations mostly informal happen all the times in personal and business life. But in long-term business relationship problems simmer and boil to the surface, when they surface those involved on either side "in dispute", typically use of one of the three styles of negotiation.
  - Problem solving - parties try to find out the solution that works best for each side.
  - Compromise – where both parties give in more or less equally regardless of how that serves their needs; and
  - Aggression – where one party forces unilateral concession from the other side. Threats and demands poison the process of negotiation and thus dead lock happens.

Negotiations are most often non-coercive, given the desire for a long-term relationship and their mutual dependence, a spirit of cooperation always works best.

Negotiation is the ability to accomplish objectives. It is equally important to bear in mind that in order to accomplish objectives in negotiation you must motivate others. All negotiations must in the final analysis, involve some form of contact between two or more persons. It is therefore, clear that the definition of negotiation is concerned essentially with your ability to motivate others. Hence, it can be defined as the ability of the negotiator to motivate other party in a manner that is favourable to the negotiators negotiating objectives. The key words are "motivated" and "favourable" to the negotiators objectives. A motivated person is one that is acting but one that must be acting in a manner favourable to the negotiator's negotiating objectives. An essential element in any negotiation process is the ability to discover sometimes instantly during the heat of negotiation, precisely how your negotiating opponent is attempting to use negotiating power against you. Use of negotiation can sometimes be the art of persuasion at it subtlest. At these times, your negotiating opponents never fully realize that they are being "persuaded". At other times, negotiating power can be the art of persuasion at its bluntest.

TIPS ON NEGOTIATION

It is said that our negotiating opponent is our true helper. Understanding opponents habits, his personal contacts, his written work, oral statements, talking with others with whom he deals provide helpful hints to know better the other party – opponent.

- Good source of knowledge – His habits – A person who dresses sloppily lacks self-confidence. A person who drinks coffee heavily undoubtly nervous or edgy because of excessive intake of coffee. These outward manifestations are nothing more than a reflection of a person's habits.

  And it is relatively simple process for the negotiator to arrive at an intelligent determination of an opponent thinking based largely on observing the opponents habits.

- His personal contacts – Personal contact with opponent does not occur until the first time the negotiator sits down with the opponent. This is often negotiator's earliest real opportunity to learn on the opponents habits. It is therefore important for the negotiator to be particularly alert at this stage of negotiation in order to be able to gain valuable knowledge about the opponent as early and as accurately as possible. This knowledge helps negotiator in planning and executing negotiating strategies and techniques and will increase negotiating power.
- Talking with others – Attempting to learn about opponent by conferring with others who have preciously negotiated with that opponent can be productive, particularly if those approached have had considerable experience with the opponent.
- His writing work – The negotiator should, whenever the opportunity present itself, read any of opponents written work or oral statements. Oral declarations often are made on the spur of the moment by a speaker who has not had the opportunity to rehearse, prune or edit. Negotiator may develop his countering strategy and prepare to provide facts and argument against what he says and what he said in the part is contradictory.
- His probing – Probing during the negotiation, especially during its early stages is one of the best ways to obtain reliable knowledge about the opponent. Watching the opponents actions and deducing from those actions the nature of opponents habits and equally important, listening to every word the opponent says.
- Another good source of knowledge – **Using leverage** – It is the process of increasing negotiation power to attain the desired result. It is therefore, important to, negotiator, to fully understand what leverage is and how it can and should be used in negotiation. In order to succeed in the negotiation, you must move your opponent favourably towards your negotiation objectives. Your tool for moving your opponent is, figuratively, a lever. It is your responsibility to create a lever long enough and stronger your lever, the greater your leverage, and the greater your leverage, the greater your negotiation power.
- Good source of knowledge – **Fact finding** – Get the facts or the facts will get you. And when you get them right or they will get you wrong. A very common error and great source of loss of negotiating power can be your failure to get complete and accurate facts relative to the subject matter of the negotiation. To negotiate without complete and accurate facts are to be very much like have it fall when exposed to water and wind. Just as the house fell, your negotiating power will dissipate once your opponent discovers that you lack complete and accurate facts. Again please note you must distinguish between facts and hearsay.
- Good source of knowledge – **Keeping silence** – One of the most important attributes of silence is that it forces the opponent to draw conclusions based largely upon the facts and circumstances of the particular situation. Since a person is normally motivated more by his own conclusions than those advanced by others, the "silence" technique is a very effective negotiating technique. Use of the "silence" technique requires strong self-control. Frequently, either party in negotiation may feel that failure to speak out some how indicates weakness

on his part, perhaps thinking that by remaining silent the party will construe the silence to mean lack of knowledge. Skilled opponent often advances propositions for a variety of reasons (other than for the substance of the proposition), reasons such as attempting to probe, attempting to confuse, or even attempts to delay. Each of the opponent's propositions should therefore be carefully weighed by the negotiator before he decides whether to respond, to remain silent, or to avoid the proposition by tactfully but purposely going on to another phase of negotiation. The negotiator should also weigh carefully the opponents silence to be certain that the opponent is not attempting to use the "silence" technique to draw the negotiator into conclusions the opponent desires the negotiator to make. Too often in negotiation an opponent silence leads the negotiator to jump to conclusions that will damage his position. Rather than jumping to conclusions the negotiator should be given due consideration and thought towards discovering the reason for the opponents silence and a proper strategy and technique to counter it. So, in the final analysis, the common misconception that negotiators negotiate by ceaseless talking should be put to rest once for all. Only "fools" talk when they should be listening and contemplating. And if there is doubt as to whether to speak or remain silent. It works that way in negotiation.

- Good source of knowledge – **Gear shifting** – The truck driver, of course, know precisely what gear he would shift into the driving situation, to negotiate his road journey. Gear shifting in negotiation, that is shifting the subject matter of negotiation from one issue to another, if done as smoothly as the truck driver shifts gears, can be a very effective negotiating technique in negotiation of al kinds. When you employ the gear shifting technique you not only know which subject to shift into but also when to shift. The other party can only anticipate or guess. The usual effect is to throw the opponent off stride to disorient the opponent mentally to such an extent that his negotiating power is diminished.
- A good source of knowledge – **Language** – Words is more powerful drug used by mankind (R. Kipling). Spoken and written words are the primary instruments of reaching the opponents main arteries of gaining information. Persuasive words, whether they are spoken or written will motivate the recipient. Language is therefore a great source of negotiating power. In every negotiation, it is your spoken and written words that will ultimately be the factor that determine whether or not you accomplish your negotiating objectives. Therefore, language is what you should spend the greatest portion of your time perfecting so that your effective use of it becomes as habitual as walking, sitting or eating. How it is said is an important as what is said. The negotiator's language should enthuse – not confuse the opponent. The negotiator's language is the vehicle of negotiating power. To get your ideas across, use small words, big ideas and short sentences. At the same time the negotiator's language should fit the circumstances of the negotiation.
- A good source of knowledge – Facial Expressions – "A flicker of the eye lids, a wrinkle of the brow or a twist of the lips, all are so revealing to the trained eye". The most important point to remember about facial expressions is that they "talk' just as effectively as the

spoken words. It is therefore, essential that your facial expressions be compatible with the impression that you desire to convey to your opponent. People are accustomed to gaining knowledge and drawing conclusions from that knowledge merely by watching the faces of others. A smile usually indicates happiness, a frown, displeasure. In most cases the conclusions drawn that are based upon the person's facial expressions may be correct. Skilled negotiator's are fully aware of the fact, facial expression "talk" just as plainly and persuasively as the spoken word and they therefore consciously make certain that their facial expressions convey only the impressions that they wish to convey to their opponents. Thus, motivating an opponent through your facial expressions is one of the effective techniques in negotiation.

Negotiation skills provide the tools you need for sharpening your beat-the-system skills. These are helpful to you to become a more powerful negotiator in any negotiating situation.

CHAPTER 19

Creativity Skills

The outstanding creative thinker in any field differs from other men in degree, not in kind. Great discoveries of science, arts were not the discoveries of great solutions but of new ways of asking questions. Creativity thus implies to newness in our approaches of doing things from bad, better to best. Creative people can't do different things they do the things differently. Creativity is thinking up new things and an ability of an individual or a group to discover new relationship, pattern, process, to look at subjects from new perspective and to form new combinations from two or more concepts in mind or in existence or newly discovered.

Process of creative behaviour involves perceptions, thinking, learning and motivation. Creative behaviour relies on the ability to transform or find new and unexpected relations among pieces of information. Creative behaviour is that mental process in which past experience is combined and re-combined frequently with some distortion in such a fashion that one comes up with new patterns, new arrangements that better solve some needs of mankind. The product of creative behaviour includes invention, discoveries, theories, excellence and innovations. Creative ideas are new to us even though the same idea may have been discovered by someone else. A product of creative behaviour must be novel or unusual. Creativity uses what is existing and available and changes it in unpredictable ways, producing unexpected results. Creativity can be facilitated through conscious thinking and follow-up action persistently. You as a creator of creativity become trailblazer, path-finder to others. You open new possibilities, new territories, new continents, so that others can follow you.

Creative thinking is largely a function of divergent thinking – the discovery and identification of many alternatives. Creative individual that promote divergent thinking include: knowledge, imagination, evaluative skills, awareness, sensitivity, memory, fluency, flexibility, self-discipline, persistence, adaptability, tolerance for ambiguity and self-confidence. We often try to enhance creativity by developing these characteristics through exercise and practice. Environmental factors such as organizational policies, systems, working conditions, equipment and employees affect creative behaviour positively or negatively.

WHY CREATIVITY?

Human being can live without air for some seconds, without water for some days, without food for week and without ideas for years, but organization cannot afford to such without because of global market competition, ever demanding customer's demands, ever increasing self-awareness of employee on his standard of living and changing values of society at large. Hence, organizations are rather compelled to change their behaviour, culture systems. They have to think of employee's creative thinking power for the betterment of workplace. They have to encourage to creative, innovative ways to manage product, processes, people and service to reduce the cost of operations. It is company's responsibility to create awareness among employees to undertake waste elimination, arrest the cost of doing wrong things and thus conform to requirements. Unless people at work are creative, such programmes implementation is next to impossible. The company has to involve and empower employees to discover and rediscover new ways of work improvements. The company has to welcome innovative ideas for reducing overall manufacturing cost and improve quality. Hence, managing creative people with the aim to draw upon their potentials, creativity, initiative and dedication in making things happen is management's responsibility. The management of company has to create positive environment to recognize creativity of their employees. Quality circles, kaizen teams, five 's' teams, smart working teams, think-tank, etc., are the routes through with employee present their success stories, excellence and innovations. These team uses to generate creative ideas which significantly bring organization the status of best from bad to better conditions.

Employee's new ideas are like new born babies, who are small, immature and shapeless. They are promises rather than fulfilment. The management must be respective, adaptive to those ideas for tomorrow's great contributions to the company. Creativity a new born idea can be nurtured, socialized and cared provided an attitude of openness to adopt new avenues; new possibilities of improvement are there in management, managers and managed. No company can change faster than it can change the hearts and minds of its people and the people who change fastest and best are those who are creative and committed. An employee role is to make people and company change at faster pace than they would have chosen. It is he who by his creativity can change the company and people from bad to best. Whether you are CEO, manager, employee or union leader, you have creative behaviour, provided the company gives you freedom without fear, involvement rather than intimation, encouragement rather than encroachment.

CREATIVITY PROCESS

Since, creativity is an ability of an individual to discover new things, new combinations, they must be acquainted to creativity processes. The processes are:

- **Preparation stage**:- Study of element of the problem, preliminary attempts to solve it. If problem is complex reach to the dead end, takeover further or burn it.
- **Incubation stage**:- Unconscious mind churns all information and assimilate for framing the thinking process.
- **Illumination stage**:- We inspire for clear solution and think dwelling in our conscious minds and collect seemingly, accidently.
- **Verification stage**:- We test and evaluate the proposed solution, considering its feasibility and acceptability. Thus, creativity can be facilitated through these stages with conscious thinking.

CREATIVE ORGANIZATION AND INDIVIDUALS

Creative organization and individuals have strong following attitude, beliefs and understanding:

- Managing people with the aim to draw upon their resources, creativity, initiative and ingenuity in making things happen.
- Technology, finance, material have presence over people but people are after all most valuable resource.
- Development of inter-personal relations has the potent capacity to make an institutions capacity to withstand stress to mark ahead in critical situation.
- Individual behaviour which facilitates people to orient for team development, informal groups cohesiveness, togetherness is an important factor to bring ownership with job and organization.
- Self-interest is a storage emotion, acts as a powerful tool apart from commitment in the development of mutual trust and faith while working together.
- Positive 'strokes' is a propellant to an individual's self-confidence which favourably influences performance. The self-worth feeling is a strong human desire.
- Honest appreciation devoid of flattery or sycophancy, satiates the crazing for recognition, arouses enthusiasm, and provides encouragement.
- Clear use of words, presence of mind, flexible and adoptive attitude, all geared towards influencing human behaviour is a favourable way in building positive human relationships.
- Such relationship recovers the sting from offensive interaction, prevents ill-will and lubricates positive interactive balance.

- Speaking well with others, helping out in work and personal issues and refraining from capitalizing on it. Proves sincerity of purpose – a value which enhances inter-personal equations.
- Empathy, selfishness facilitate growth in personal relationships, fortifies friendship and develops faith and trust beneficial for work performance.
- The culture in an organization flow from values, belief and mission. It inculcate, display unified "we stand" culture. An organization's strength lies in the people within. Creative individuals and organization with these beliefs keep their learning alive for the betterment of all in workplace. Once creative mind of set up creating innovation and excellence at work is easy as well as encouraging.

CHAPTER 20

Innovation Skills

Innovation means not merely introducing novelties but making of changes to something already established. Innovation is an act that strives to produce small improvements on what is accepted today. Innovation requires a certain amount of humility. We have to build upon others contribution and allow our own to be build upon by others in turn. Innovation is not for people to accept ideas, but how to get old one out. The greatest difficulty in the world is not for people to accept ideas. Therefore, if you change yourself you will trigger off change about you. Develop an atmosphere of trust and warmth, a supportive and constructive climate where individuals are encouraged to think of themselves.

- Innovation means a change in an old custom, rule and method.
- New practices implementation.
- Bring in novelty in work areas.

It is an act of removing *status sqo* situations for betterment of the company or self. Innovations occur when individual learns to do something it did not know how to do before or learns not to do something that it formally did. Innovation can include any improvement due to change in an old procedure, system, practice, productivity and work improvement initiatives, prevention of non-conformance by root cause elimination, new idea implementation, etc.

But innovation does not mean invention. Invention means discovering something altogether new, which did not exist. Innovation means rediscovering the new and fruitful way/ideas of doing the things. Innovation can be in any field of work, manufacturing, quality service, commercial, human resources areas. Innovation is an act that endows resources (men, material, method and money) with a new capacity to create wealth. Once upon a time bauxite mineral oil were nuisance to the mankind, as they were troublesome to agriculture. Today, they are resources due to their innovative uses. Innovation that way indeed creates a resource out of nuisance.

Innovation is important to make work improvement small or big. Revenue enhancement is the ticket for innovator while relative cost must remain under control and cost is kept to a minimum. It is innovator in the long haul who reaps the rewards. Innovative and creative thinkers are different from the rest of us. They do not do different things, they do the things differently:

- They see what we overlook;
- They turn the ideas into what others can't.
- They lead us on a path of discovery, rediscovery and reinvention and majority ideas come from people at work, as they are professional service providers and receivers. Make people vital centres of intellectual capital accumulations, rather than the prime source of bureaucratic systems followed under centralized governance. Wealth in the new era flows directly from innovation, not optimization only. That is not gained by perfecting the known, but by perfectly seizing the unknown – new ideas, rules, methods, etc. In today's competitive marketplace the company has to survive, it has to keep pace with the technology advancement with conducting innovative uses of technology to better the results. Hence, innovation and innovators are important.

YES INNOVATION CAN BE PLANNED

Systematic innovation consists in the purposeful and organized search for a change and in the systematic analysis of the opportunities which need continuous monitoring of sources.

- Unexpected events – unexpected success or failure in work activities gives an opportunity for an innovation.
- Incongruity – it is a discrepancy between what is and what ought to be.
- Process – need is a source of innovations.
- Change in perception – how we see the same situation, half full glass or half empty glass. Our observations into situation may give an opportunity for innovation.
- Climate for innovations is management responsibility – systematic policy of abandoning out dated systems, practice, products and services. Regular business activities x-ray to check how product and services need innovation, measuring innovative performance by proper feedback, systematic review and recognition.
- Innovation is conceptual and perpetual: go out to look to ask, to listen; meet customers and users to see what they need ; expect simple: start small and achieve big gain is the starting point for creating day-to-day innovation.

INNOVATOR'S SKILLS

For innovator, innovation, reinnovation signifies the rebirth of things, which are more efficient and acceptable.

- For them, good, better, and best never rest till their good is better and better is best. Their innovative mindset forces them to view their jobs in a different ways.
- As long as an individual continues to learn and produce new ideas and insights and incorporate them into their work, they provide a lasting source of competitive advantage.
- For them new ideas do not get off the ground because they were never given a chance until it is brought to fruition.
- For them every new idea has innovative value, convert it into money, time, efforts saving device.

If you talk to the people who work for you, you will discover that there is no shortage of creativity or creative people at workplace. The shortage is of innovators. People believe that creativity automatically leads to innovations. It is not. Creativity is thinking up new things. While innovations are doing new things – a powerful new idea can kick around unused in a company for years together. Not because its merits are not recognized, but because nobody has assumed into responsibility for converting it from words into action. Ideas are useless unless used. The proof of their value is only in their implementation. Until then they are in limbo.

- The innovator may not be an intellectual guy. He may be even an idea thief. But above all, he is the pragmatic one who grabs on to someone else theoretical construct if necessary and bullheaded pushes to the fruition.
- He is company's champion and allrounder making sure that his potential comes forward, grows and flourishes for bringing, new things in the company.
- He is someone who has courage into taking on the task to make it new.
- He is that champion pivotal and potential to the innovative process. Innovator, the champion is sometimes obnoxious, impatient, egotistic and perhaps a bit irrational in organizational terms, regarded as not disruptive person. Hence, the company tolerates such creative, fanatic who perhaps driving force behind major innovations.
- Entrepreneurs often need a sponsor for numerous projects; it is innovator only who pushes innovation forward. Innovators are pioneer and have rich support network so they flourish in implementing new things. If no support no innovation occurs.
- Innovator, being enterprising individual involves in new or alternative ways and thinking other thoughts while remaining in touch with reality.
- Innovator is sometimes called researcher whose unauthorized research can pay big dividends in the form of improving the systems.

The best thing any CEO can do for his company is to allow its employees to discover and re-discover their own greatness: knowledge, skill, expertise, competitiveness for renewal of the company systems, practices on continual basis. They must adopt 5% technology and 95% psychology and attitude approach. He must unlock the power of ideas by educating employees giving them an opportunity to develop their skills, creativity and innovative attitude. Ideas from grassroot employees hold tremendous money and service potential because they are the programmer, service providers and receivers at each stage of work processes. When people put their mind to it, there is no limit to the novel ideas they can create. The challenge is how do get whole organization to think outside the box. Remember people in organization are like diamond, have a basic value. But it is only after they have been polished and that the world will understand their real value. Innovators are company champion who are pivotal and potential in establishing innovative work processes.

CHAPTER 21

Work Excellence Skills

Changing or creating the culture within an organization is formed by number of components like: behaviour based on people interactions, norms, values resulting from different work group, dominant values adopted by the organization and overall climate of company. Culture in the organization is defined as the beliefs which pervade the organization about how business should behave and should be treated. Attempting to control performance through systems, procedures or techniques external to the individual is not an effective approach since it relies on controlling other. Individuals should be responsible for their own actions. When individuals are stimulated to commit themselves to a goal and where personal pride and self-esteem are at stake, then the level of motivation is at a peak. For most people the toughest critic and the hardest task master they confront is not the immediate boss, but themselves. So to say, excellence at work is thus user-driven. It can't be imposed from outside. That means ideas for improvement must come from those with knowledge and experience of the process activities and tasks, the process owner handles.

Excellence is not cost-cutting or productivity improvement device alone. It is more concerned with changing attitudes and skills so that the culture of organization becomes one of the preventing failure – doing the right things, right the first time, every time and as per conformance to requirements will establish the culture of preventing failure. Obviously, then it is true that creating excellence in work and excellent organization is collective responsibility lie with management, manager and managed in general and in particular lie with individuals/process owners. Managers are in control when their subordinates can exercise self-control. The only efficient way to tackle process, activity improvement is through teams, which allows individuals to grow. Of course, employees will not engaged continual improvement without commitment and an effective mechanism for capturing individual contributions. For any individual or team to succeed, team need to be facilitated through the stages of becoming AWARE, needing to ACCEPT, ADOPT and a ADAPT in order to ACT to achieve desired goals. In such circumstances problems are exposed to a greater diversity of knowledge, skill, and experience and are solved more efficiently.

Knowledge is very much like organic manure – if it is spread around it will fertilise and encourage growth, if it is kept closed in, it will eventually fester and rot. Teamwork throughout organization is an essential component of organizational excellence as it builds trust, improves communication and develops inter-dependence. This enable people to feel, accept and discharge responsibility and accountability, foster pride, job satisfaction and better work and people themselves expand their knowledge, skills and ability to give more to the company. They themselves ask:

- How can I be worth more to the company?
- How can I help it to achieve more in less time?
- Are there some ways that I could help cut out cost and increase productivity, quality and efficiency?
- What new system could I develop?
- What new product/service/method/practice could I use that would allow the organization to produce it products/services more effectively? If organization can help people to do more with less then we truly are empowering people. They will take the organization at the peak of excellence. Excellence is nothing but work improvement and outcome of involvement, participation and empowerment.

WHAT IS EXCELLENCE

Thousand things, a thousand and thousand of times done a tiny bit better is excellence. The emphasis is on doing not one thing or few things but on doing thousands of things better. Excellence means doing the right things, right the first time and all the time. It is a continuous process and requires continuous adaptation. The core of excellence must be the customersupplier interface. The vehicle for achieving this interface is the involvement of the entire organization, all the people and in all the functions is necessary.

- Providing motivation through leadership.
- Recognizing internal customers and discovering their needs.
- Controlling processes including systems and improving their capability.
- Empowering people at all levels to make improvements.

Thus, excellence is built upon built-in-quality through management of the inputs of processes. Following are the prerequisites of excellent organization and individual.

- The organization/individual must have long-term commitment to constant improvement. There must be a consistancy of purpose and commitment to improve organization and people therein.
- Adopt zero defects attitude to change the culture to right the first time, conforming to all requirements all the time.
- Educate individuals to understand the customer-supplier relationships. Customer orientation internal and external must be achieved for each and every individual employee.
- Recognize the improvement of the system need to be managed. Defining performance standards expected and the system to achieve them. The system has to be in line with the shared needs and expectations and will be part of continuous improvements process.
- Adopt modern methods of supervision and training – eliminate fear. It is easy to critics mistakes, but it often seems difficult to praise efforts and achievements. Recognize and publicize efforts and achievements and provide the right sort of facilitation, supervision and training.
- Eliminate barriers between department by managing processes, improved communication and teamwork. Remove the system of silo management. It is advantageous to build teams and improve communication around the processes.
- Eliminate barriers to pride of workmanship and fiction; get facts by using the correct tool. Adopt the principle of fact-finding not fault-finding.
- Encourage employees to measure their own performance and benchmark their performance against the best practices.
- Constantly educate, retrain and develop employees on their skills. The energy which lies within them can be released into the organization through education, training, encouragement and involvement.
- Develop a systematic approach to present organizational and individual excellence by way of presenting success stories, innovations, excellence, story telling, breakthrough people have achieved.
- From various teams like kaizen, quality circle, think-tank, task force, smart working teams, project teams, giving them small project on work improvement.

Achieving organizational excellence often requires a mind – set to change old practices with new practices replacement. Creating excellence is more an attitude of mind. People's attitudes and behaviour can be changed by communication and the essence of changing attitudes is to gain acceptance through excellent communication processes. Good leadership is mostly about good communication, the skills of which can be learned through training but must be acquired through practice. Once people understand the strategy, the management must establish the infrastructure.

CHAPTER 22

Communication Skills

The most important sale in life is to sell you to yourself. Communicating effectively with people is important part of your life and is also important for building your career. A well informed employee is the best salesperson a company can have. Employees value the opportunity to influence their company, peers, and superiors to have voices heard and see changes as a result of their input. Effective communication process is built on the words, messages, body language. These processes transmit communication content and intent between sender and receiver. If content and intent is well structured, harmonious, smooth then it establishes effective communication. If not distortion, misunderstanding is created and it results in poor communication. Poor communication sometimes prevents anyone to do their best work.

When you communicate openly, you open people energy, creativity. If you don't people just feel like trapped and unhappy. Here are some of the skills individual must develop, understand and implement while communicating with others.

❖ Inter-personal relations –

The crucial dimension in communication is the mutual relationship. Many people trouble some knots develop in communication because of poor inter-personal relations. When relationships are poor, people become suspicious and distrustful. On the other hand, when relationship is unified and harmonious, we can almost communicate without words. Hence, the key to effective communication is the one-to-one relationship. The moment we enter into the positive relationship with another person, we begun to build trust and confidence. Your attention is focused upon the person, his interest, concerns, and need, etc.

Building harmonious relationship and achieving mutual understanding is difficult without changing ones perceptions, assumptions. Therefore, in fact, person's behavioural change is a must for establishing effective communication. You need to adopt the attitude of wanting to improve your skills of empathy. The foundation of communication lies with people and their relationship. When we ignore the foundation, our improvement will fail. Effective communication is built on the cement of trusted relationship and trust is based on mutual trustworthiness.

❖ Skills of empathy –

Attitude of empathy is enormously attractive because it keeps you open and others feel that you are learning to listen. When you finally learn to listen, you learn more about communication. So, if you want to be really effective in the habit of inter-personal communication you cannot do it merely with selective listening. You have to build the skills of empathic listening. Empathic listening is so powerful because it gives you accurate data to work with. It gives you the reality inside another person's head and heart. You listen to understand, you focus on receiving the deep communication of another human. When you listen with empathy to another person, you give that person psychological air. Once, that vital need is met, you then focus on influencing or problem-solving. This need for psychological air impacts communication in every area of life. If you want to interact with anyone, to influence him you first need to understand him. "In empathic listening, you listen with your ears, but you also, and more importantly, listen with eyes and with your heart. You listen for feeling, for meaning you listen for behaviour" (Stephen Covey in the "seven habits of highly effective people".)

❖ Attitudinal skills –

- I assume good faith. I don't question your sincerity or your sanity.
- I care about relationship and want to resolve this difference in perception.
- I am open to influence and I am prepare to change.

Such type of personal construct helps an individual to prepare responses to situation. Personal construct forms the basis of individual's attitudes and underlying value system. They become deeply ingrained and can become enmeshed as part of the individual personality. Our attitudes grow out of our personal construct. The habit we develop to see the thing is the source of the way we think and the way we act. Our communication with other persons, correct or incorrect, is the sources of our attitudes and behaviours, and ultimately our relationship with others. Therefore, if you want to be an effective communicator you have got to change your attitude positively and proactively. Positive attitudes people are caring and confident. They have high expectations of themselves and others. They always anticipate smooth and effective communication. Ultimately, your attitude decides your altitude. We can alter our lives by altering our attitudinal framework. Formed from the combination of experience, social conditioning and personality, attitude can be demonstrated in behaviour. Change in behaviour induces attitude change and it is socio-psychological in nature.

❖ Behavioural skills –

Attitude has power to affect behaviour. A change in behaviour leads to change in attitude. Therefore, if we change our behaviour, that will change our attitude. And we can change our behaviour following these behavioural skills;

- Listen to understand.
- Speak to be understood.
- Start dialogue from common point of reference or point of agreement and move slowly in to area of disagreement.

When such behaviours are developed almost any perception or credibility problems can be solved to establish effective communication. Behaviour is the manifestation of personality and attitudes demonstrated as individual interacts with the environment and the other people. We build our relationship without making any fundamental change in our behaviour, conduct or attitude and win friends. Show consistency and sincerity in behaviour whenever you communicate with others. Your power to distinguish between person-to-person to communicate your intrinsic worth flows naturally out of your own sense of intrinsic worth. We all want to have positive behaviour with people in our personal and professional lives. Our motive is to win change behaviours or improve relationship. Most personal communications are governed by our behaviours. Positive and proactive behaviours and attitudes make us perfect and proven while dealing with people and or interacting with them.

Logic and Emotion – Your two-way communication between sender and receiver demands the skill to capture both content and intent and then learn to speak the language of logic and emotion. Emotion is far more motivational and powerful for establishing effective communication. That is why it is important to listen primarily with our eyes and heart and secondary with our ears. We must seek to understand the intent of communication without prejudging or rejecting the content. We can do this being patient, seeking first to understand, and openly expressing feelings.

Sympathy and Empathy – Giving tall attention, seeking to see things from another's point of view demands courage, patience. It takes moving into minds and hearts of others to see the world as they see it. It does not mean that you feel as they feel. This is sympathy. Rather, it means that you understand how they feel based on how they see the world. That is empathy. An attitude of empathy is enormously attractive because it keep you open and others feel that you are learning. We will learn that the language of logic and language of emotion – and that people behave more on the basis of how they feel than on how they think. We will learn that unless there are good feelings between people, they will find it almost impossible to reason together because of emotional barriers. Successful communication demands logical skills and appropriate emotional awareness while communicating with other people.

An organization achieves continuity of purpose towards improvement of product, service, and relations, if clear communication among all level of employees is clear and consistent. Otherwise, how can the organization motivate employees to work to accomplish the transformation? If communication is unclear they will not understand organization's mission or mistrust the desired transformation. Poor communication prevents anyone to do best job, effective communication rest upon the ability to clearly and accurately interpret content and intent, the interaction of people with each other with the systems in which they work and grow. Among managers, communication competence strongly distinguishes star performers from average or poor ones; lack of this ability can demoralized person.

- **Listening well**, the key to empathy is also crucial to competence in communicating. Listening skills asking astute questions, being open minded and understanding, not interrupting, seeking suggestions account for about a third of people's evaluations of whether someone they work with is an effective communicator. Listening is among the most frequently taught business skill.
- **Being in control** of our own mood is also essential to good communication. Handling our own emotions determined the degree to which those around us preferred to deal with us. Therefore, while dealing with colleagues, subordinates, superiors; calmness and patience are key. One must keep his mood cool. It makes us an emotional clean slate and allows to adopt to whatever the situation calls for. A neutral mood leaves us ready to be fully involved, present, rather than emotionally removed.
- The ability to **keep cool** helps us to put pre-occupations aside, staying flexible in our own emotional responses is the positive traits admired by all. In contrast, people who have pre-occupied mind, are burdened by their emotions are much less available for whatever the present moment demands. Best communicator are rated best for their shared ability to adopt a calm, composed and patient manner, no matter what emotional stake they are in. They are able to put aside the imperatives of their own feelings. As a result, these people are able to take time needed to gather essential information and find a way to be helpful including giving constructive feedback. Instead of being dismissive or attacking they tend to be specific about what went right, what went wrong and how to keep the good things while fixing what was off. They exercise emotional control keeping cool so as to stay open to what they were hearing, fine-tuning their responses of taking one-size-fit all approach.
- People with this type of communication skills listen openly and send convincing messages.
- They are effective in give and take, registering emotional clues in attuning their message.
- They deal with difficult issues straightforwardly.
- They listen well, seek mutual understanding and welcome sharing of information fully.
- They foster open communication and stay receptive to bad news as well as good.
- They keep control of own moods. It does not matter what mood they are in. Their challenge is to stay cool and collected. Aiming at neutral mood is the best strategy in anticipation of dealing with someone.

The essence of changing behaviour in business is to gain acceptance for the need to change, and for this to happen, it is essential to provide relevant information, convey good practices, and generate interest, ideas and awareness through excellent communication processes. Communication can be a powerful stimulus to personal development at the workplace. To understand communication methods such as verbal, written, visual communication necessary skills can be developed through relevant training to individual.

COMMUNICATION SKILLS

Communication is a prerequisite to the problem-solving and one of the most fundamental skills in life. Communication is mutual understanding. The main problem in communication is the "translation" problem. Translating what we mean into what we say and translating what we say into what we mean. The first challenge, therefore, is to learn to say what we mean; the second challenge is to learn to listen so that we understand what others mean. Stephen Covey has rightly said that "the key to accurate translation of effective communication is high trust". You can communicate with someone you trust almost without words. When trust is high, communication is easy, effortless and accurate. When trust is low communication is extremely difficult, exhausting and ineffective. Effective communication requires skill and skill development takes practice. Therefore, Stephen Covey says that "seek to understand before being understood" – The principle of empathic listening is the most powerful principle of all human interaction. Genuinely seeking to understand another person deeply before being understood is return. At the root of all inter-personal problems is failure to thoroughly understand each other. Therefore, through empathic communication we gain not only clear understanding of others need, ideas and basic paradigms but also assurance that we accurately understood as well. True empathic communication shares faithfully not only words, ideas, information, message but also feelings, emotions, attitudes, behaviour and sensitivities. In other words, we may look at the communication skills as we look at an iceberg at two levels. The small visible part of the iceberg is the skill level of communication. The great mass of the iceberg silent and unseen beneath the surface represents the deeper level, the attitudinal, motivational, behavioural and social levels. To make improvement in our communication abilities we require working at both the levels.

Communication skills are vital and very important at workplace. Because there is a direct correlation between employee communication and business results. The best business is meaningless unless everyone is aware of it and pulling together its objectives. Good communication is the life blood of any organization. It is essential to keep the entire organization functioning at maximum levels. How we can improve our communication skills. One way to understand and use the process of communication.

WHAT IS COMMUNICATION?

The process of transferring information, message and understanding from one individual to another is known as communication. Sender and receiver are the two prerequisites of communication process. Communication involves: transmission of information, receiving information, understanding, acceptance and action. The understanding is the main building block and critical part of communication process. for effective communication the processes involved are:

- Sender should have well thoughtout message,
- He should put in writing, or
- He should transmit it using appropriate communication channels (memo, circular, report, presentation, audio-visual aids, e-mail, internet, telephone, etc.)
- The receiver should receive the message and should understood and act on it.

Thus, the communication is the capacity of an individual or group to convey ideas and feelings to another individual or group to evolve a desired response. 70% of our active hours are spent in communication either orally, listening, reading or writing.

PRINCIPLES OF COMMUNICATION

For establishing effective communication, following principles need to be followed:

- **Principle of clarity** – You be clear, precise and specific in your communication. Get informed. If you don't know and understand, you can't communicate, prepare and learn what to communicate.
- **Principle of integrity** – Which supports understanding of sender and receiver to attend desired goals?
- **Principle of strategic use** – Communication when, how and why should be observed to avoid misunderstanding.
- **Principle of appropriateness** – Timely communication to take timely decisions, results or its reaction.
- **Principles of positiveness** – Develop positive attitude while communicating good or bad messages.
- **Principle of planning** – Plan for communication agenda. Since people likely to be told in advance about changes that affect them; communication must be at the beginning or in advance. Plan agenda, data, time, action, presentation, role play, etc.
- **Principle of quality** – The key to effective communication is quality not quantity. Overloading of communication shall cause ineffective communication. Enormous of amount of information inputs cannot be processed at a time.

THE COMMUNICATION PROCESS

Business executives spend most of their time on communicating than doing any other activity. Other people may also need to develop their ability to communicate more effectively when they worked under such executive. Research shows that people spend about 45% of communication time at listening. Despite this average listener understands and retains about half of what is said immediately after a presentation and within 48 hours, this level drops off to 22%. Listening is one of the most critical skills in the communication process. It helps manager and managed to determine needs, problems, moods or level of interest of each other. Effective communication requires responses that demonstrate interest, understanding and concern for each other.

Communication effectiveness is also dependent upon the message through words:

- **Words** – That we select to express the thought that we intend to communicate include – vocabulary, language, phrases, sentence structure and sentence clarity. Words can insult, injure or exalt. They can lead to costly error, false hope, disillusionment and disappointment. They can evoke pride, loyalty, action, or silence and are critical to influence the process.

Communication effectiveness is also related to:

- **Paralanguage**- The characteristics of the voice: rate of speech (speed); diction; tone and rhythm; volume. Your voice is highly versatile instrument in communication process. Through voice you can convey enthusiasm, confidence, anxiety, urgency, serenity and other state of mind and intent. The ability of the voice to effect how something is said is known as paralanguage. Timing when you increasing and decreasing voice, intensity, pausing, varying pitch and other aspects of speech patterns can increase your ability to influence. By closely attending other person's paralanguage, you can pick up clues about his intentions. Thirdly, your non-verbal behaviour also effects communication process.
- **Non-verbal Behaviour (body language)** – It is anything than can be seen by the other person, such as gestures, facial expression, eye-contact and body language, positioning, etc. How you support your message through gesture and facial expressions, how you imply interest and vitality through eye-contact and other non-verbal behaviour affect other peoples reaction to you. In turn the non-verbal clues of person serve as windows to their emotions, desires and attitudes. Changes in body postures and gestures often signal a change in readiness. It is also important to monitor how you position yourself in relation to other person. People have levels of comfort when it comes to how close they want you to be. The general rule is, if you are making them uncomfortable, and then change. Many of these non-verbal's under your direct control. You can make them what you want to be. Your attire and general appearance should reflect a sense of personal dignity and self-worth. They should be appropriate to the other person's environment and should reflect your personal values.

You need to practice and learn to become proficient in all these representations at system. The kind of behavioural adaptability will help you to improve your communication ability; increase your effectiveness and build ongoing relations with others.

COMMUNICATION BARRIERS

Sometimes communication is obstructed, misunderstood. Words, messages, conversation, information are broken down at individual level as per individuals perceptions and the whole process gets distorted. This is normally called communication break down. At the root of most communication problems are perception or credibility problems. Unaware of break down or distortion in your own perception, your attitude is "If you disagree with me, in my eyes you are automatically wrong, simply because I am sure that I am right". Such type of perceptions greatly influence our feelings, beliefs and behaviour and we will not be released our intent of communication. In general, following major communication barriers are identified:

- **Psychological Distance** – We see and hear what emotionally turned to "See and hear". So, communication can't be separated from our personality. Individual perception acts as filter in communication. For example, to an engineer who is watching a group of laughing employees; for one, who is personally insecure, weak in his job or relations, the laughter communicates that employees are ridiculing him. For other engineer, who believes, the laughter communicates that he is who knows joy and sorrow of his working group. It all depends how you perceive the situation. We interpret everything we experience through our mental maps and we seldom question their accuracy; we are usually even unaware that we have them. We simply assume that way we see things is the way they really are or the way they should be. And as a result our attitude and behaviours grow out of these perceptions. Our perception, correct or incorrect, is the source of our attitudes and behaviours and ultimately our relationships, interactions with others. We cannot act with integrity outside them. We simply cannot maintain wholeness if we talk and walk differently we see. This perception demonstration shows how our thinking affect the way we interact with other people. In short we develop our thinking like this; when somebody disagrees with you, you immediately think something is wrong with the fellow. These state of mind distort the communication process between two people.
- **Physical Barriers** – Interferences that occur in the environment for example, distracting noise, telephone/mobile conversation, distance between people, partition walls are also responsible for distorted communication.
- **Semantic Barriers** – Semantic is the science of meaning, symbol suggests meaning, words and map, and it denotes meaning. Symbols usually have a variety of meaning and we choose one meaning from many.
- **Wrong Meaning of Words** – Sometimes we choose the wrong meaning/interpretation of words and misunderstanding occurs. For example, Airplane pilot sends e-mail to his office expressing his inability to attend flight duty. The message he writes "Wife is unwell, send a substitute". This type of version carries different meaning to different people. Likewise 'dummy' is unparliamentarily word in office but respectable in film industry.

- **Body Language** – Unappopriate and nonlogical body languages are also sometimes put barriers to communication.
- **Context** – We use certain words in a certain environment. Good morning is not acceptable in afternoon. Greeting or congratulation on promotion, birthday requires context with proper environment.

Effective two-way communication demands that we capture both content and intent and learn to speak language of logic. We must seek to understand the intent of communication without prejudging or miss-interpreting. We can do this by seeking first to understand and then express feeling. Communication, after all, is not so much of a matter of intellect as it is trust and acceptance of others, of their ideas and feelings and from their point of view they are logical and correct. This mindset will help you eliminate the barriers in communication.

CHAPTER 23

MBWA – Visible Management Skills

Mutual commitment exists between leader and followers or manager and his subordinates. You must have mutual commitment to goals. How do you get it? By spending time together. The more time you spend with someone, the better you can identify with his abilities and vision. You must spend time, share goals, problems and victories. Mutual commitment develops only through time and effort. It all come back to the MBWA principle. Manager's involvement in workgroups is perceived by people as "caring". Management expert Tom Peters in his book "*In Search of Excellence*" came up with a concept called – MBWA. This means simply being with people. It means getting out from behind you desk – being available – asking questions about people and their projects. How are your people doing, is there something you can do to improve a process? etc. The more you get involve with people, the more they feel involved with your goals – the goals of the organization. When you choose to get involved with team members, you are saying you care. You are saying each member is valuable to you and to the organization. Once you start getting involved with the people who work with you, you will find that the next step to filling the coaching, counselling role comes very naturally.

WHAT IS MBWA?

Management by Wandering Around (MBWA) has same policy. Once the organization has developed a plan of setting objectives, it is important for leaders to keep it in the operating condition. There is where observation, measurement, feedback, guidance, participation, involvement, empowerment come in. By wandering around your offices/shop floor, you find out whether your plans are on track and heading at the right speed and in right direction. If you don't constantly monitor how people are operating, not only will they tend to wander off track but also they will begin, to believe you are not serious about the plan in the first place. So, management be wandering around is the business of staying in touch with the people all the time. It has extra benefit of getting you off your chair and moving around your area: wandering around means moving around and talking to people. It is all done on a very informal and spontaneous basis of course, it is vital to keep people informed about what is going on in the company especially those things that are important to them. If you maintain good working relations, contacts with people, you should not have any trouble. Nothing more effectively involves people, sustains credibility or generates enthusiasm than face-to-face communication. It is critical to provide and discuss with all people about all the results. They widely will share information and prevent secrecy.

Not surprisingly, sometimes the mental map of employees presents a unique view of management training terrain. To them much training is not needed in the quantitative, theoretical business areas but in the human aspects of managing people, sharing information, listening, trusting, understanding employees job, integrating with them and praising their work are not complicated concepts, yet these are the very areas in which many leaders, managers today are seen as needing help. By learning how to affirm, exhibit fair treatment, listen and view situation accurately and by recognizing employees as responsible people. Their new management map might provide better guide for getting along in a territory that employees often see very differently. MBWA provides the ability to get along with others.

The key to get out of office to listen to what employee have to say, is terribly important for everyone to get involved. Best ideas for improvement may come from workers, clerks, supervisors or engineers.

Our businesses learn from each other and they use that learning, sharing of company information, both – up and down as well as across the organization, leaders have to develop means to tap into some of the more informal sources of internal and external information. The leader is a person who listens. The value of listening is clear: you can't succeed in running a company if you donot hear what your people, customers and suppliers are telling you. Poor listeners do not survive. Listening and understanding well are key to making good decisions. How do some executive glean key information, especially from more informal sources. It is by practicing a well-known and often effective skills of MBWA. It is a part of everyday life. Get out of your office for a brief time and have interaction with shop floor/office people, eat with them in canteen, arrange get-together with them, discuss official, non-official and personal issues with them, you will find employees are very open to chatting. MBWA is critically important for two reasons: it shows people that you care about them as individuals, not just employees and it provides wonderful opportunity to hear what is on people's minds. It is a great way for leader to motivate people and to learn from them at the same time.

SOME TIPS ON MBWA

- Wander frequently especially in the areas of your responsibility.
- Wander aimlessly without work agenda.
- Be consistent, be spontaneous, schedule time for this spontaneity if necessary.
- Be a good listener. Don't try to steer the conversation. Let the other person do most of the talking.
- Be open and don't argue. The goal is to provide an open environment of trust.
- Talk about non-company matters to really get to know your employees.
- Wander about even if you are introvert, it gets easier with time and practice.
- Remember, this is not waste of time, personal involvement is essential to good management.
- Ask open-ended question: Are you happy here? Do you like your job? What would it make more meaningful and productive? How is your family? How was the vacation? How are your colleagues? Are they happy with their work, bosses, work environments, etc?
- Talk with all employees, not just the ones who are easy to talk with or who have similar interest.

It is an indispensable hour/s of unmediated interaction. At times, you find there is an inconsistency between what his executive or policy say are doing or practicing and what is actually happening. It gives you gap analysis, its causes, grassroot problems to find out easy and amicable solutions.

WHY MBWA

Trusting, helping and sharing while recognizing a job well done undoubtly will bring some welcome sunlight into the lives of people at work. Trust people to do what is right. Few less things can help an individual more than to place responsibility on him and let him know you trust him. Find a way to provide constant formal and informal feedback to all employees. Try to give personal recognition to employees. This is the easiest form of recognition. Consistent recognition and feedback instill a sense of belonging for people in obscure positions. The secret of leadership is to stand behind people and try to catch them doing things right. The old way of thinking about leadership was to try and find people doing things wrong and get on them about it. That is easy to do compared to trying to stand behind people and trying to find things they are doing right and help them.

If you want to make the relationship work, you will catch the other person doing things right. But if you don't want to make it work. For whatever reason, you can easily undermine another person's best effort to please you. No matter what that person does right you will say, yes but – you did not do this or that right. Wander around your operational area and catch people doing things right and tell them about it. Try it. You will like catching people doing things right. It will put a spring in your step and a sparkle in your eye. And just imagine what it will do for the people you catch. When you do, give them a one minute praising that is immediate and specific. Praising is the most powerful activity a leader can do. Praising focuses on reinforcing behaviour that is moving am employee closer to goals.

Remember people are ok. It is just behaviour that is sometimes a problem. The proper use of MBWA will help communicate and get information necessary to get poor performance back on track. By doing MBWA, at times, you are dealing with prevention rather than prioritizing crises, and the best way to do this is to recognize your some specific time slot to meet people at their work stations.

Through MBWA, we just talk each other a lot without a lot of paper or formal rigmarole. All this add up to a virtual technology of keeping in touch, keeping in constant informal contact. Informal communication leads to more action, more experiment, more learning and simultaneously to the ability to stay better in touch and on top of the things.

The underlying principle of MBWA is catching important trait of interaction and action orientation. This strengthens breaking the formal things to facilitate organizational fluidity. Task force, small groups, smart working teams, quality circles, kaizen teams prove real building blocks of the company. Usually, we focus on higher level of management, department, division or strategic business units as building blocks of the company. These are the ones that appear on the organizational charts. But the small groups are critical to organizational functioning. These groups do not wait for executive orders but take the initiatives. They achieve this through long experience and years of discussions with others at all level.

While wandering around, you must be good listener. You get a benefit from your office / shop floor people to know closeness of the problems/perspectives that are for you truly unexpected. Unexpected, that is, until you think about it. Most of the real feedback comes from these people. Whether it is policy, people, product or practices of the company.

We assume people at work are adult, keep telling ideas, know the grassroot business issues well and can go for innovation and improvement. These people will flood you with ideas if you let them. Hence treat people as adults, treat them as partners, treat them with dignity, and treat them with respect. Treat them not capital spending and automation as primary source of productivity gains. If you want productivity and financial reward that goes with it, you must treat your employees as your most important asset. People want to do job, creative job and that if they are provided with the proper environment they will do so.

The achievements of an organization are the results of the combined efforts of each individual. Give people the freedom to work toward objectives in ways they determine best for their own areas of responsibility. In instilling critical business values, there is no alternative but to speak with people with one voice. An important principle of wandering around is the creation of a homogeneous staff. The development of derived policies and detailed applications will be guarded by shared and general perspectives. MBWA skill or a tool of social technology is good to develop individual ability to get along with others.

No organization or institution can realize its potential unless its entire people are in tune with and committed to the main business issues. To succeed, organizations, need to spot light more than stars. When backstage (office/shop floor) contributions are respected and recognized, employees will respond in terms of hardwork, dedication and a commitment to an excellent performance. We believe that giving people more attention will help restore organizations ability to complete in a global scenario. MBWA is one of the methodology, tool, social technology, which help find out what is in employees mind at workplace. Remember! If you are a jerk in one relationship, you will probably be a jerk in your next relationship as well unless you learn the basics of human interaction.

PRINCIPLES OF MBWA

❖ Finding champions

Champions can provide much needed lines of communication between upper management and other employees. Advocate in order to acknowledge the needs, problems and accomplishments of people. This champion can highlight, support and give purpose to the important roles people pay in offices/shop floors. Recognize and praise them for doing the things right.

❖ Link people to the core mission

People who understand the end result work harder and smarter than those unable to see how their efforts contribute to the big picture. Presenting and reinforcing an organization's core mission and value in easily understood language give employee more meaning. Mission and values must become an integral part of an organizations daily operation.

❖ Customer-service orientation

Front line people are taught to please the customer. Hidden efforts are equally important and contribute indirectly to top quality customer-service. The concept of internal customer will help support handling external customer. All employees need to be taught the art of customer-service.

❖ Broadening the base of ideas

Every employee, views business processes, procedures and practices from a slightly different vantage points. Every one has ideas that can contribute to the company's well being. Placing a premium on suggestion, success stories presentations is an important source of continuous improvement. Employee always have ideas for performing their jobs better, regular solicitation of ideas lets people know that they are an important part of the company.

❖ Trusting while helping

It is important to trust employees to do what is right. But constant feedback, continuous improvement and reward for a job well done are important for people. It is important to maintain a balance between giving people autonomy and trust and providing evaluative feedback for them. Employing trust, feedback employee feel they are worthy, valued and needed members of the ensemble.

❖ Right things, not tight rules

There is tension between individual and established rules. Effective people have little tolerance for filling out forms and dealing with excess red-tape. Emphasis on doing things right rather than on doing the right things can shift attention from an organization's more important vision and values.

❖ Don't steal the show

Providing visibility and applause to employee is important, as long as it does not take the spotlight away from others. By providing ample recognition to all employees, organization can create and maintain an enjoyable, satisfying workplace for everyone.

❖ Celebrating achievements

Regulatory and publicly celebrating accomplishments conveys a sense of appreciation. It also lets others know about important contribution that enhances the performance. Celebrations are more important to people because they often provide the only occasions where their efforts are recognized.

Practicing MBWA, a leader knows all people by name, behaviour and attitude. They all work together to get the job done. The people need him and he needs them. Without people leader can't deal with other employees, customers. Every one is important to him, is the feeling binds him with working group.

CHAPTER 24

Customer-service Skills

Generally, customers are typically seen as the actual buyers of certain product or service. In our context, the term is expanded to encompass customer within an organization. Under this definition, employees are considered as internal customer to the organization. Terms such as customer-service, customer-supplier relations, customer satisfaction are related to an employee as an internal customer of enterprise and what skills are required to satisfy the customer is the only subject matter of this chapter.

Helping others is the primary goal of those who want to reach their own potential. Just as companies need to make their employees, suppliers and customers successful, individuals need to do that with their co-employees. They have to recognize in a real way fellow-employees and their companies are their suppliers and customers. Thinking this way makes customer-service more obvious and subtle. The key to having a successful customer is in determining what the customer – internal or external want and then arranging the operation to produce the product or service. Any individual or organizations that actually use others output (product or service) that we are going to depend on it for our survival and prosperity are our suppliers. Whatever your job is, you have got a supplier and a customer. All goods and services flow through a series of internal suppliers and customers to the ultimate buyer, our external customer.

Good customer-service requires paying attention to every link in the internal system of transactions that ultimately produces products or services for delivery. If one part of the system goes down, the whole system goes down. It is up to every individual to maintain the standard of product or service. Therefore, always mindful of managing a creative environment at work. If customer-service is to be priority of an organization and the focus of organizational productivity and improvement then conceivably we see the function immediately involved with customer-service tier. Services and products need buyers. Unless service and products can be delivered to customer satisfaction, financial success is a fleeting pipe dream. Everyone in the world is customer or supplier. That does necessarily make their beginning of a relationship. In any business enterprise, management-employee relations are also based on customer-supplier relations. They are service provider and service receiver to each other. It is of prime importance of utilizing the incredible power within people to solve problems and create innovative new ways to do business and it is the central tenet of any business enterprise. But of all things, perhaps the most important is a fundamental understanding of internal customer – an employee.

Real excellence at work arrives when each employee from lowest to highest level of organization understands as a basic rule that everyone with when he comes into contact during business hours is a customer. In almost every fraction is at one point or another is a customer. "Let me know your needs, and I will endeavour to fulfil them." This definition is applicable to all jobs in the organization marketing or customer-service department. The enterprise has to achieve a deep sense of the importance of satisfying all their internal customers, not just ultimate external who pay the bill for our finished products or services. Each of the employees is a customer and supplier to many others within the organization. Your secretary, whose need might include an accurate and timely schedule for your future business trips so that your reservation and travel can be properly orchestrated. The customer may be your boss, who may have some specific needs about the report you are preparing. Each of such customers has a set of MUSTS and WANTS. Must are those needs that are non-negotiable, mandatory and measurable. Wants are negotiable, often subjective and usually weighted. The organization must accept the fact that customer needs will be changed as the time changes. What is done today to meet these needs will not be accepted later. Organization then must implement the means to continually change the things they are doing and the ways of doing them to adjust to the changing needs. Therefore, to achieve customer satisfaction, it is important to provide quality services so that their MUSTS and WANTS are fulfilled. Improve employee motivation and morale; make decisions that are based on looking at the customer – the employee. The more they understand business priorities and mission of the organization, the harder they seemed to work, regardless of their limitations. When stressing customer-service don't expect what you don't inspect. Keeping customer happy requires a commitment of the total organization. Successful organization stress and train all employees in service orientation, team efforts and customer service attitudes.

❖ Organization – Employees – as Customer-supplier

The organization, considering its employees as customer must develop the house of quality mindset. The complete house of quality should include:

- Understanding of customer needs and wants, define their functional characteristics and relative inter-relationships of the factors in workplace.
- Listen to the voice of the customers needs and translate those into service requirement at the workplace.

- Specify customer requirements and characteristics of his role play.
- Develop inter-relationship between all factors: individuals, departments, jobs effectively to achieve smooth working results at work.
- Define and determine the results of performance, measure, manage it and communicate.
- Undertake performance and personal development of individual to acquire new skills, re–skilling to meet changing job requirements.

On the other hand, every employee as an internal customer in the organization must focus on improving personal quality. Personal quality pertains to:

- Passion for self-improvement and work improvement.
- Demonstration of right attitude and behaviour toward the next customer, supplier, process owner, the job, work team and support the organizational customer satisfaction objectives.
- Personal quality also relates to how well an individual knowledge, skill and experience are used to produce excellent goods and services.
- Improving personal quality requires emphasis on personal traits as well as technical and other social/soft skills and capabilities.

The organization climate affects personal quality. Therefore, participative management is conducive to improvement in employee personal quality. Based on this premise the customer satisfaction can be achieved through partnership between organization and individuals as they are each others customers-suppliers. Successful partnership results when management and employees are willing to take responsibility for results: workplace improvement. Understand that "WE and THEY" in the organization have obligation and responsibilities resulting from each others dual role as customer and supplier. Ultimately, customer satisfaction is nothing but an agreement based on trust and reliance with the commitment to satisfy mutual requirements and more importantly requirements of external customer – your buyer.

TYPES OF CUSTOMER

In any enterprise there are three types of customers: Self-customer, Internal customer and External customer.

(1) **Self-customer** – is an employee himself. All individuals in the organization are self-unit customer of themselves. Self-inspection, a disciplined attitude and desire for improvement should be the way of worklife for everyone.

(2) **Internal customer** – are those individuals, departments who receive output from one or more internal process owners.

(3) **External customer** – who receives the finished final goods/services from the enterprise as a whole.

The outputs of all above said customers must be considered as customer-supplier chain management to achieve total customer satisfaction, the needs, wants, priorities. Attitude of customers can be affected positively or negatively depending upon management created antagonistic, supportive or right environment.

- **Customer-supplier relationship chain** – There are three roles the organization as well as individuals plays in the world of work:
- **Customer's role** – Any person or organization who receives outputs from processers.
- **Supplier's role** – Any person or organization who provides inputs of some nature (material, information, report, policy, etc.)
- **Processor's role** – Any person or organization that takes inputs and performs work processes or through puts on them, with the intension of adding values and satisfying the need of internal (employees) or external (product buyer) customers.

The improvement system of any organization is founded on the basic premise that your customer's expectation is everything of organization does. The only reason organization exists is to satisfy your customer. Excellence, innovation or high performance comes from moving beyond customer satisfaction to customer delight. The organization must learn to think of itself not as producing goods and services but as buying customers, as doing those things that will make people want to do business with it. Broadly, to us in our context, quality means quality of work, quality of worklife, information, processes, people, processes of manufacturing/services, quality systems. To control quality in its every manifestation is basically (organization and employees) collective approach. This makes clear that everyone in the organization has internal suppliers and many employees serve internal people as their next immediate customer as well. Focus on customer-supplier chain helps all teams and individuals trace how, what they do affect the organization's ultimate purpose – continuously more satisfied customers at continuously lower cost. Then external customer needs become the unifying focus of all objectives, priorities and measurements. At the other end of the chain, supplier management becomes a key part of ensuring that the information, materials, policy, expertise or whatever is brought into the organization to help produce, deliver or support the organizations core product and service contributes to ever higher service/quality at ever lower cost.

This brings us to important personal skills everyone in the organization need to push service quality level ever higher. Customer-supplier skills.........

- Identifies key customer and suppliers for each major products or service being provided.
- Clarifies, weighs and quantifies customer expectations for each major product or service.
- Works with customers to resolve areas of dissatisfaction and set a plan to better meet their expectations.
- Works with key supplier to clarify his or the team's needs and expectations of that supplier.

The internal customer-supplier chain as a part of the upside down organization, rests on managers effectively serving the need of those within the chain. Without the kind of management support, the internal customer-supplier chain pulls apart.

The organization as well as employees (as internal customer) must ask themselves over and over again:

- Are we doing right?
- Is there a better, using less time, resources, money or efforts?
- Can we streamline the work processes that we are performing to achieve or better output quickly?
- Can we identify way in which our suppliers internal as well as external can modify their output to us so that we can better meet the needs of our customers?
- Can we suggest to our customers either internal or external changes to our output to meet their needs better and at the same time make us more cost-effective?

We have seen the importance of recognizing that we have many customers. They are co-employees as well as external – who purchase our products/services. We have to understand and meet their changing needs. It does not hold goods to meet those needs with no profit. It violates the purpose of being in business. Therefore, continual improvement is the only way to grow our business. Management of the company must first record its thinking to final within itself the ability to change old ways of thinking about and running the business. It must be genuinely believe that quality of product/service or quality of worklife equals profitability and there are no other ways we do it. It must insist on the conversion of all the company employees to the complete belief in quality.

AN ENVIRONMENT

Quality antagonistic environment, in which managers are sometimes unaware promote the policies of "Do what you are doing until we tell you to stop or change" or "We know what is best for our customer" or "we have always done this way attitude" spoils the team spirit, initiative, ownership and pride in workmanship.

A supportive environment, coupled with the specific skills that will enable people to perform the job of meeting customers needs will greatly enhance quality within the organization. Investment in people is assurance of the viability of the company and it is not one time effort. It is a way of life, a culture of constant-analysis, problem-solving and restructuring for change.

The right environment that will support effective quality and quality of workforce efforts requires management excitement in the company's improvement and that will be only effective way to tap the incredible store of knowledge they have been carrying around them. Keep employees inform that company needs their help and that it believes the process will be personal win for each of them. Tell them new skills applicable to everyday life and will enrich them with skill mastery. Convince and counsel them that company's profitability will bring prosperity in their working life and in workplace. Treat people as if they were what they ought to be and (the company) helps them to become what they are capable of being. Knowledge is the only instrument of production that is not subject to diminishing return – all the training, teaching, learning, mentoring and counselling at workplace should be appropriate mixture of technical skills (how to do) and social skills (how to relate, especially in team). This combination will provide the bang for the buck – antagonistic environment. Please remember! There are only three issues critical to business success: innovation, productivity and total quality. These are not programmes imposed by the management. Rather these are the demands straight way from the customer (external). The best way business can protect its future is to focus on the customer and his needs, whether he is internal or external.

CUSTOMER-SERVICE — CHANGING PERSPECTIVES

Nature of Customer-service

Serving the customer is everyone's business and all people need to understand the importance of customer satisfaction in any business. They also need to know how their specific job can positively or negatively affect customer. They need to make sure that their daily deeds make keeping customer happy. Paying attention to customers is an attitude that should pervade any organization. Frequent two-way communication between organization and employees is required to create awareness and understanding of customer-service. Many top service providers have been successful because they made their particular service activity unique and not simply the normal drudgery that most services seems to be. They changed their attitude, way of treating their customer with the changing nature of customer-service from time-to-time like this village barber. "The old village barber used to make his customer sit on gunny bag and used to shave him with a dull razor simply with water application. Resentment was not there between service provider and service receiver. Because culture of service had its traditional base. With the changing nature of customer-service, today the village barber shaves his customer making him sit comfortable in a cozy chair and in air-conditionly room, shaves him with sharp razor applying shaving cream before and after shaving lotion, to make him satisfied." Why this drastic change of attitude between service provider and service receiver is witnessed?

The change has occurred because customer-service, treatment and satisfaction are redefined by both. With the change of time they changed their way of doing and treating each other. This has happened because:-

- Customers today are getting more and more critical of the service they accept and receive.
- Many customers are not only wanting but expecting better service.
- Quality service is becoming a more and more important issue in today's service economy.
- If any service provider goes into business with only the idea of making a lot of money, chances are he won't. But if he puts service and quality first, money will care for itself.

Like village barber, human resources treatment pay me well; treat me well; and use me well has also brought revolutionary changes in management-employees relations.

Today's knowledge workers are much more aware of their competencies, skills, knowledge and contributions. Employees not only expected to know more about the company that employ them but also wanted to know its problems, successes and objectives for the future than ever before. Again, importantly they will be called upon to act on that knowledge to continually improve their own performance, the performance of the company as a whole. Customer-service altogether has changed its basics form bad to better and better to best. Customer-driven attitude is a watch-ward in today's competitive business. Organizations have to make decisions that are based on looking at their internal customers – their employees.

POOR CUSTOMER-SERVICE

Management spends more time trying to automate, eliminate and simplify the technical skills needed rather than developing customer-service skills. If there is training it is more likely to be on mechanical or technical nature rather than geared to providing customer satisfaction. It is any wonder we can't get good service. Service providers are not taught to think, react and communicate. The end result is poor customer-service.

- The employee may be most visible aspect of poor service. But the system in which the employee functions is the primary culprit. Given the same working conditions, most of us would behave in the same manner.
- Service stinks because the job stinks. Lack of basic skills of service provider, lack of product, service knowledge and skills, lack of motivation and interest affects service to customer. Poorly paid for their efforts, combined with lack of career path make the job unrewarding.
- 'You will have to see our manager's attitude shows bureaucratic approach to service. Red-tape, rules and regulations detached employees from developing his service-oriented approach. Instead of flexibility and accountability we often have bureaucratic approach to service.
- Service is cultural. Interior or superior service begins at the top. Those who wanted to earn money by pushing the unquality products, offering heavy discount are careless about customer satisfaction. They give little attention to service after sale.
- Poor service has its root in poor management. They demonstrate their learning disabilities by sticking to old ways of doing business and management of internal customer- employees.
- Because of inferior customer-service, the organization loses its existing, potential and prospective customers. Opposite to this, superior customer-service providers are flexible. Involve their employees in day-to-day decision-making. They trust their employees; give them freedom as well as authority and responsibility to deal with customer. They demonstrate customer-oriented attitude.

SUPERIOR CUSTOMER-SERVICE

The management knows the science of superior service. Approaching is scientifically begins with the definition- quality first.

- Superior service providers know that quality service can't occur unless we know the art of people management. It takes deeds, not talk to prove to the customer that they are getting what they expect.
- They believe a motivated, knowledgeable and caring employee is an invaluable asset, who improves services.
- Efficient service providers are those people who are most important. For them technology is secondary to quality service. If people can't provide services, machines surely not.
- Demonstrating management support is a fundamental principle of superior service providers to customers.
- Superior service providers don't assume customer requirement. Instead they make sure they mesh their personal views with those of customer. They are aggressive about listening to customers.
- Superior service provider believes that if there is no way to assess the service then there is no way it can be improved. Customer survey, self-assessment, opinion survey are the measures they use for monitoring customer feedback for undertaking corrective actions.
- Superior service provider believe that quality service is not based on assumptions, it is based on accurately reading the customers pluses through the vide variety of customer feed-back. They make it easy for the customer to tell them what is right and what is wrong.
- Superior service provider stays in close contact with their customers. They see their services from the customer's eyes.
- Superior service providers encourage respect and sometimes nurture employees as equal partners in delivering services. Hence, customer satisfaction tends to take care of itself.
- Lastly, superior service providers are decidedly people-oriented companies. They recognized that service is people not just customer but employee as well.

CUSTOMER SATISFACTION

Keeping buyers happy requires a commitment of the total organization. Likewise keeping internal customer – an employee satisfied is management's obligation. If customer-service is the priority then focusing organizational development, along with individual's development is management commitment. To reinforce the service value, the organization must have people-oriented approach, people-oriented organization develop service-oriented employees by creating employee profile of effective customer service standards. Contrary to this if you don't listen you can't involve people. If organizations don't listen, they know organization think they are not important.

Are you listening and involving your employees? It is observed that thirty-four per cent (34%) of organizations do not. Their listening disabilities spoil the spirit of togetherness at work. Deming – quality Guru narrates that "Most trouble and most possibilities for improvement belongs to the system which is controlled by the management". Centralization of decision-making, love for *status sqo* operating systems are the main culprits; discourage employees involvement. Eighty per cent of the damages done by poor quality/service are traceable to management action. If you put a skilled, knowledgeable employee into bad system, the system will win most of the time. Therefore, it is only management responsibility to make learning organization happen and allow people to learn new skills in business areas.

The message is very clear. If organization wants to satisfy their external customer, first of all it must take care of its internal customers – its employees. Our forefathers were fine craftsmen with mastery on their skills, were committed to produce quality products/services. They taught us that the team of skilled employees, motivated and with the opportunity to contribute can turn products/services of highest excellence, achieving customer satisfaction, assuring that customer's will come back again and again. Thus achieving customer satisfaction is not an accident. It is a continuous process established by traditions. Today, it is management commitment to make it happen. Management has to support its people so that, in turn, they support external customers. Management must take care of its people because it is people who take care of company customers.

Management must believe that their people who make the difference and it is management attitude make these people different. Management's ultimate objective of quality service is to make employees satisfied to satisfy company's external customers – company's product/service buyers.

Customer satisfaction

Following are some of the tips on skill development for achieving customer satisfaction:

- Training and motivation is essential if employees to understand their role in achieving customer satisfaction.
- Employee's involvement is the key to the success of any organization. If employees are motivated and interested in the organization they are more likely to offer friendly service and find ways to increase productivity, profit and customer delight.
- The quest to become a customer-oriented enterprise requires more than speeches and good intentions. Well defined continuous strategies for quality improvement and customer satisfaction. There must have mutually committed partnership among internal customers and suppliers. Lack of partnership to achieve customer satisfaction produces real liabilities and this is a fact that business can ill-afford to ignore. That is why organization must invest heavily on employees training, perks, benefits, etc., employee must be trained in their new skills required in the new areas of business. Customer satisfaction gets enhanced because employees understand the art of customer-service and the ways of satisfying them.
- Dedicated people with right skills, traits are crucial if business hopes to obtain the quality in service. Organization looks for people who really enjoy helping customers.

- Employees do not believe in a stop-watch approach. They believe with an emphasis on extending quality service to customer on time and all the time.
- Helping employees achieve job mastery, multi-tasks skilling with proper coaching and mentoring will help employees to serve their customer defect free.
- Providing successful role models, allowing them to observe peers who are already performing job successfully, supports fast learning of skills.
- Using social reinforcement and persuasion, giving praise, encouragement and feedback designed to raise self-confidence.
- Giving moral and emotional support, providing reduction of stress and anxiety through better role assistance, task assistance, honest caring and empathic listening, help employee develop loyalty to his job, co-employees, workplace and organization at large.
- Monitoring the quality of relations and service is important to customer satisfaction. Services are not generated by machines, they are produced by people. If employees are not cared or are not appreciated, employee's loyalty to organization and external customers will soon disappear.
- A positive climate existing between employees and management is also essential. Employees are not necessary evil; they are the solution to customer satisfaction. Service needs dedicated people. It is difficult, may be even impossible, for employees to be unhappy on the job and still give the necessary efforts to ensure customer loyalty. Management has to support its people so they in turn can support their customers.

Attracting, managing and nurturing today's knowledged employee are the single most critical issues with the new people's management. People are crucial to every work operation because best products/services, best price, best technology are managed by people only. All this is with the aim for attracting, retaining company customers – buyers – who are the ultimate factors in keeping our business alive. The people-oriented companies have deeply, ingrained philosophy that they in effort "respect for individuals", "make people winner", "let them stand out", and "treat people an adults" – (Tom Peters – *In Search of Excellence*). Marshall Field very rightly observed on customer-service and satisfaction. He states "Those who enter to buy support me, those who come to flatter, please me, those who complain, teach me, how I may please others so that more will come". Customer satisfaction does not just occur. It takes close follow-up and a perfectionist's attitude. Make customer satisfaction does not just occur. It takes close follow-up and a perfectionist's attitude. Make customer satisfaction focus at the corporate level. Involve managers in monitoring and better understanding the customers. Openly share information about the company and the need for service. Show support for and faith in the service providers – manager and managed.

CHAPTER 25

Trainer's Skills

Learning process can be nerve-wracking experience, especially for new learners. New employees may think that they will be unable to perform tasks and as a result may lose their job. People have been conditioned to believe that training will be limited or they will be shown the job only one time. On the other hand, teaching/training people are one of the most challenging tasks because of the variation in each situation of learning or teaching. Training sessions, contents of training will vary because of the complexity of the jobs, the learning capability of the learner or a number of other factors that may arise. And, the challenge to trainer is that he must be able to continually adjust his methods as challenges occur. The technology for developing people is not new or remarkable. The commitment to do it consistently by individual and organization is remarkable. There are many companies that have committed to develop exceptional skills in their employee to create skill bank of their own. You too can do it if your company and yourself are truly dedicated to people development.

The first requirement of successful trainer is that he must be good learner and then successful trainer. Many people make the incorrect assumption that the most skilled person will be the best person to train others. Unfortunately this is not always the case. The reason for this disparity is the difference in skills sets required for each task. Therefore, while selecting a role of trainer you must consider the requisite skills required for the trainer. It is experienced that there are some intuitive abilities and fundamental skills are necessary to be a trainer. It is then true that trainer and the company must understand the company's needs for people development. In the company both trainer and learner should feel encouraged to excel in their abilities to create a very special learning experience.

Trainer should be cautious, have a thirst for knowledge and seek to be inspiring of training and development of people. As a trainer, you may be required to take on a number of roles within the company. These may be trainer, coach, facilitator, innovator, etc. By identifying which role you play and where you excel, you can then focus on developing the skills required by you. Operating as a trainer requires the ability to help people learn. If you are going to provide training you need to consider carefully your own development, as any trainer knows it is important to keep developing your own skills. If you want to develop training excellence you need to present the best yourself. The only way to do this is to constantly keep developing your own skills and awareness. Lifetime learning gives us the opportunity to explore the dimensions of ourselves and we build layers of knowledge as we work with others. The trainer should lead the way, supporting and helping others to achieve their full potential.

Skilled trainer does not have to be the fastest person at the task in order to effectively teach others to be fast and competent. The trainer only needs to know how to teach the techniques that allow people to be efficient in their movement. With time and practice the well-trained employee can master the skills and become proficient trainer. Natural talent is necessary to be effective trainer. All jobs are made up of fundamental skills, core-jobs specific knowledge and accumulated know-how. In addition, there are personal traits each person has, that also help in the performance of any task. These traits are hard to quantify and sometimes are referred as natural talent or intuitive ability. Successful trainer must also learn the following skills.

❖ Willing and able to learn

Teaching others is as much about learning as it is about teaching. The trainer must have the desire and ability to continually learn and grow and to reinvest his own learning into teaching. This trait is generally observed in people who make efforts on their own to learn and accept new challenges.

It is therefore, said that the true master trainer is also a master student. It would be insane as a teacher to expect different results without ever adopting to varying situation.

❖ Adaptable and flexible

As a trainer you will face different circumstances while training in action. There will be differences in the material covered, the ability of the student, the condition of workplace, the amount of time set for training. Skilled trainer must have core competence in the training methods, but he must also be adaptable to the moment. It is not always possible to approach the varying conditions in the workplace with the same teaching style and method every-time and except a successful out-come. Hence, adaptability and flexibility are the most important skills trainer should possess.

❖ Genuine caring and concern for others

Trainer must genuinely want the student to become successful in the task. Hence, he must care about the student. This desire includes respecting others and the ability to be empathetic to each person's situation as a student. Make efforts to help others learn without being asked to do so.

❖ Patience

Conditions for the real training situation rarely occur and the challenges are plentiful. Each student will have different abilities and some will need lot of practice to master the skill. A skilled trainer must be able to put trainees at case prior to beginning of the training session. Training to others requires a great deal of patience.

❖ Taking responsibility

There are many persons who try to do a job of training, but not all are willing to take responsibility. But the responsibility for successful training outcome rests with the trainer. In case of training, if trainee fails, the trainer has failed. If the trainee has not learned the trainer has not taught. Hence, the trainer is a decision-maker throughout training process. If decisions lead to undesirable outcomes, the trainer must take responsibility and accordingly develop a new plan in order to obtain best results.

❖ Confidence and leadership

Trainer should be confident and self-assured. He should have confidence when challenged in terms of his capability. Trainees view trainers as the subject expert and seen as an authority but not necessarily as an autocrat. Trainer must lead by example in that they should demonstrate proficiency in the subject they are training. Trainer need to provide some guidance without being too overbearing or too tax. Nothing is more frustrating to a trainee than a trainer who does not know the material.

❖ Questioning nature

They must know that trainees are full of questions and the trainer have already asked the questions and pursued the answer on their own and are willing to share what they have learned with others. Therefore, the first characteristic that trainer should have questioning attitude. He must question why there was particular outcome of the training and what must be changed, if a different outcome is desired.

❖ Mastering fundamental skills

Following fundamental skills and abilities that can be mastered by the trainer:

(a) **Observation and job analysis ability** – The ability may require observing trainees during training session and to detect problems. It may happen that trainee is not grasping the concept and the trainer needs to break the content into smaller pieces. Or perhaps the trainee is struggling with a particular step and then trainer must adopt and concentrate on that single step.

(b) **The ability to analyze** – The final result determine the effectiveness of the method and to incorporate the learning into subsequent training session. Trainer must continue to observe the trainee until they are certain that the training is complete and has been effective.

(c) **Communication skills** – Go well beyond the ability to speak clearly. Communication is also about body language, gestures are the key component of communication for successful training. A trainer must demonstrate correct posture and positioning by pointing, posing and emphasizing certain work movements. Of course trainer must have the ability to speak clearly and concisely. Moreover, the ability to listen effectively and to interpret questions accurately is the other side of the communication equation. This is often called active listening – the ability to go beyond taking in the words, to actively interpreting what is being seen and heard.

❖ Attention to details

It is related to keen observation ability; however, attention to details is also about being thorough and complete. Although attention to detail may reflect personality characteristic, it can be sufficiently for people to make it a part of how they function.

❖ Knowledge of the job/subject

A trainer must have a solid knowledge of the subject at hand. He must have subjected understanding that is deeper and is developed overtime with experience. Knowledge of part issues helps trainers to identify the correct key points that are necessary to prevent defects. Trainer must have an understanding of knacks that are used to perform the work efficiently. They must be able to draw from variety of knacks that are used by others to complete the task successfully. Again demonstrating adaptability is also a must in training.

❖ Respect for others

People are more likely to listen to and accept feedback from someone they respect then from someone they don't respect. Respect is earned and given if a person possesses the traits and abilities. If trainer is not hardworking, knowledgeable and caring, they are not likely to earn respect and will not have credibility with others.

❖ Relationship network

If you are giving others you need to be able to take from others. You need a network of people. You meet people who will have a significant impact on you. They may be colleagues, teachers, trainers, speakers, executives or clients. It is important to stay in regular contact with these people. They can help you to develop new skills and to grow. Joining professional organizations, attending conferences, committee meetings which also influence your training career positively. They may provide you with the opportunity to gain first-hand information in the field.

❖ Your creative attitude

One of the greatest skills a trainer can possess is the ability to think creatively. If you expose yourself to richness of experience you can stimulate your creativity by drawing down from external stimuli and other pleasurable experiences. Often people find that by doing something completely different (non-routine) their mind will suddenly start generating ideas. Generating new ideas and being creative takes tremendous personal discipline. Being creative and open to new experiences is an important part of trainer's self-development. As a trainer, if you really want to make a difference, it is important that you achieve a greater understanding of what stimuli you and your participants need to help you operate at optimum performance. Understanding your own creativity is important part of your role to create opportunities for participants to bring new ideas of improvements in workplace.

Smart trainer knows that employees who are learning and growing are happier and more productive and perfect in their acquisition of skills. People with greater skills and abilities are able to support the leader, their team and the company more effectively. When employees are able to utilize their skills, they provide greater benefits to themselves, the company and to their work team. Smart trainer will achieve great success when they pay attention to the development of complete individual beyond basic job skills. In the long-run you as a trainer will be doing everyone a great service.

Finally, to say, the true trainer is also a master student, learner. A trainer must have desire and ability to continually learn and grow and to reinvest his own learning into teaching others. This trait is generally observed in people who make efforts on their own to learn and accept new challenges.

Above are some of the fundamental skills and abilities that must be mastered by anyone with the desire to be a successful and effective trainer. Some people possess greater natural abilities, but with continued practice and guidance from an experienced mentor, nearly everyone can become proficient trainer. Being cautious and open to new experiences is an important part of self-development.

CHAPTER 26

Time Management Skill

Self-management is the bricks and mortar for the strong foundation of time management. Self-management really makes a difference in human interaction and relationship and is almost naturally flow from a truly independent character. So the place to begin building any relationship is inside us and insiders are our circle of influence and character. As we become proactive, centred ourselves in correct principles, values and able to organize and execute around the priorities in our personal and professional life with integrity, we become capable of building rich, enduring and highly proactive relations with people at work. So, time management is actually self-management. The barriers to its accomplishment are chiefly negative mental attitudes. If you never learn self-management while young, you may considered yourself naturally disorganized person. The truth is, however, that anyone can learn to organize and manage their time, at any age. All it takes is a readiness to make changes in your life, together with knowledge of where, when and how these changes need to be made.

In today's pressurized society managing your time efficiently is not merely useful, it is essential. On this time management skills depends:

- Whether or not you achieve your goals in life.
- Whether or not your deadlines are met.
- Whether your work is proactive and fulfilling or pressurized and frustrating.

The secret of managing your time is to work not harder but smarter. Until you manage your time it is impossible to manage anything else (P. Drucker)

People who complain I have not got the time… are mistaken. Since time can't be stretched, stored or supplemented, our only solution is to manage it sensibly. On this single time management skill depends not only your success but conceivably your mental and physical health. To organize yourself and manage your time effectively and successfully it is essential to know:

- How did you spend your time at work?
- What goals were you able to accomplish?
- Which one did you fail/achieve?
- How often were you interrupted?
- What were the most frequent interruptions?
- How long did it take you to refocus on the task at hand?

Unless you are truly exceptional, the likelihood is that you will have only the vaguest recollection of how your time was invested. It is only time tracking technique will identify regular patterns of activity. And to create priority task efficiency scale. You need to master the following skills:

- ➢ Self-discipline
- ➢ Identifying key areas of result
- ➢ Controlling interruptions
- ➢ Planning and prioritizing
- ➢ Avoiding procrastination
- ➢ Attending and/or organizing effective meetings
- ➢ Focusing and concentration
- ➢ Delegation

For improving your time management skills, let examine where you are at low level and consider how these skills can improve your present attitude, mindset, working methods and practices. At the heart of effective time management lie specific and well-defined life goals. Without these you will never really know how best to invest your time or whether that investment is proving worthwhile.

Evolutionary stages in time management

The essence of the best thinking in the area of time management can be captured in a single phrase, "Organize and execute around priorities". The phrase represents the evolution of three generations of time management theory. In this theory each stage builds on the one before it. Each one moves upward greater control of our lives.

Ist stage is characterized by **notes and check list**, an effort to give some semblance of recognition and inclusiveness to the many demands placed our time and energy.

IInd stage in characterized by **calendar and appointment book**. The stage reflects an attempt to look ahead to schedule events and activities in the future.

IIIrd stage reflects the current time management field. It adds to those preceding stages the important idea of prioritization of clarifying values and of comparing the relative worth of activities based on their relationship to those values. It also focuses on setting goals toward which time and energy would be directed in harmony with values. It also include the concept of **daily planning, of making a specific plan** to accomplish those goals and activities determined to be of greatest worth.

IVth emerging evolutionary stage in time management is quite different. It recognizes that time management is really a misnomer – the challenge is not to manage time, but to manage ourselves. Rather than just focusing on things and time, fourth stage expect focus of preserving and enhancing relationships and results. The essence of fourth generation time management is framed in time management matrix describing basically, how we spend time in one of four ways:

TIME MANAGEMENT – MATRIX

URGENT	NOT URGENT
I – Activities – Crises, pressing problems, dead line driven projects.	II – Activities – Prevention, relationship building, recognizing new opportunities, planning, recreation.
III – Activities – Interruptions, some calls, some mails, some reports, some meetings, some pressing matters, popular activities.	IV – Activities – Trivia, busy work, some mails, some phone calls, time workers, pleasant activities.

Urgent – means it requires immediate attention. Urgent things act upon us. Urgent matters are usually visible. They press on us, they insist on action. They are usually right in front of us. We react to urgent matters.

Not urgent – are important matters and has to do with results. If something is important. It contributes to your mission, your values, and your high priority goals. Important matters that are not urgent require more initiative, we must act to size opportunity to make things happen.

- Quadrant I from matrix – comes under both urgent and important. It deals with significant results that require immediate attention. We usually call the activities – crises or problems. We all have some such activities in our life. People in this quadrant are crises managers, problem minded people, dead line driven producers.
- Quadrant II – it is the heart of effective personal management. It deals with things that are not urgent, but are important. It deals with things like building relationships, long-range planning, and preparation. All such things we know, we need to do, but some how seldom get around to doing because they are not urgent.
- Quadrant III – under this an individual reacts to the outside forces. Thinking they are urgent, assuming they are important. But the reality is that the urgency of these matters is

often based on the priorities and expectations of others. Effective people stay out of quadrant III, because urgent or not, they are not important.

- Quadrant IV – some people are literally beaten up by problems all day everyday. The only relief they have in escaping to the not important, not urgent activities. People who spend time exclusively in quadrant IV basically lead irresponsible lives. These people manage their lives by crises – stress, burnout, crisis management, etc.

The essence of effective time management is to organize and execute around balance priorities. If you were defaulted yourself in these areas would convey your inability to prioritizes, inability to organize around those priorities, the lack of discipline to execute around them.

The way you spend your time is a result of the way you see your time and the way really see your priorities. If your priorities grow out of a principle centre and personal mission, it is almost impossible to have effective time management. Your self-awareness, imagination and conscience to create a new, unique principle centred thinking to which you can say 'yes' – only then will you have independent willpower to say 'no', with a genuine smile, to the unimportant.

Identify your time zone and your choice of zone

What we are exploring are ways of managing yourself and as far as this is possible – your surroundings, with maximum effectiveness, because time management is self-management or personal management. And to check your own attitude and your general outlook on life affects the way in which you perceive and seek to manage time – Dr. Philip Zimbardo of Stanford University suggested four zone people can live and live in one or two of four different time zone and how and what your choice reveals. The assessment below allows you to identify which ones you prefer to spend your life in. You may find more than one of these profiles/zones apply in different situations.

ZONE	YOUR CHOICE REVEALS
Zone I – Individual prefers a quiet life, free from too much pressure: likes to work at his own pace and adopt relax attitude towards deadlines. His view is that if something does not get done exactly on time, does it really matters? He is seldom on time for appointments.	Individuals in this zone adopt relaxed, laid back attitude and prefer to delay decisions as long as possible. **If you placed yourself** in this zone, an obstacle to better time management could be an inability either to get started or, having begun, to persist in your goals.
Zone II – Individuals in this zone have greatest pleasure is being sociable to friends, dining out, going to parties and so on. They often act on impulse and may not always think through the consequences of their actions sufficiently. They would far sooner behave in a spontaneous way than trying to plan every details of their	Individuals living in this zone are termed 'present domestic' because they are motivated by the needs for rewards and enjoyment. **If you are placed yourself** in this zone, a possible barrier to time management is your dislike of planning & organizing. You may postpone urgent but disagreeable tasks in favour of lower priority but more enjoyable activities.

life. They prefer a job with plenty of variety and where they can see the results of their work fast.	
Zone III – These individuals prefer to organize their life carefully and prefer routine to variety. They are careful about their diet, take regular exercise. They think through their actions carefully before proceeding.	Individuals who choose this zone are said to be 'future-oriented' because they plan and set long-term career and personal goals. **If you place yourself** in this zone, the chances are that you already manage yourself and your time reasonably, effectively. It will still be possible however, to fine tune your skills, to manage time even more efficiently.
Zone IV – individuals in this zone enjoy working to fight deadlines and pride them selves of their punctuality. They generally are well organized and work best under pressure. They admit to having difficulty relaxing and enjoy taking a variety of challenges. They tend to arrive for appointments on time but at the last minute.	Individual in this zone are termed 'time conscious'. They enjoy working to deadliness and demand punctuality from themselves and others. **If you place yourself** in this zone, you may find it difficult to deal with people who are less punctual or show less urgency in meeting deadliness. An obstacle to improved time management could be the addictive nature of the deadline high prescribed above.

It is you to decide in which zone you classify yourself. However, quadrant II and zone III are having more or less similar time management attributes. You must consider in terms of effectiveness rather than efficiency in yourself. Quadrant II and zone III encourage you to understand and centre your life on principles, to give clear expressions to the purpose and values you want to direct daily decisions. It helps you to create balance in your life. It empowers you to use self-awareness in your life. It empowers you to use self-awareness and your conscience to maintain integrity to the principles and purposes you have determined are more important in your life. Lastly, it gives you the opportunity to recognize your life to the best of your ability in harmony with your values. The practical thread running through three quadrant II and zone III is a primary focus on relationships and results and a secondary focus on time. People are more important than things.

CHAPTER 27

Etiquettes and Manners Skills

Like enhancing any other soft-skills, developing your etiquettes, manners take practice and hard work. Personal involvement is absolutely necessary to learn this skill. Our manners, our behavioural style and related attitudes advertise our personal image in public. Your silent messages through these channels are the signals you send to others. May you look people right in the eye to others, or may stare at your shoes when you talk to them. May be you don't smile naturally or shakehand firmly or you dress in a way that is not you. These can all shape your image in the eyes of people, through which you create your impression. The first impression is the only impression that counts and the only one that lasts. Therefore, to be successful in professional and personal life, you must cultivate good and positive etiquettes and manners to win over people around you. Etiquettes are the virtues and abilities of individuals to influence others positively by connecting with socially and emotionally. It is what makes people like you even when they don't know much about you.

WHY ETIQUETTES ARE IMPORTANT?

As business today becomes more globalised, developing and training people for working across cultural boundaries is becoming increasingly important. Culture and societal values of any country are the important determinants of beahviour and manners of people. Not being sensitive to these differences can often result in misunderstanding and embarrassment, even in loss of efficiency and goodwill. Therefore, an understanding and sensitivity to cross-cultural differences in behaviour and its orientation is necessary pre-requisite for developing cross-cultural competencies. However, by just understanding the differences in behaviour, etiquettes and manners, one only scratches the surface of the cultural iceberg. This is even more relevant when we try to understand the differences in business cultures and practices across the countries.

The roots of cultural differences in business etiquettes and practices lie much deeper. These are moulded not just by the behavioural orientations, but also are the products of social institutions; public policy, legal framework, political system and cultural specific values in which business is conducted. These issues as such more important in understanding differences in business practices, etiquettes and beahviours. Therefore, developing people to adopt and to operate across business culture of different countries require an appreciation of aspects which are deeper and more pervasive that just cross-cultural differences in behaviour. While understanding of differences in behavioural orientations and etiquettes help people truly to get cross-culturally educated and it is essential to provide an understanding into deeper structure which moulds the culture. This demands intensive training to employees in the areas of cultivating good etiquettes, manners, behavioural patterns and image-building.

Cross-cultural training socializes individual to assimilate cultural values of other countries. Cultural values have a major influence on the way people relate to each other and what they aspire for in the job or personal life. For example, in hierarchical cultures like India and Japan, the meaning and values of job lies in the status, more than in the pay packet. In these cultures, people also expect to be recognized for their seniority or age. On the other hand, in more egalitarian culture like United States, Germany, people expect reward and compensation for their performance than their seniority. Similarly, work is not equally central to life in all cultures and countries. For example, in many European and Scandinavian countries, work is only seen as just another part of life. In these countries 5 to 7 weeks of annual vacation is normal and acceptable. In sharp contrast, in countries such as United States and Japan, work is an essential part of one's personal identity and a quest for leisure would be perceived as unprofessional.

In conclusion, the most pervasive impact on business culture, practices, etiquettes, manners and behaviour comes from broad cultural and societal values of any country. These values influence business behaviour in different ways and at different levels.

IMAGE-BUILDING

Nothing good comes easily. And while you have skills, developing it is not automatic. You must be motivated and prepared to spend time and make the effort to sharpen your skills. As you know, doing well in life does not hinge solely on merit and hardwork. Your image especially when backed up by performance is a powerful force. And it is also negative first impression: saying wrong thing at wrong time and place, wearing the wrong clothes are not good etiquettes or manners. Uncaring and inept attitude creates roadblocks that can cut-off relationships before they get started. Some of the feedback from business community is down to earth true and disliked by people. And at the same time simple to correct too.

- Some employees have body odour unacceptable.
- Some don't shave everyday.
- Some talk too loudly.
- Some even don't wish good morning or other type of situation-oriented greetings.
- Some drink excessively alcoholic beverages in business meetings/parties.
- Some burp loudly which is considered very bad manner.
- Some don't know when to wear informal dress and when to wear formal dress.

These are some of experiences people witnessed in business workplaces. Preparing self to handle such etiquettes, manners to establish personal positive image, rapport and interaction building is immensely important to all of us. Your first impression, your positive image, your acceptable self-presentation is in your hand. Preparing yourself for successfully interacting with people of different origin and values and cultural background is very similar to the other knowledge, skills and attitudes required for an effective performance. Most importantly, learning and acquiring a cross-cultural mindset that enables a person to embrace a different culture without any bias or judgement. If we match with their mindset positively, we can imaginatively leverage our business or customer relationships and do wonders for our business success.

The point is people with presence of mind; enthusiasm and energy are able to maintain an excitement about them that starts with a favourable first impression. Many of us carry around an image that does not really jibe with the facts. For example, you could be holding a negative self-image that you subtly communicate to others you meet. If you are short height or overweight or unattractive someway, you will lack self-confidence and others will catch on or you have overly positive image of yourself. You may think you look terrific, when in fact you are a sloppy dresser, who is underweight and badly in need of a haircut or a makeover. In either case, analysis by yourself is needed. Your image is important factor while you present yourself to others. Understanding and adopting right and positive image to create style or etiquette is an important key to attract people's attention, right the first time.

You might have experienced that sometime we admire people before even we know much about them. Because they win over admiration so quickly and effortlessly, as they possess an enormous advantage in establishing a bond with people. And building that bond, forging these relationships is what helps them give charisma. People admire them because they cultivated their self in emotional, psychological, intellectual physical and social areas. Together, these 'self' comprise the silent messages you send out to the surrounding world and suggest different ways you can deliver your messages to others.

Emotional self – Energy has many components, but for our purpose, the most important are the positive attitude, enthusiasm and self-control. They embody the basic values of optimism. Optimists believe the power or control comes from within them. They feel they are ultimately responsible for their own success. They view most problems are solvable.

You generally wear positiveness "inside". But your enthusiasm is how you show into the world by your face, your voice, and your gestures. Sometimes, we feel enthusiastic about our ideas but we are afraid to show it. Those are able people to express on the outside what they are feeling on the "inside". Most people like to be around those who radiate joy and interest, whether at work or at play what is more, enthusiasm is infection. It spreads. But so does the lack of it. The choice is yours.

For a sustained good image and rapport building, you also must master emotional self-control "those who command themselves" is now saying "commanding others" is today true, and it means being disciplined enough to put your personal feelings on hold.

If your overall approach is cheerful, hopeful, positive and tolerant of differences, you send out a positive message. On the other hand, if you are critical, pessimistic and intolerant of anything unfamiliar, you convey a negative outlook. Guess which attitude gets better results when you are trying to interest people?

Psychological self – There is some overlapping between the emotional and psychological self. But for our analysis, the emotional is how you feel about yourself and your objective, and the psychological is how you think about them. Do you think of yourself as a 'can do' person? How you think about yourself directly affects yours ability to exercise your skilfulness. Sometimes you have to do a mental spring cleaning to get rid of ingrained attitudes and negative thinking. Stopping self-destructive thought is like stopping any other bad habits. Among the most effective ways to do this are visualization and affirmations. Affirmations are positive statements about yourself that you repeat over and over in you head. Visualization is imagineering. It is mentally picturing yourself the way you want to be: I will see it when I believe it. Affirmation and visualizations may not feel true at first. They may not even be true! But they can become so.

Intellectual self – How well you have developed what is inside your skull. This is your intellectual self. This refers to your depth and breadth of your knowledge, your mental fitness. Most of us were given plenty of basic intelligence. We alone decide whether we will use it to capacity or let it get flabby or stiff from disuse. Training your mind to take on longer-term and more demanding tasks gives you the stamina you need when mental marathons come up. What you don't know can hurt you. And depth of knowledge means, how well you understand you are an expertise. The more you know about your subject, the more power and influence you will have. Skillful people often make good first impressions not because they are smarter than others but because they prepare better. Acquiring depth knowledge can help make you an exception to that cynical rule. And in some cases, it may even help overcome an initially bad impression. Breadth of knowledge is what enables you to engage in meaningful small, small talks. It is a social lubricant that looms large in all human exchanges. The more people feel they in common, the better they like each others. So, by increasing your breadth of knowledge, you will be able to project a favourable impression.

Spiritual self – It has nothing to do with religion. Spiritual self is dynamics between you and those you are seeking to influence or interact positively with others. The bond of trust you are able to create, the level of caring and the attitude of service you convey, and the sense of higher purpose or greater good that you communicate. It is opposite of self-centredness. So to be skilful as you can, to send out the best silent message you can, you need be alert to the emotional state of others. It requires sensitivity. It is a definite spur to your skill as well as a sign of character and decency.

Physical self – we all carry around with us a bundle of opinion about what we like and expect and what we don't like or expect about others appearance. If that appearance is out of sync with our opinion, it will create distractions in the communication process, making it difficult for the other person to hear what you are saying because they are distracted by, say, your ill-matched clothes, so it is with physical image. Clothes don't make the man or women. They make the message about the man or women. Few are going to be a nice wardrobe and a good sense of grooming, a pleasant smile and a firm handshake, a smattering of knowledge, enthusiasm, and sincerity. But failure to attain those could be easily undercut all your other skills and virtues. These things don't go unnoticed: limp handshake, the shifty eyes, uncommon facial expression or body language, the unpolished shoes or shabby dress. Our appearance is an advertisement to the world. It is not just as that people see but also the statement we chose to make about ourselves. Besides clothes, other aspects of personal appearance can make or break your first impression.

The social self – man is a social animal. He is socialized by the family, society and nation at large which culture to follow or adopt to be an individual choice and cannot be forced by anyone. However, what matters is what you practice in public, at workplace and how it creates barriers in interaction. Not being aware of the cultural values, norms and practices with whom you are working, not understanding them and not being sensitive to be, the impact of your behaviour creates in the work environment can very adversely affect the business or customer relations as well as service. Cross-cultural knowledge is a must in today's globalised scenario. Therefore, preparing yourself for successfully interacting with people of different origin, values, traditions and cultural background is very similar to the other knowledge, skills and attitude required for an effective performance. Most importantly, it is acquiring a cross-cultural mindset that enables a person to embrace a different culture without any bias or judgement. If we match their mindset, we can imaginatively leverage our business, customer relations and do wonders for our business success.

PUTTING ETIQUETTES IN PRACTICE

Now you are well-known to various self and their attributes thoroughly. These self-emit different kind of energy and power in you in different degree and in different situations. How you are going to sell it to people your customer, or your co-employees. You need to know that customer don't buy because they made to understand the details of the product or service. They buy when they feel understood. Likewise, like a salesman you must show that you understand (them customers, guest, co-employees) by giving them what they expect? Respect for their etiquettes, manners or behaviour style. Adjusting your etiquettes to there is called adaptability. It is key to successful relationship to all sorts. Adaptability comes from understanding people's needs and expectations and then working to meet them. By choosing how you act, you can encourage others to respond more positively. Thus, you can enlarge your skills in etiquettes or your personal magnetism. This works in the workplace, in family, in public or other areas of work. By dealing with people as they want to be deal with, you will make them more comfortable with you and heighten the chances for win-win relationship. Being the best person you can be by treating people the way they want to be treated, pay-off enormously.

But the truth is, most of us don't try very hard to understand others and when we fail to understand others, when we just assume they ought to be more like us, we create tension and discomfort known as personality conflicts. You can reduce these conflicts by learning to understand people behavioural style, etiquettes of others including your own.

Cultural Differences – People can generally be classified into two major categories "contact" and "non- contact". Contact people sometimes view non-contact people as cold and impolite, on the other hand non-contact people may feel that contact people are aggressive or even rude. Arabs, Latin American and Italians normally use a lot of contact in their conversations. On the other hand North Americans and Northern Europeans typify the non-contact group and employ smaller amounts of touching. Violation such as unwanted touching occurs, non-contact people may have feeling that something is not right. Violation in either case, attention shifts to the behaviour and away from conversation at hand. This interferes with effective communication.

Keeping Social Distance – Initially, when meeting a new person, you will get best rapport by establishing a social distance and then slowly moving as the relationship develops, to a personal distance. Whatever the distance, body language also needs to be appropriate during the conversation. Standing or leaning over someone who is seated does not convey power, but it can be intimidating for the sitting person. On the other hand, leaning back and appearing too causal can foster a feeling of superiority or lack of caring again creating a possible negative reaction. In a good interactive relationship, both parties respect space and use it effectively. The net result is more attention, better communication and better chance of a successful relationship.

Using Your Time - Your use of time is an expressive language: To whom give time, how much you give, and when you give it convey important messages. Treat other people time as if it is a precious as yours and you will increase charisma. Waste others time especially if they are time-conscious individuals and you will squander their respect. When your superior keeps you waiting he sends the message that your time is not as valuable as his. When co-employee is frequently late for meeting, he implies that company time is not valuable. Generally speaking, inaccuracy with time creates a bad impression. Our accuracy with time often broadcasts a signal about our priorities. Time also can be used to demonstrate how we feel about others in terms of their status and power. Secondly, for the longer time people are kept waiting, the worse they are likely to feel. This may affect relationship negatively. Therefore, the longer a person is kept waiting, the more reassurance is required to neutralize the irritation. If you are frequently disorganized or late, you may be a liability to your organization and an embarrassment to your associates. Improving your time management etiquettes can boost your productivity service to attain a better balance between you work and your personal life.

Be Quick to Compliment - A really good, honest compliment shows that you appreciate the person you admire. People who say nice things when they genuinely feel them. Compliment is a kind of feedback through which people want and need to know how they are doing. Be on the lookout for positive act and attitudes worth noting. You will convince the other person that you care and you will convince yourself as well.

Using Space or Territory – In office people value their territory and privacy you can use space to your advantage, or disadvantage, in communicating with others. When you are conscious of what others have defined as their space, you give them a sense of control. Violating their boundaries will cause anger, while responding them may gain points. If you are talking someone and inadvertently violate his personal space, he may not say anything to you directly, but internally he may be so upset that he does not hear a word you say. Similar reaction might occur if you sat in your co-employees chair, used his pen, telephone without permission. So, if you are attempting to build rapport with some one, don't violate his territory, even if you are the boss. Trust is based on honouring a person's territory, his privacy and promoting mutual respect. So to increase trust, get in habit of knocking before entering anyone's office. These etiquettes are important while interacting with co-employees or external company customers, delegate.

Gender Consciousness – Gender also play a critical role in the areas of etiquettes and manners. The role of touching in the workplace is increasingly emotion-filled. While touching can underscore much of what we wish to communicate colleagues-friendliness, consolation or excitement. Research shows that male employees permit female employees to get closer to them than male employees. But female employees display no difference in the space they permit between themselves and their supervisors, whether male or female. People like to be closer to people of the opposite sex than to those of our own gender. Touching female, for example, can easily send the wrong signal and be interpreted as sexual harassment. Thus, men touching women that can lead to misunderstanding. Cultural differences often come into play with regards to touching.

Other Physical Signs – Besides clothes, fitness, other aspects of personal appearance can make or break first impression. Your body language communicates your manners and etiquettes to others. Your handshake should be strong and firm. A more subtle element is your eye-contact. Think for a moment about what a powerful force it is. By be-holding eye-contact, we signal others that we lack interest in, or even disbelieve, what they are saying. Thus, eye-contact can be a potent tool for building a bond or for damaging one. Body posture is also important too. Not only do you look better to other if your posture is good, you feel better too. Like eye-contact, a smile is a small gesture, with a powerful impact. Your eyes, face, hands, arms, legs and posture are powerful non-verbal communicators to project positive emotions such as openness, readiness, enthusiasm and thoughtfulness. In our culture, we have come to expect likable, approachable people to smile when we meet, greeting someone with a warm smile is the best manner/etiquette to introduce yourself, and it sets the stage beautifully for any discussion that follows.

Avoid Annoying Mannerisms – Rarely do impressive people cover their mouths or noses, scratch their heads, chew on pencil, and twist rubber bands around fingers. Tugging at clothing, drumming fingers on a table, tapping pencils or clicking pens, doodling, jangling keys or biting nails, cleaning teeth's are bad habits. Not only do these habits make it more difficult for other person to hear you, they also detract from your image.

Don't Just Say It, Do It – Credibility is gained by backing up those words with action. Especially if you are in a leadership position, be very aware that you set the style, both in appearance and integrity cultivate a do-as-I-do, not as do-as-I-say philosophy. You can show your sincerity by practicing what you preach on a daily basis. The ability to speak confidently is not only one of the major personal manners; it is also one of the most acceptable skills.

Good Presentation – Can provide an opportunity for growth, recognition and prestige. Effective public speakers establish themselves as experts to whom others turn for advice. Thus, being able to stand on your feet confidently and express your thoughts clearly and logically is a major building block of your etiquettes or manners.

Listening Others – When you want to win someone's attention and gain his confidence, listening is just as important as speaking. Good listening draws people to you; poor listening causes them to drift away. Learning to listen better can transform people and relationship by helping solve problems more quickly or making others feel appreciated and valued because you make the effort to share their excitement and ideas.

It is said that success is getting what you want, but happiness wants what you get. So, by all means, seek to develop your good etiquettes. Try to become the most effective person you can be. Work at making a good first impression and positive image and also try to retain self-awareness. Look around you; think how you appear to others; be alert to the impression you are creating, or trying to create. The best impression and the surest way to building etiquettes and manners often just means putting others first. Always do right things because it will gratify some people and astonish the rest.

CHAPTER

28

Customer Relationship Management

"Most human organizations that fall short of their goals do so not because stupidity or faulty doctrines, but because of internal decay and rigidification.They grow stiff in the joints. They get in a rut. They go to seed".

– James Gardner

The survival of such organizations depends on events. For example, survival might be the result of a lack of serious competition or the company's product is presently so important to the customer that some degree of tolerance of manufacturing imperfection and poor service is acceptable. If you believe it is reasonable for any modern business to stay, it is difficult. Even today, in reality many organizations have such day-functional assumptions on customer-service relations and their satisfaction. No Action Talk Only (NATO) approach to customer-service underlies the common failures of quality service.

To say:

- They talk of quality service while personally avoid customer contacts.
- They talk of teamwork while behave like lone ranger.
- They talk about people as our most important asset and then do not exploit the value of this asset. They neglect the innovative ideas of people.
- They talk of improved communications and then do not inform concerned people.
- They talk about human resource development and then cut the training budget.

Such or similar NATO approaches spoil the very spirit of customer-service, relations and their satisfactions. Those are so much ingrained that they always demonstrate organizational culture and values.

Customer-service, satisfaction does not happen without change and sometimes considerable change, especially in the attitudes of senior and middle management. But it is possible. More important, it is necessary for success in our future of global competition. Good and quality service to customer is an investment, not an expense. It will provide lasting dividends to the visionary leaders who make tough choices and move forward total operational performance excellence and or total quality management in their companies. They focus on total customer-service and satisfaction should be integrated into accepted management processes and the enterprises culture. Everyone must be made aware of internal and external customers. Each individual customer of a product or service is in turn the customer of people working in different jobs in various departments. Therefore, total employee involvement is recommended at all levels of the organizations. A customer based measure of performance should be included in the reward and recognition mechanism of the enterprise. The continuous improvement focus on cost reduction and improved performance and quality can help position an enterprise for long-term profitability and desired performance. In competitive world economy, a dissatisfied customer – internal as well as external will look for an alternative source of products and services. A satisfied customer will recommend excellent products and services to a friend and help the company increase its market share and profitability. What is needed to deal with these seemingly needs is the ability to work smarter, not harder. Easily said, less easily done. But effective quality management processes help companies do just that.

WHO IS CUSTOMER?

In almost every transaction in business each party to the transaction is at one point or another customer which is simply to say "let me know your needs and I will endeavor to fulfil them". The customer is a person, department or organization that receives the work output. The work output may be product or service. Within an organization, customers are recipients of process outputs performed by suppliers. Each customer then becomes suppliers in subsequent process steps. Ultimately, the output of this network is a product or service provided to external customer.

The customer is the final arbiter of quality, value and price of products and services. And there are three types of customer in any organization: self-unit customers; the internal customer, and the external customer. The inputs of all such customers must be considered in the management processes to achieve total customer-service, relations and satisfaction. Therefore, customer needs, wants and priorities are the part of manufacturing, service departments. Therefore, on their part quality in product, service, delivery, cost and professional courtesy is a must for achieving customer satisfactions. A satisfied customer brings additional revenue to the organization. While dissatisfied customer quickly advertise your poor product and service standards in the market. Hence, the major challenge in the satisfaction of customers is deciding how to provide the right product/service in the right quality, quantity at the right time and right price is the subject matter of right organizational performance.

WHAT IS CUSTOMER SERVICE?

"Getting close to the "customer" is not enough glue yourself to customer, distributors and suppliers; make relationship management your motto."

– Tom Peters.

Top service providers to customers know the science of service. Approaching it scientifically begins with a definition itself. Service is people-oriented function and management must nurture employees; teach them how to and allow them to solve problems; find ways to measure their efforts. If you can't measure, you can't improve. People at all levels have to do their jobs right and develop an interface with customers – internal as well as external customers. This will not happen unless management understands their customer needs, and it takes deeds, not talk, to prove to the customer that they are getting what they expect. In service, it is the people who make difference.

Positive changes in customer-service will occur through a regular, proactive focus on opportunities for improvement and action on the opportunities. For this activity to occur, employees must understand the required service optimization process and techniques. The improvement process should focus on effective ways of integrating product and service development objectives with manufacturing and marketing capabilities. It also involves institutionalizing total performance and improvement in the product and service life cycle from concept to commercialization. To understand this more clearly we must review PEAD model developed by Edosoman. His model captures the requirement of the customer and supplier, and such requirements can be incorporated to produce excellent products and services. Total process performance is then visible for establishing desired customer-service.

PEAD MODEL FOR CUSTOMER-SERVICE

Pay attention to the voice of the customer and supplier:

- Identify their needs, wants and desire.
- Obtain marketing information on customer and supplier perception for existing products and services.
- Translate the needs, wants and desires into product and service requirements.

↓

Evaluate the effectiveness of mechanism in place to satisfy customer and supplier requirements:

- Focus on product, service and processes characteristics.
- Specify requirements by operational needs.

↓

Analyze customer and supplier requirements and market information and synthesize data for relevance:

- Develop inter-relationships between product and service characteristics.
- Select the requirement that depicts customer and supplier input.

↓

Develop product and service characteristics and technical measurements that meet the customer and supplier requirements.

- Review final specifications with development teams.
- Implement the recommended product and service specifications.

Managing the product and service improvement process not only requires pushing the frontiers of technology but also involves the use of continuous improvement, evaluation, control, planning, improvement and monitoring. Total customer-service and satisfaction can be achieved only through partnership between supplier, process owner and customer. From the above we can review what is customer-service?

- The customer defines quality in service.
- Your customer's perception of the value they are receiving must become the common yard stick against which all activities throughout your entire organization are measured.
- Customer does not buy a product, they buy what the product/service does for them.
- Quality is product/service is not what we think it is. It is what our customers perceive and what they need and want.
- If you give them more than they expect, they will perceive it as an excellent service.

An employee being internal customer serves the company's external customer – buyer. Hence, the quality of external customer relationship is a direct reflection of the quality of service provided to internal customer – an employee. If the organization provides the best services to the bottom line, they take care of every external quality services. Hence, when managers lead, service excellence is within reach and when manager do not, excellent service becomes a pipe dream. Therefore, employee's involvement is a must for improving external customer-service. The magic of employee involvement is that it allows individuals to discover their own potential and put that potential to work in creative way. People develop pride in workmanship, self-respect, self-reliance and heightened sense of responsibility. In fact, majority of service improvement efforts owes much of their success to effective employee involvement. It has been proven time and time again that internal service providers treat their external customers in the same way as they are treated by the company. If they are treated well, they in turn will treat external customers well.

CUSTOMER RELATIONSHIP

Through the network of relationship with employee (internal customer) and our product buyer (external customer), the company develops its customer relationship network. These relations are built-up on certain mutually agreed upon requirements between service provider and service receiver, on the foundation of customer- supplier relationship.

The company or department or individual play **THREE ROLES**:

A. THREE DIFFERENT ROLES

- **Supplier:** Who provides INPUT for product/service in the form of material, information, report, procedure, etc.

- **Processor:** Who takes INPUTS and performs work process with the intention of adding value and satisfied needs of customer.
- **Customer:** Who receives output, product/Service from processor or supplier.

Quality in the workplace and worklife comes from the understanding of their role play, their inter-relationship for meeting customer needs – internal/external. Through this role play, company, department or individual works at three levels in a given organizational network.

B. THREE LEVELS OF CUSTOMERS

1. **SELF-UNIT CUSTOMER:** Employee himself/company itself or department itself. Self-inspection, Self-discipline. Disciplined attitude, values and desire to improve way of working life for individuals and others is their prime responsibility in quality improvement. Their focus must be on personal quality, performance and value systems.
2. **INTERNAL CUSTOMER:** Those who receive output, company, department, and individuals from one or more process owner, their focus are on providing defect-free quality product/service to the customers.
3. **EXTERNAL CUSTOMER:** Those receive the finished product/service from the company, department, and individual. Their focus is providing defect-free product with excellent service support to the ultimate and final customer, the judge of our products/services value, quality and excellence.

Thus, fulfilling external customer requirement through quality improvement at every stage is the basic responsibility of self-unit customer and internal customer – may it be company, department or employee on their positive and proactive attitudes and values the business cycle can race with customer cycle, if not unquality in business peeps in.

C. THREE BASIC CUSTOMER BUSINESS CYCLE – SUCCESS

The Business Cycle – It is the cycle begins with the strategies and mission. The company may spend a lot of effort prior to start-up quality improvement or performance improvement in business.

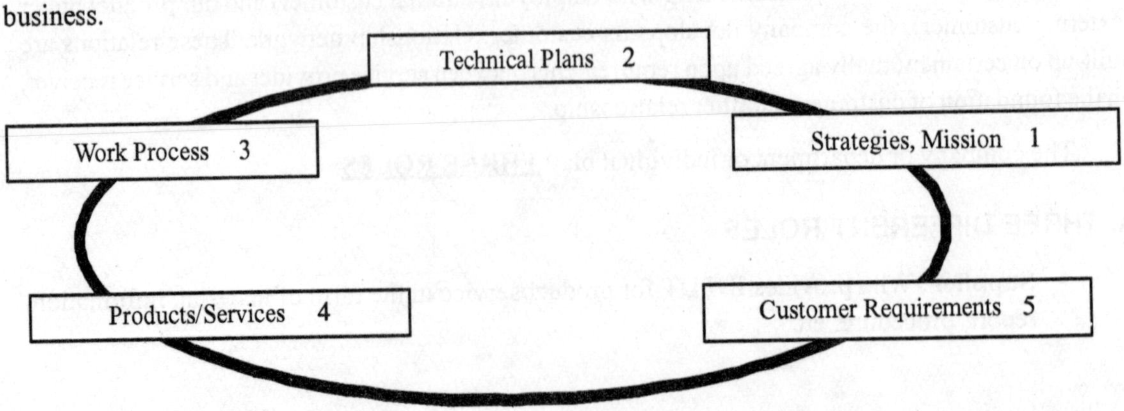

Technical plans are decisions about facilities, employee skills, annual budgets, RandD, advertisement plans, public relations and other things to begin to translate the strategy of business into the final products or services.

Work processes or employees daily activities are designed to enable the company to achieve its tactical and strategic plans may it be related to men, machines, method or money.

The resulting product/services hope fully meet the needs of the external customer. Hence, the unending effort is to identify new or changed customer needs so that strategic tactics and work processes can be modified to continue to meet their needs. Then, it is of primary importance to go for continuous quality improvement.

The Customer Cycle: Customers (internal and external) relationships with business are also cyclic. New or returning customers receive products/services have some degree of low, average or high satisfaction with company, department or employee. High satisfaction means customer's requirements were largely met which determines whether the customer will return with new customer with him.

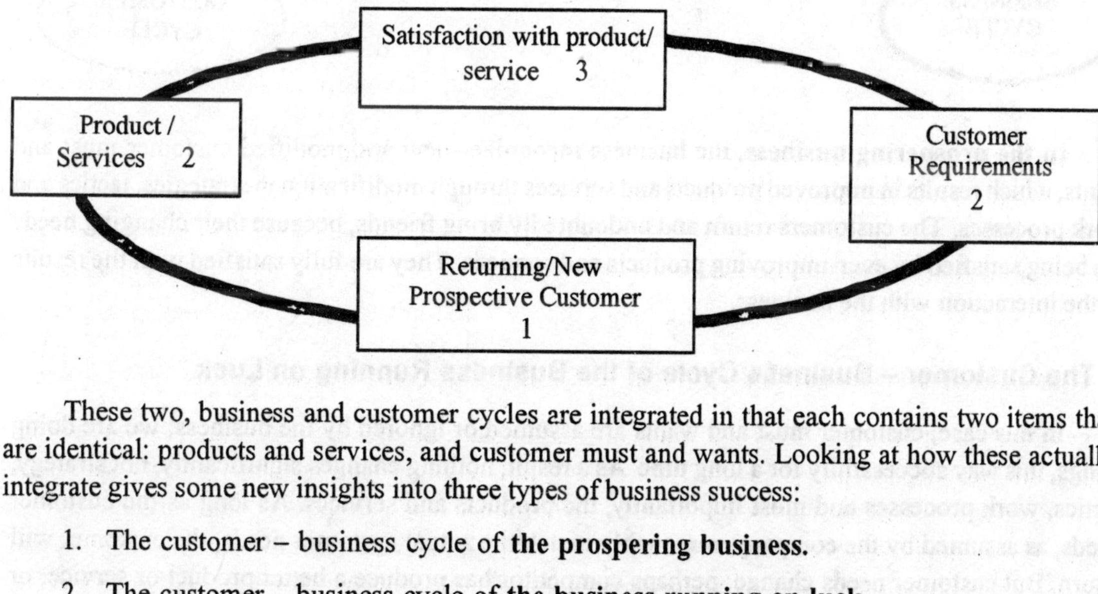

These two, business and customer cycles are integrated in that each contains two items that are identical: products and services, and customer must and wants. Looking at how these actually integrate gives some new insights into three types of business success:

1. The customer – business cycle of **the prospering business.**
2. The customer – business cycle of **the business running on luck.**
3. The customer – business cycle of **the business doomed to failure.**

1. The customer – Business cycle of the Prospering Business

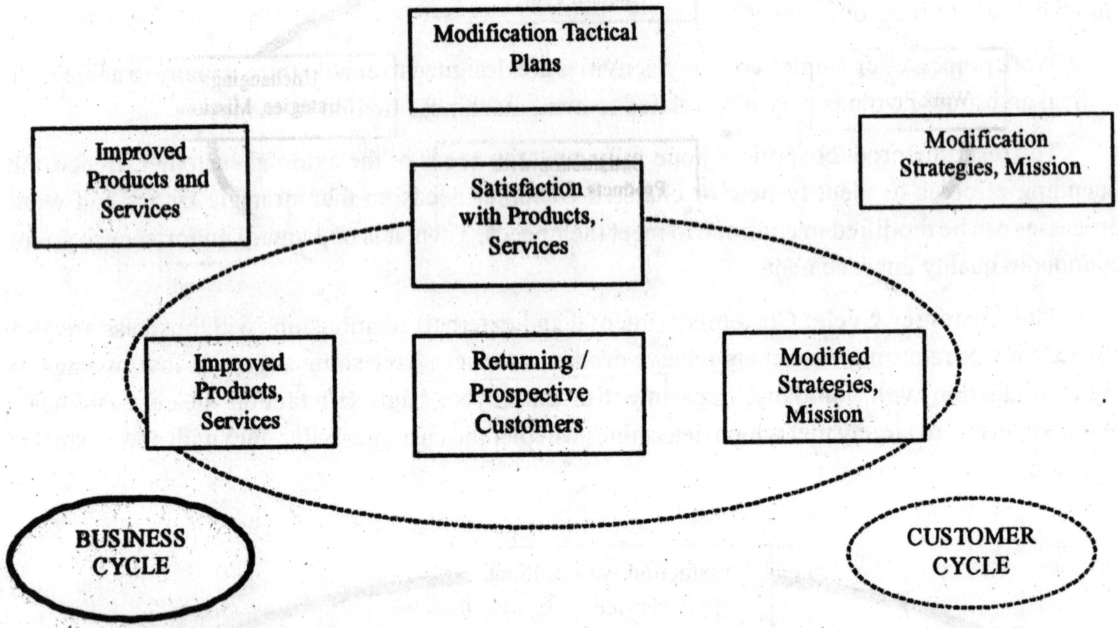

In the prospering business, the business recognizes new and modified customer must and wants, which results in improved products and services through modification in strategies, tactics and work processes. The customers return and undoubtedly bring friends, because their changing needs are being satisfied by ever-improving products and services. They are fully satisfied with the results of the interaction with the business.

2. The Customer – Business Cycle of the Business Running on Luck

In this case, customer must and wants are assumed or ignored by the business; we are doing things, this way successfully for a long time. As a result, nothing changes significantly, not strategy, tactics, work processes and most importantly, the products and services. As long as the customer needs, as assumed by the company, reasonably match the actual customer needs, the customer will return. But customer needs change; perhaps competitor has produce a better product or service, or figured out how to provide the same product at a lower cost. This business is running on luck because it has no control over the satisfaction of its customers.

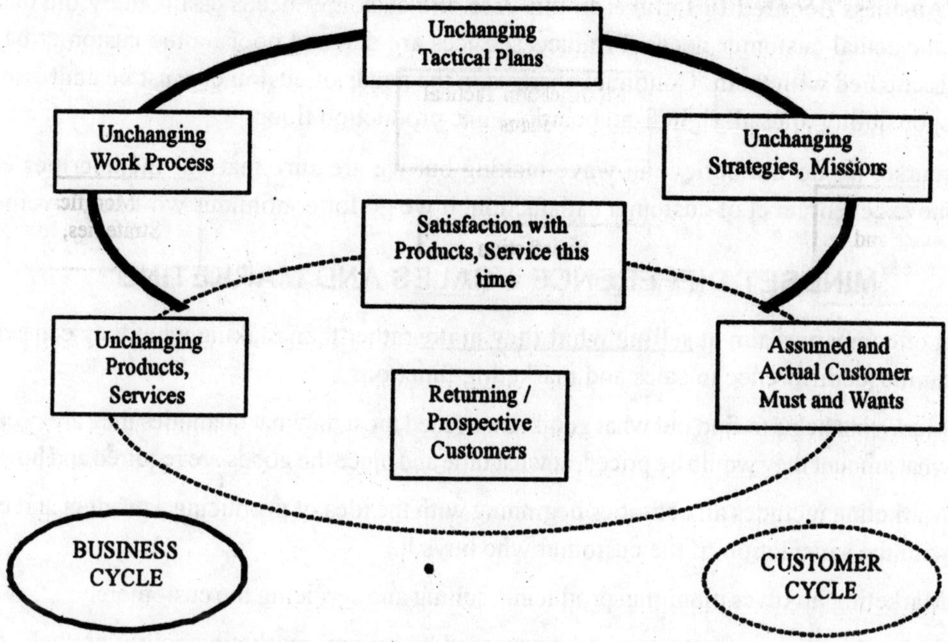

3. The Customer – Business Cycle of the Business Doomed to Failure

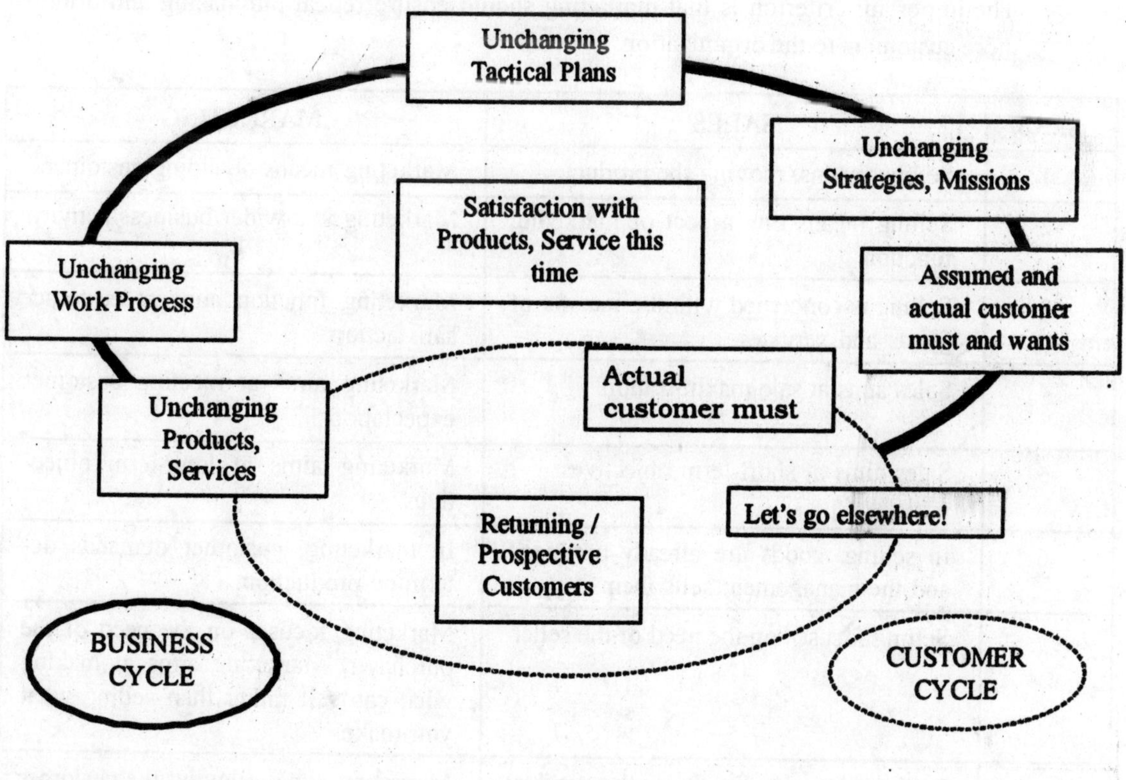

The business doomed to failure. In this case, the customer needs assumed by the business no longer the actual customer needs. Products/services are deemed poor by the customer because they are dissatisfied with them. Continual changes in the needs of customer must be addressed and it is the responsibility of us all right from boardroom to production floor.

Of course, we do not believe in wave-making but we are sure that our mediocrities can be raised to the excellent level of customer satisfaction, if we go for continuous work improvements.

MINDSET DIFFERENCE – SALES AND MARKETING

Most of companies aim at **selling what they make** rather than making what they can sell. Lét us see the mindset difference in sales and marketing functions.

- Marketing helps to find out what goods are needed most, in what quantities they are needed, at what amount they would be priced, at what time and place the goods are required and how soon.
- Marketing includes all activities beginning with the idea of producing a product and ending with the satisfaction of the customer who buys it.
- Marketing involves planning, producing, selling and servicing the customers.
- The selling to be effective must be preceded by several marketing activities such as need assessment, marketing research, product development, pricing and distribution.
- The important criterion is that marketing should ensure repeat purchasing and bringing more customers to the organization.

Sr.No.	SALES	MARKETING
1	Selling means, moving the product.	Marketing means obtaining customer.
2	Selling means one aspect of marketing function.	Marketing is a wider business activity.
3	Selling is concerned with the transfer of goods and services.	Marketing function aims at customer satisfaction.
4	Sales aims at sale maximization.	Marketing aims at meeting customer expectations.
5	Sales aims at short-term objectives.	Marketing aims at long-term objectives.
6	In selling, goods are already produced and the management sells them.	In marketing, customer demands determine production.
7	Selling focuses on the need of the seller.	Marketing focuses on the need of the purchaser. Marketing aims at making what can sell rather than selling what you make.
8	Selling aims at disposing the product than caring the customer.	Marketing aims at loving the customer more than the product.

CUSTOMER SERVICE

❖ SEVEN LAWS OF SATISFACTION

(1) Treat the customers you have as though they are prospects.

(2) View customers as partners – members of your team.

(3) Consider recruitment as serious business – and hire only the best.

(4) Give your staff members the tools they need to build skills and develop professionally. And evaluate them on what they accomplish, not hours worked.

(5) Prepare for the inevitable conflicts that arise in any customer relationship with this thought in mind. "IT'S HOW YOU HANDLE THEPROBLEMS THAT SETS ONE PROFESSIONAL OR ORGANIZATION APART."

(6) Invite customer complaints instead of just responding to what comes in.

(7) Foster exchanges among your organization's groups and individuals to get their ideas on how to better satisfy customers. And test what you assume is working even your best programmes.

❖ STAY FOCUSED TO GET THE MESSAGE

Here are some ways that can help you stay tuned in when you are meeting with a customer or client in your office:

(1) Have phone calls held or picked up by voice mail. If you can't do that, go to a conference room where there is less chance someone will call you.

(2) Get rid of papers on your desk if you know you have a lengthy discussion. When they are there, you are tempted to look at them even though you try not to.

(3) Sit on the edge of your chair. This keeps you from getting so comfortable that you might daydream. Also, lean forward. When you do, you will find that you are more attentive and can maintain eye-contact more easily.

(4) Show that you are tuned in by paraphrasing. "So, the way I understand it is that" or by asking specific questions about specific points. This, too, will help keep you alert.

(5) Take notes, but don't try to get all the details down. If you do, you can't pay attention to what is being said. Write only key words, phrases and numbers – just enough to remind you of the speaker's main points.

AVERT TROUBLE WITH CUSTOMERS

Don't wait customers to call you when their orders have been delayed. Reasons: A phone call from you can prevent an angry call from the customer, build customer loyalty and provide a cross-sell opportunity. When you call, be sure to:

(1) State the order's status and explain why it is late.

(2) Extend your regrets for any inconvenience.

(3) Reconfirm the order.

(4) Set a new due date for the order.

(5) Offer to substitute a similar product that you have available now.

(6) Follow the phone call with a written note, e-mail, if the original order came electronically – confirming the new due date.

Customer relationship management starts with people in the organization and ends with them. It is therefore necessary to understand relational network within, before undertaking any project on performance improvement.

CHAPTER 29

The Soft Technologies Revisited

Soft technologies at work are the products of social/soft skills acquired, demonstrated and implemented at workplace. There is fundamental difference in hard and soft technologies. In examining the soft technologies, it is useful to look at some of the way that the hard technologies have been misapplied to soft technologies probably the most important is in the area of measurement. The hard technologies (processes, products, tools, equipments) are based on objective measurement derived through statistical techniques and other methods. The primary use of measurement in the hard technologies is to control and reduce variability in products, processes. Accuracy of measurement and the use of proper statistical procedures are essential. Products and processes can be measured as often as one likes and the results will only show normal operational or measurement variation. But with people this is not the case. The difficulty occurs when we mistakenly try to equate the human system of organization with production processes. People are not machines or parts. Products/processes can be measured for variation, now and then. Machine, equipments and products do not care what is done with measured information, people do. Rather, in the soft technologies; it can't be assumed that the familiar understandings of the hard technologies will apply. Yes the pattern of variation though unknown can be changed based on motivation, experience, skills and abilities of individuals. Soft technologies will enable to better express their values, purpose and beliefs in creative ways through the production of goods and services. Because here the focus is on the person, team building, inter-personal relations understanding people are the kind of processes mainly means of improving the employees internal quality and productive capabilities. Quality in products/services is an outcome of human endeavour, which is the real aim of human happiness, satisfaction of achievement, the good feeling of cooperation the pride of being recognized and the joy of personal growth. These are clearly the dimensions of inner quality and the cornerstones of the soft technologies.

In the soft technologies, the main objectives are to improve customer satisfaction internal as well as external and quality of service and worklife. Within the organization everyone is both customer and supplier. Each person is a supplier to someone else and is also someone else's customer. Thus, improving the internal quality of person accomplishes both objectives. However, in improving the internal quality of the person, we are not trying to reduce variability; we want to increase the capabilities of each person to express his unique set of values, purposes, intents and creativity within the organizational context. When seen in this light, we are actually trying to increase variability in the human system through the teaching of soft skills.

To conclude, by sharing a vision that soft technology enhances the existing hard technologies by placing them on a foundation comprised of the inner or soft dimension – soft skills, the needs and priorities of any person or organization. I believe it is a vision worthy of any progressing organization. In social technologies paradigm, skill development will begin internally as a vision, as an awareness of creative impulse to express values and ideas. Soft skills will become the manifestation of human intellect and ability in its myriad forms. And we will know the soft skills are the creator of quality products and services – the truly visible and tangible expression of human excellence at the workplace.

BE AWARE OF THE MONSTERS OF FEAR

Many of the problems that we face in the business world today are directly attributable to our traditional management thinking and its systems. We fear that developing employees skills and their involvement in management activities will rob the organizations of its existing values and beliefs. Thus, fear a major reason for the difference between the fullest potential of the people and the current achievement of the organization. If fear limits the collective potential capability of the people that means it also restricts the capability of both the processes and products of the organizations. This type of fear propagates "old ways" and limits ability to change in a responsive manner. It robs an organization or its potential. Such monsters of fear are everywhere, but they can be defeated. Quality Guru Deming has rightly stated that "It is necessary for better quality and productivity, that people feel secure – secure means without fear, not afraid to express ideas, not afraid of asking questions, not afraid to ask for future instructions, not afraid to report equipment out of order, or material that is unsuited to the purpose, and other working conditions that impair quality and production. Now to drive out fear and to achieve a culture of transparency and togetherness, the only solution is awareness building on how learning of soft technologies brings required change in organization and individuals. To change a culture requires that the environment be seen to encourage learning and learners. It is management obligation to establish the learning environment by providing necessary training facilities. Unless management and managers show a commitment to learn, they will not demonstrate a commitment to improve. In the tradition of culture, management beliefs need to be supported by management systems and practices. And for this 'Change management attitude'. There are three major interventions where change can happen, changing management practices, changing management systems and processes and changing people's attitudes.

(1) Changing management practices

Management beliefs are reinforced by management practices. Managing is like holding a dove in your hand. Squeeze too hard and you kill it; not hard enough and it flies away. Employee responsibilities must be reinforced by supportive actions if fear is to be driven out of an organization. The supportive practices include additive instead of subtractive management. Additive management is finding things right, praising action beyond the call of duty, looking for what is good in an idea and critiquing by asking how can we further improve management practices that support a culture of collaboration and are those actions that promote cooperation instead of confrontation and teamwork instead of adversarial relationships. Management must learn and let learn employees; team-building, influencing, communication skills. This approach gradually will ensure full and equal participation of all concern.

(2) Changing management systems and process

Management belief need to be supported by management practices that in turn need to be reinforced by management systems and practices. An important system is the way problems are identified, documented, communicated and addressed. For example – problem-solving team, will initiate corrective action and communicate situation that will preach people doing their job right the first time and prevent wrong doing of employees, corrective action through problem-solving will effectively foster open two-way communication between management and employees. Meetings shall provide an opportunity to share the state of the business, understand employee concerns and encourage open discussions on problem-solving. Performance development system should be nurture and sustain individual employee contributions to the continuous improvement of the organization as a team and to provide an assessment or evaluation of performance for employee and management.

(3) Changing people's attitude

Change in people's attitude, will be greatly facilitated by the training and development programmes. The learning environment created by management is one that should be a team effort. If our organizations are to survive and grow, individuals must learn soft skills and use their own thought, power to work, communicate and trust in the workplace, the works community. The changes in management beliefs, practices and systems will help improve the fear of management can be trusted and make employee feel more secured in their jobs. However, in order to participate, the employees will need to feel more confident in their own ability to contribute. They will have to create more positive self-image assuming positive attitude at work, their peers and people in the organization. The transition process can be expedited by using the open communication, by overcoming our own personal resistance to change and by being believer in management's efforts to change. We must willing to participate in the corrective action process and deal with facts without emotion. We must overcome our own personal resistance to new change. We must be willing to make the improvement journey and not be complacent with current conditions. We must eliminate our own blind spots and prejudices. Instead of looking for reasons why the change won't work, we must be willing to listen and change.

Let's look for what is right with our management, our people, our processes and practices and build upon the good things we have already put in place.

It is important to realize that there are no great people. There are just ordinary people with great ideas and great courage. We must have the great courage to change our philosophy, our beliefs, and our old ways of doing business. We have to retool our way of communicating, our belief in ourselves and management, employees and companies. Imagine a company where the managers are teachers, helpers and coaches instead of just bosses, where the purpose of our business is to create a customer as well as to make profit. Build an environment on trust and respect, where everyone's ideas are welcomed and used, where employees are valued for their thinking as well as their labour.

In conclusion, ask yourself this simple question, can an organization improve without first learning something new? Whether solving difficult problem, introducing a new product/service or re-engineering a process to improve productivity, they all need to see the existing situation in a different way and then act in an appropriate manner. Continuous improvement requires continuous commitment to learning, unlearning and relearning. In the absence of learning, companies and individuals simply repeat old practices. This is obviously not good. As knowledge becomes more central to competitiveness the ability of individuals and organizations to learn becomes a primary means of winning in the market-place. Learning is really about the enhancement of our capacity to take action. We need learning in organization as well as at personal level. What we need to do is to give people the ability to adopt and learn. The organization that will survive and thrive in today's chaotic period would be as observed by Peter Senge, "Where people continually expand their capacity to create the results they truly desire, where new and expensive patterns of thinking are nurtured, where collective aspirations are set free, where people are continually learning how to learn together. The ability to learn faster than competitors will be the only sustainable competitive advantage in emerging knowledge economy." Soft technological tools-skills as narrated in this book, shall make you learn as organizational professional to upgrade quality of worklife and to produce quality goods and services. We believe that it takes quality people to do quality work. And quality is the expression of human excellence.

This book does not purport to be a definitive guide on the skills covered but only present the basic concepts and techniques that will enable you to employ soft skills more effectively in your work-place and ultimately help you become a knowledge employee. If you wish to learn how to improve your soft skills, you have to take active role in your learning process. you should identify yourself the skills that you need to develop and the specific activities that will help you develop those skills.

BIBLIOGRAPHY

Sr.No.	Author's Name	Book's Name	Publisher's Name, City and Year
1	Marsha Sinetar	The Mentor's Spirit	St. Martins Graffin, New York,1998.
2	William G. Dyer	Team-building	Addison Wesley, Longman, INC, New York, 1998
3	Dr. William Hendricks	Coaching, Mentoring and Managing	Carter Press, New Jersey
4	J. H. Boyett and H. P. Conn	Workplace	Penguin Group, New York, 2000
5	Top Peters and R. H. Waterman	In Search of Excellence	Harper and Row Publisher, London, 1904
6	K. H. Blanchard and Paul Hersay	Management of Organisational Behaviour	Arintice Hall of India, Delhi, 1988
7	Margaret Dale	Developing Management Skills	Kogan Page Ltd., London, 1998
8	J. K. Liker and M. Hoseus	Toyota Culture	Tata McGraw-Hill, New Delhi, 2008
9	Stephen R. Covey	The 8th Habit	Free Press, New York, 2004
10	Daniel Goleman	Working with Emotional Intelligence	Bantam Books, New York, 1999
11	Ronnie Lessen	Total Quality Learning	Beacon Books, 1997
12	D. Keith Denton	Quality Service	Universal Book Stall, New Delhi, 1995
13	Stephen R. Covey	Principle Centred Leadership	Semon and Schuster London, 1993
14	Philip B. Crosby	Completeness	A Plume Book, New York, 1994
15	Anthony Robbin	Awaken The Gaint Within	A Fireside Book, London, 1992
16	Stephen R. Covey	The Sevan Habits of Highly Effective People	A Fireside Book, New York, 1990
17	A. Hardinghame and J. Royal	Teamwork in Practice	Jaico Publishing Hse, Bombay, 1995
18	Tony Alessandra	Charisma	Warner Books, New York, 2000
19	G.G. Dess and J. C. Picken	Beyond Productivity	A. M. A, New York, 1999

20	T. E. Deal and W. A. Jenkins	Managing the Hidden Organisation	Warner Books, New York, 1994
21	John Rich	Power Negotiation	Playboy Publications, New York, 1982
22	John Okland	Total Organisational Execellence	Butterworth, Heinmann, 1999
23	Dr. V. R. Khatkhede	Human Relations in Industry (Phd Thesis)	Marathwada University, Aurangabad, 1977